None Dare Call It
EDUCATION

By

John A. Stormer

Liberty Bell Press
Florissant, Missouri

None Dare Call It Education
A Liberty Bell Book

ALSO BY JOHN STORMER

None Dare Call It Treason
The Death of a Nation
Growing Up God's Way
None Dare Call It Treason—25 YEARS LATER

LIBERTY BELL PRESS
Post Office Box 32
Florissant, MO 63032

Library of Congress Cataloging-in-Publication Data
John A. Stormer
None Dare Call It Education
Includes index.
1. Education 2. Schools 3. Title
LA209.2
ISBN 0-914053-14-0
PRINTED IN THE UNITED STATES OF AMERICA
Hardcover Edition - October 1998
Paperback Edition - September 1999

ABOUT THE AUTHOR

In 1962 John Stormer left a successful career as editor and general manager of a leading electrical magazine to write. His first book, *None Dare Call It Treason*, was a runaway best-seller in 1964. It was widely distributed by those supporting the Presidential campaign of Senator Barry Goldwater. His four books have sold over 10-million copies.

He was called to preach soon after trusting Jesus Christ to be his Savior and Lord in 1965. As a best selling author, pastor and Christian school superintendent, John Stormer has encouraged many to fulfill their responsibilities to their families, the Lord and America. His *Growing Up God's Way* is a guide for getting children ready for school and life from birth on. Published in 1984 it has become the most widely distributed book on marriage, family and child rearing from a Biblical perspective.

He was president of the Missouri Association of Christian schools for ten years. Since 1977 he has conducted weekly Bible studies in the Missouri Capitol for members of the legislature.

He publishes *Understanding The Times*, a periodic newsletter analyzing significant news developments in foreign policy, politics, education, religion and economics. He speaks regularly in Bible conferences and *Understanding The Times* seminars.

A native of Altoona, Pennsylvania, he attended the Pennsylvania State University and graduated from California's San Jose State University after Korean War service as an Air Force editor and historian. He is a member of the American Legion and the Council For National Policy. He has honorary degrees from Manahath School of Theology (1965) and Shelton College (1976). He and his wife, Elizabeth, are 45-year residents of Florissant, Missouri, a St. Louis suburb. Their daughter, Holly, is married and the mother of their four grandchildren.

CONTENTS

I'M THANKFUL

DURING THE YEARS I was growing up I couldn't understand why my mother was always questioning teachers and school administrators about changes being made in education. Her questioning started over fifty years ago. Mom didn't know what or who was behind the changes, she just knew that some things didn't make good sense. She continued to ask questions as a concerned parent and dedicated PTA worker at the local, county and state levels for over 25 years.

On New Year's Eve 1960 I learned why Mom was concerned and what and who caused her concerns. I spent the last night of 1960 and the first hours of 1961 reading *Bending The Twig —The Revolution In Education And Its Effect On Our Children*. Written by Augustin Rudd it was published in 1957 by the Sons of the American Revolution. It opened my eyes.

Shortly thereafter I met a man who suggested, "If you ever get the opportunity, ask your state or local superintendent of schools these two questions." The questions were:

What do you see the nature of man to be—and what should be his purpose in life?

He said that invariably an educator will answer, "We don't deal with questions like that." The man then pointed out that it is impossible to construct a system or philosophy of education without consciously or unconsciously making a definite determination about a child's basic nature and what his purpose in life should be. Those answers ultimately control all other education decisions.

I'm grateful to that man and to the state legislators, state and local school board members, teachers and other researchers in a dozen states who have related their experiences, documented "horrible examples" and given access to their files. Without their help it would have been impossible to produce this book.

*Theoretically a society
could be completely made over
in something like 15 years,
the time it takes to inculcate
a new culture into a rising crop
of youngsters.*
—SPECIAL COMMITTEE TO INVESTIGATE
TAX-EXEMPT FOUNDATIONS,
83RD CONGRESS, 1954

WHAT'S HAPPENING TO OUR SCHOOLS AND TO OUR CHILDREN?

The predominant value system of an entire culture can be overturned in one generation, or certainly in two, by those with unlimited access to children.
— **Dr. James Dobson**

MOST OF US would like to think today's schools provide the same education we think we received. We've heard about "dumbing down," high school graduates who have trouble reading their diplomas, drugs, unmarried teenagers having babies, and the violence and killings in inner city schools or in far off little towns like Paducah, Kentucky; Jonesboro, Arkansas or Springfield, Oregon. Even so, many feel or hope that the schools our children or grandchildren attend are doing a good job—although they may be somewhat different from those we attended.

This book is filled with examples of horrible and outrageous happenings in America's schools. The "horrible examples" were collected from teachers and parents, state and local school board members, state legislative files, a U.S. Senate speech about new-new math which would be funny if not so tragic, newspaper articles about moral outrages in the nation's schools and illustrations from school textbooks.

As you read you'll understand why the nationally syndicated columnist Thomas Sowell says:

> If every parent in America knew what was really going on in the public schools, there would be a revolution.

The "horrible examples" won't be found in every school. However, they result from a faulty philosophy of education which influences all public schools (and many private institutions). That faulty philosophy (1) has produced schools which are failing children academically, (2) is subjecting children to wrong moral influences, and (3) establishes the foundation from which education "reformers" are working to remake our children, our society and our culture.

That word *culture,* as it refers to the "culture of a nation," is defined by the 1951 *American College Dictionary* as...

> ...the sum total of ways of living built up by a group of human beings, which is transmitted from one generation to another.

America's culture—the values and traditions which determine the way we live and the way of life we will hand down to our children and grandchildren—is being transformed.

Periodically America gets a "wake up call." While the first edition of this book was being completed, twenty-one students and teachers were gunned down and killed in schools by fellow students. Fifty others were wounded. On May 22, 1998, a *St. Louis Post-Dispatch* editorial said of the ongoing killings:

> We can ask ourselves over and over why these tragedies happen. What leads these kids to kill? A screwed up home life? A psychological disorder? An innate evil? We can speculate, but we can never know for sure.

The following day President Clinton in his Saturday radio address said of the rash of in-school killings:

> We must face up to the fact that these are more than isolated incidents. They are symptoms of *a changing culture*...

Our culture—the sum total of the ways of living built up by one group of human beings which is transmitted from one generation to another—has been changed as President Clinton acknowledged.

Our nation and many of its laws, our ideas about family and marriage and our attitudes toward life, liberty and property have changed drastically. In effect, America has lived through a revolution. It's been a revolution which has been unfolding slowly, step-by-step for several generations. The revolution has changed what too many Americans think about school, work, sex, responsibility, right and wrong and the importance of spoken or written agreements. Consider how America has changed. In 1960...

> ... a radio or TV station was in danger of losing its operating license from the Federal Communications Commission if it permitted the words "Hell" or "Damn" to go out over the air waves...prayer and Bible reading were permitted in America's schools...it was safe to walk even big city streets at night...there was no drug problem, no X-rated, R-rated or PG movies...there were no co-ed dorms on college campuses or in Army barracks, no birth-control pills (they were introduced in May 1960) and no legalized abortions...homosexuals hid their sin rather than parading it openly and proudly in demonstrations and on TV (perhaps that's why there was no AIDS or HIV).

America has changed! People under age 50 have a hard time comprehending the changes. They haven't known any America other than today's violent, sex-crazy, drug-dependent world. Because the changes happened little by little, even older Americans who lived through them didn't notice what was happening. However, what must be characterized as a revolution has produced a different America and a different way of living than that which existed before 1960.

The changes produced a "collision of two worlds" in the library of Columbine High School in Littleton, Colorado on April 20, 1999. The two worlds which are in conflict all over America today were represented by executioner Eric Harris and martyred Cassie Bernal.

In the library that day, Eric Harris announced, "I am the law. If you don't like it, you die." Harris had written the same words in a classroom essay a few weeks earlier. Martyred Cassie Bernal represented the "other world." With a gun pointed at her head, she declared for her world, saying, "Yes, I believe in God."

The world of Eric Harris is a world where man is the law—the ultimate authority. For Cassie Bernal, God is the lawgiver—the ultimate authority. The conflict which produced the tragedy in Columbine High School is manifested today in every area of American life, its families, its economics, its churches, and its politics.

How has it all happened? The disruptions of several wars, the TV and the entertainment media, the government and changes in the doctrine and practices of many churches have transformed how Americans think and live.

No influence is greater than that of America's schools. Children spend over thirty hours a week in school during thirteen of their most formative years. Educational goals and what is taught and how it is taught have changed in the last 65 years. It was done by a group of education "reformers" who over 65 years ago said they would use the schools to produce "a new social order." The changes have transformed how we think and live. That's what this book is about.

In succeeding chapters you'll see "horrible and outrageous examples" described and documented with details. In Chapter 1, titled *What Are Schools Doing To Our Children Academically* you'll read...

> ...how children across America, instead of being taught to spell, are encouraged to use "inventive spelling" *and parents are instructed not to correct them.* "Educators" say spelling isn't necessary because "spell-check" on computers will do the work.

You'll read how...

...official state Outcome-Based Education guidelines instruct teachers to encourage children to guess at words and meanings from pictures printed with the stories *rather than teaching them to sound out words phonetically.*

You'll learn that...

..."new-new math" books tell students that math isn't too important anymore because computers do the work and then instructs them to "guess and check" until they get "right" answers.

Chapter 1 also gives the details on how when Massachusetts started testing incoming teachers in 1998...

...56% of the college graduates being tested for teaching jobs flunked. To help more pass, the State Board of Education lowered the "passing grade" for the eighth-grade level test. The governor was outraged. He expressed concerns that "perhaps thousands of teachers in the classroom today are not meeting the standards." Similar alarming reports are documented from other states.

CREATING NEW PEOPLE

Falling academics—the dumbing down of our children—is not the only problem. Some kids do learn and excel. Chapter 10 documents the techniques used to manipulate the thinking and values of the very smart kids. They are taught to base their thinking and decisions on faulty, humanistic, God-is-not-relevant foundations. They are being trained and prepared to be the leaders of "the new social order" which education "reformers" say they are working to create.

Not all the atrocities are in the area of academics. Chapter 2, titled *What Are Schools Doing To Our Children Morally?* details how the Illinois State Board of Education had 61 Illinois high schools give a test to 11th grade students. Questions asked students which types of sexual activities are least likely and most likely to expose people to HIV and what are the best ways of avoiding pregnancy, HIV and other sexually transmitted diseases. The multiple choice questions had students choose between...

> ...anal and oral sex, mutual masturbation, French kissing, having vaginal sex with or without a condom, and having sex only with people you know. <u>Students weren't given an opportunity to choose abstinence or answer "None of the above."</u>

No one, including the state supervisor who signed the letter which sent the test to the 61 schools, admitted to having seen the questions. The State School Superintendent Joseph Spagnolo issued a public apology.

In response to his official "explanation" the *Chicago Sun Times* editorial on June 5, 1998 carried the headline "Excuses, excuses." The paper said that blaming "an unnamed bureaucrat for this *egregious error* was not good enough." The editorial said that the questions were no mistake, but rather they are...

> ...a window into the mind-set of educational bureaucrats and assorted activists determined to force their vision of permissive sex education on parents and students—even when the vision conflicts with Illinois law.

The Illinois State School Board indicated that they had received the controversial questions from the Council of Chief State School Officers, the organization to which the top education official in each state belongs. They indicated the questions had been used in many other states as well. The four actual questions and the choices they offered students are printed in Chapter 4—along with a host of other moral outrages to which other students, including even those in kindergarten, are subjected in state after state.

Chapter 4 is titled, *Textbooks Destroy The Foundations of America's Way Of Life*. Examples from textbooks used in America's schools over a 40-year period show how schools have undermined the twelve basic foundational concepts of American life. Those foundational concepts are being replaced with the false teachings of *Humanist Manifestos I and II*. The examples show how textbooks have been changed to...

...(1) weaken marriage and family life, (2) downgrade parental authority, (3) change traditional attitudes toward sex, morality and life, (4) substitute situational ethics for absolutes of right and wrong, (5) deny the importance of spoken or written contracts, and (6) undermine national independence and sovereignty.

There are multitudes of dedicated teachers in the public school system. But they teach in schools controlled by a faulty, flawed humanistic philosophy. It is a philosophy constructed years ago by "reformers" who redefined the purpose of education and based it on an incorrect view of the nature of children and their purpose in life.

I'm not writing about a conspiracy. Conspiracies deal with what is done in secret. The education "reformers" who have made America's schools the primary agency for changing our culture and our way of life wrote and spoke *openly* about their dreams and their goals. The tragedy is that for too long no one noticed—or no one took their words seriously. Now we are reaping the harvest in a serious academic decline and a changed national culture—a changed way of living. It's time to look deeply into their goals to see how they are achieving them in the lives of our children.

How they laid their false foundations for what is happening to America's way of life today is detailed in Chapter 3. Without a knowledge of what they planned, it is impossible to understand how American society and its culture have been transformed—or where we are headed. What those "pioneer" reformers started planning for our children and our nation over 65 years ago, their present day successors in education and government are implementing *now*.

Chapters 6, 7, 8 and 9 tell who the new reformers are and what they are doing through Goals 2000 and School-to-Work laws which Congress passed and President Clinton signed. Those laws will make School-to-Work mandatory in all public schools by 2001.

What is School-to-Work? You'll read a U.S. Department of Education document which says that...

> ...School-To-Work changes the purpose of education from intellectual development to vocational preparation.

By 7th or 8th grade "assessments" will be made which will determine what job a child's future education or vocational training will prepare him for. It's already happening. The 1997 Annual Report to Congress by the Secretaries of Education and Labor says that...

> ...as of June 1996, 23 percent of the 115,000 elementary and secondary schools in America were engaged in STW....and all 50 states have applied for and received STW planning grants.

You'll learn that a top education official has told state governors and cabinet level officials that...

> ...We no longer see the teaching of facts and information as the primary function of education...Building a new kind of people must be part of the curriculum.

What kind of "new people" do these "educators" have in mind? Representative Henry Hyde is Chairman of the U.S. House of Representatives Judiciary Committee. In a letter to his congressional colleagues he said:

> Behavior modification is a significant part of restructuring our schools. School children will be trained to be "politically correct," to be unbiased, to understand diversity, to accept "alternative lifestyles..."

The Outcome-Based Education process described in Chapter 8 is the method for doing it. The man credited with being the brains behind Outcome-Based Education and many of the on-going school "reforms" says:

> The purpose of education is to change the thoughts, feelings and actions of students.

How will it be done? Lamar Alexander told the 1989 Kansas Governor's Education Conference that schools should be open from 6 a.m. to 6 p.m. daily, year-round and serve children from age three months to eighteen years of age. Shortly after he made that proposal Alexander was named U.S. Secretary of Education by President George Bush. You'll read Alexander's actual words in Chapter 6.

Many who have read even this far will say, "It could never happen in America!" It is happening. Under the guise of "education reform" our nation and the way we live and think is being transformed. In the process academic excellence has disappeared and new attitudes and values are being implanted into our children's minds and hearts.

Even if you are sure that your children and grandchildren are not being affected, they will grow up to live in a world where a majority of the people are products of schools which are greatly different from those we attended.

Read the rest of this book to see *the details* and *the proofs* of what is happening *now*. Then read Chapter 12 to see what some communities are doing about it—and what you can do to restore America's traditional values and culture for our children and our grandchildren.

John A. Stormer
Florissant, Missouri
July 4, 1999

*We no longer see the teaching
of facts and information
as the primary function of education*
DR. SHIRLEY MCCUNE
1989 Kansas Governor's Conference

WHAT ARE SCHOOLS DOING
TO OUR CHILDREN ACADEMICALLY?

If every parent in America knew what was really going on in the public schools, there would be a revolution.
> —*Syndicated columnist Thomas Sowell*

NEW TEACHING METHODS used in some schools would be funny—if the results were not so tragic. Succeeding generations of Americans have been "dumbed down." Some "horrible and outrageous" examples have resulted.

A textbook widely used in something called "new-new math" was the focus of a lengthy June 9, 1997 speech in the United States Senate.[1] Senator Robert Byrd (D-WV) said:

> Over the past decade I have been continually puzzled by our Nation's failure to produce better students despite public concern and despite the billions of Federal dollars which are appropriated annually for various programs intended to aid and improve education.

Byrd asked whether a new approach to teaching math could be why U.S. students rank 28th in the world in math. Byrd said:

> Apparently the concept behind this new-new approach to math is to get kids to enjoy mathematics and hope that the "enjoyment" will lead to a better understanding of basic math concepts. Nice thought, but nice thoughts do not always get the job done.

Byrd then told of a professor at Arizona State University, Marianne Jennings. She found that even though her teenage daughter was getting an "A" in Algebra I, she could not solve a simple mathematical equation. Curious as to why, she checked her daughter's algebra book. Titled *Secondary Math: An Integrated Approach: Focus on Algebra,* it was produced by Addison-Wesley, a major publisher of textbooks. The book has 25 authors and contributors plus four "multicultural reviewers." Byrd commented:

> Why we need multicultural reviewers of an algebra textbook is a question I would like to hear someone answer.

Byrd said the opening section titled, "Getting Started," confirmed his suspicions about the "quirky fuzziness of this new-new approach to math." It tells the student:

> In the twenty-first century, computers will do a lot of the work that people used to do. Even in today's workplace, there is little need for someone to add up daily invoices or compute sales tax. Engineers and scientists already use computer programs to do calculations and solve equations.[2]

Byrd then asked and commented:

> What kind of message is sent by that brilliant opening salvo? It seems to tell students, "Don't worry about all this math stuff too much. Computers will do all that work for us in a few years."

Byrd said, "Can you imagine such a goofy passage in a Japanese math textbook?"

The "algebra" book has "lectures" on endangered species, air pollution, facts about the Dogon people of West Africa, chili recipes, a discussion of hot peppers and the role zoos should play in today's society. Page 5 has its headlines written in Spanish, English and Portuguese, a map of South America showing which language is spoken where, followed by the United Nations *Declaration of Human Rights* in three languages. Byrd adds:

By the time we get around to defining an algebraic expression we are on page 105. But it isn't long before we get off that boring topic to an illuminating testimony by Dave Sanfilippo, a driver with United Parcel Service. Sanfilippo tells the students that he "didn't do well in high school mathematics..." but is doing well at his job now because he enters "...information on a pocket computer..." That's hardly inspirational stuff for a kid struggling with algebra.

Byrd went on to tell the United States Senate:

By this time I was thoroughly dazed and unsure whether I was looking at a science book, a language book, a sociology book, or a geography book....The textbook tries to be all things to all students in all subjects and the result is a mush of multiculturalism, environmental and political correctness, and various disjointed discussions on a multitude of topics....This awful textbook obviously fails to do in 812 pages what Japanese textbooks do so well in 200. [That's why] the average math score in Japan is 80. In the United States it is 52.

Byrd said that having reviewed the book, "I now have a partial answer to my question about why we don't produce better students despite all the money that Federal taxpayers shell out." Byrd concluded with this word of advice for parents:

The lesson here is for parents to follow Marianne Jennings' lead and take a close look at their children's textbooks to be sure that the new-new math and other similar nonsense has not crept into the local school system.

Jennings, a professor at Arizona State and the mother who uncovered the book, had an article titled, "Why Our Kids Can't Do Math" in *Reader's Digest* in December 1997. She added to what Senator Byrd said, saying:

U.S. math educators have all but eliminated numbers. They are creating a generation of math nitwits.[4]

After five years of experimentation and drastic drops in students' math scores, California dropped the controversial Addison-Wesley text and the new-new math approach and went "back to basics." Almost immediately, the National Science Foundation threatened to cut California's $50-million federal grant for teaching math and science. The NSF letter to the California State School Board stated:

> You must surely understand that the Foundation cannot support individual school systems that embark on a course that substitutes computational proficiencies for a commitment to deep, balanced mathematical learning....The wistful or nostalgic "back to basics" approach that characterizes the Board standards overlooks the fact that the approach has chronically and dismally failed.

The NSF head apparently does not recognize that even with "deep mathematical learning," students and future workers won't get right answers without "computational proficiencies." What the head of National Science Foundation called the dismal failures of the "basics" approach was the system of teaching through which the engineers who put a man on the moon learned their math.

As California was dropping new-new math, on November 11, 1997 the Texas State Board of Education approved the Addison-Wesley text for use in the Lone Star state *even though it tells students to keep guessing and checking until they get the right answer (Page 219, 1998 edition).*

The new-new math and what Senator Byrd called "similar nonsense" is being added to math and other textbooks and classrooms across America. Here are examples reported in newspapers or revealed at education conferences across the nation:

> A New York attorney and talk show host, Bob Unger, related the struggle he and his wife had with their first grade son's *math* problem which asked: "There are ten children in the

small school Samuel goes to. There are five jars of paint. How
many children can paint?" After trying to work that *math*
problem for several hours they FAXed it to their CPA. From
the school they ultimately learned the answer was: "If they
share, they can all paint." Unger commented, "That's math?
It's a nice lesson in sharing—but does it teach students the
basic math facts they'll need in life?"[5]

A Waukesha, Wisconsin attorney and school board member,
Bill Domina, also found that the new-new math his first grade
daughter brought home was "not very parent friendly." Neither he nor his wife, who is also an attorney could
figure out her problem. He told the school board, "If we're
having trouble, it's going to be too hard for a first-grader to
understand." As a school board member he had voted earlier
to adopt the grade school math series.[6] A fellow board member suggested that the district must work with parents to find
a way to make parents "comfortable" with the new texts.
Another board member, Kathleen Briggs, who had voted
against purchasing the $250,000 math series for grades 1-5
two years before, responded: "It strikes me as absurd that
you'd have to train parents—many of whom are college-edu-
cated to help kids with a first grade math problem."[7]

When a Westport, Massachusetts mother, Laurie Andrews,
found that her daughter couldn't do simple third grade math
without using a calculator, she was told that the school wasn't
going to teach the multiplication tables. She formed a parents'
group, filed for the school board and despite being labeled a
"religious radical," was elected. She continues to serve although she says, "meetings of the board are getting ugly." She
and her husband David have withdrawn their three children
from the public school district where she serves on the board.
They'll go to a private school which teaches the multiplication
tables. She told the superintendent: "My kids are not guinea
pigs. They have one chance at an education. I can't risk
sacrificing them for your theories."[8]

In a series titled "The Dumbing Down of America,"
Washington Times education writer Carol Innerst
reported other new-new math atrocities. She wrote:

A baffled Pennsylvania parent called a member of her local school board about a math paper her child brought home. The paper explained that there were four birds in the nest and one flew away. The question: "How do you think the bird that flew away felt?"

"Who cares?" snaps Fran Bevan, the Norwin School Board member who got the parent's call. "Why even ask this question?"[9]

The newspaper's reporter wrote:

Why indeed? What do birds, feelings or nests have to do with teaching math? Yet this kind of touchy-feely question and non-academic attitude are widespread in public schools today, a special report by the *Washington Times* finds.

Another fad sweeping the country is "inventive spelling." The *San Francisco Chronicle* in a story headed, "Bad Spelling Now Viewed As Inventive," reported:

After hearing the story "Jack and the Beanstalk," 6-year-old Pablo wrote a story of his own and read it to his summer school teacher in a halting voice. "If I would have magic beans, I would save the beans. And when I save the beans, then I will give them away. The end." Teacher Michele Chabra smiled at her student's brief recital. Then she looked at what he had written. "If i wd hf mg ics I wd save the bses and one I sav the bes then I wi g thmn way the end."[10]

The newspaper article then explained:

Known as "inventive spelling," such creativity is permitted—even encouraged—in many American classrooms. Although Pablo has completed first grade, like thousands of elementary school children he has never studied vocabulary lists, never used a spelling workbook and never spent a morning at the blackboard writing corrected sentences.

The teaching of basic spelling has undergone a quiet revolution in the United States during the past 15 years. Drills are out. Learning to spell by reading is in. Teachers have become increasingly reluctant to "stifle" the efforts of young writers by correcting their spelling or marking errors as wrong.[11]

California legislative files have letters which teachers in various districts distributed to parents explaining the "blessings" of inventive spelling. Parents are encouraged and cautioned not to correct their children's spelling. This letter to parents of Crafton, California first graders is typical of letters in legislative files from the 1993-96 period:

Dear Parents:

Once we start doing more creative writing on our own, we will be using "invented spelling." Invented spelling is when the child sounds out the word and writes it as it sounds. This is an important part of fostering a positive attitude for writing in your child. Please do not correct their spelling when they write at home....Correcting all of their spelling mistakes at this point will only discourage them and keep them from writing their true thoughts.

The *San Francisco Chronicle* said "inventive spelling" has been the practice in the many school districts for years. An unusual coalition of liberals and conservatives in the California legislature united to mandate a "return to basics." The back-to-basics legislative effort was opposed by The Association of California School Administrators and many education professors. One outspoken critic of what education professors call "mind-numbing, time-wasting practice drills" was Professor Stephen Krashen of the University of Southern California. He wrote:

Learning spelling rules is of dubious value....When spelling instruction does work, it may only be helping children to spell words they will learn to spell on their own.[12]

The Middletown, California *Times Star* had already shown its readers the fruits of "inventive spelling." Middletown is a town of 2,000 people about 75 miles north of San Francisco. In October 1994, vandals did thousands of dollars in damage to classrooms, computers, televisions, etc. Students were outraged. An eighth grade class wrote letters to those responsible, expressing their feelings. The paper published 26 student letters under the following disclaimer:

> The following are some of the letters that were received by the *Times Star* from a class of 8th grade students at Middletown Middle School following the vandalism that took place this past week. The grammar, spelling and punctuation have been printed as received from the students. Because some of the signatures were not legible, the *Times Star* chose not to print any of the names.

Samples reproduced here are typical of those printed:

Dear Vandles,

> You really hiurt people at this school. I do not know how much you hurt the teacher. But your relly dont know wate you do? We just got are new cumperters. You relly dameg are thing. We do not know why uou do this to us? I have been here all my life. I have never saw like this before. I hope you suffer. We all hate you.

Dear Vandules,

> I am verey made at you and it herts to see my teacher's cry. Youhave to be a rill peep to do some thing so mean. Ther is know punishment that can fix whate hapend. I thenk that some one should go into your beadroom and do this to you but then we wold be just as bad as you and we are not. You touch awey our classroom and we are on the flour riteing thiss leter to you peeps. I hate you.

Dear Vandle,

> You know you are prittle stupid for distroying things like computers and chlak boards, students chance to learn other new school stuff. 100,000 is a lot of money I know you cant pay so why dont turn your self in.

In the 26 published letters the eighth grade students spelled "vandal" ten different ways including: *vandal, vandeliser, vandles, vandalis, vanduls, vandols, vandle, vandales, vandules, and vandallists.*

In the week that followed, *Times Star* editor Teresa Sanders was viciously attacked by teachers and school officials for printing the letters. She published the teachers' letters and replied with this editorial.

> When we received last week's "Dear Vandal" letters I was impressed by what I thought was a rather sophisticated thought process coming from elementary school students, only later to find these letters were written by middle school students. I was shocked to find eighth grade students not possessing basic elementary level English skills.
>
> We understood the intent of the letters. And the community needed to know how the children felt about vandalism....But after reading the letters it was apparent to me the students were already victims prior to the vandalism. They are victims of an educational system which has failed to do its job.
>
> We could have edited and corrected the letters prior to publication, but by doing so, a number of us felt we would be guilty of covering up a crime far greater than vandalism. Whether it was right or wrong to publish the letters "as is" is to me, not the issue. The issue is the failure of the school system to be able to teach "the basics" to our children.

A Maryland father, Leonard Gahm, objected to "inventive spelling" in his son's school. He reported the response:

> The middle school principal told me that in our society, with the advent of computers and spell check, it's not as important that children know how to spell correctly.[13]

Whenever such school failures are spotlighted, a frequent response is, "Those are just isolated cases." However, an eighteen-month study by a Presidential commission in the early 1980s concluded that the "isolated incidents" are indicative of what has happened to our schools and what is happening to a significant percentage of our children.

In April 1983, the National Commission on Excellence in Education issued its now historic report, *A Nation At Risk*. After an 18-month study the report said:

> The educational foundations of our society are presently being eroded by a rising tide of mediocrity that threatens our very future as a nation and as a people.

The Presidential Commission added these chilling words:

> If an unfriendly foreign power had attempted to impose on America the mediocre educational performance that exists today, we might well have viewed it as an act of war. As it stands, we have allowed this to happen to ourselves.

What's been done since 1983? Multiplied billions in federal, state and local tax dollars have been poured into education, but in 1997 Brunno V. Manno, senior fellow at the Hudson Institute, said:

> The fundamental indictment that came out of the *[Nation At Risk]* report was that kids weren't learning enough. Fifteen years later we're still saying that kids in this country aren't learning enough and their academic performance is still mediocre.[14]

Assessments made in the intervening years confirmed Manno's charge. During those years Americans have become accustomed to seeing on-going headlines saying:

> City Schools Get Poor Grades In Survey....SAT Scores Fall To New Low....College Test Scores Lowest Since Mid-1950s....Students Today Have Vocabulary Problems, Educator Says....City 8th Graders Slip Again In Basic Skills Test Scores....Cleveland Pupils Do Poorly On Test....Schools Brainwashing Our Children....High School Diplomas Should

Mean Something....U.S. Students Lag In Math, Science....Trouble In Schools—Will It Get Worse?

Declining SAT and ACT college entrance scores have gotten headlines almost annually since the early 1960s. However, there's been a supposed turn around since 1995. A *New York Times* News Service story told how the SAT scores have "improved." The story reported:

> The College Board "recalibrated" the scoring of the SAT to "make it easier for everyone to get higher scores." Bradley J. Quin of the College board explained that when the current scoring system was established in 1941, 500 was the average score for each test, the math and the verbal. The average verbal score by 1994 had fallen to 424 and the average math score to 478. By "recentering" the scale the average student will once again get scores of 500 in verbal and math.[15]

In other words, student achievement hasn't improved, but their scores will look better. Standardized scores or "norms" for widely used achievement tests in elementary and secondary schools have been similarly "recalibrated." Therefore, on a standardized achievement test an average fifth grade student today will get scores which show that he is working at fifth grade levels in reading and math. However, if he were to take the 1965 test [which some Christian schools continued to use for entrance tests for many years], his scores would show that he is barely working at a fourth grade level—a loss of about a full year in average achievement levels in thirty years.

The National Education Goals Panel's Annual Report grew out of the national governors education summit. It confirmed why American students fall behind. It said most students who receive a high school diploma do so...

> ...without ever being seriously challenged, without ever fully knowing what they are capable of learning and doing, and

without having gained the tools and skills they need to survive and prosper.[16]

Even with the "recalibrated" tests mentioned above, the 1993 National Education Goals Panel said that only...

...one in five fourth graders met math performance standards and only one in four eighth graders measured up. Only one in four fourth graders met needed reading standards of accomplishment.[17]

The deficiencies show up in every area of the curriculum. Recent results from the National Assessment of Educational Progress (NAEP) science exams showed that 40% of high school seniors and one-fourth of all 4th and 8th graders didn't meet minimum standards. Half of the 4th graders tested couldn't identify the Atlantic and Pacific Oceans on a map. Syndicated columnist James Kilpatrick reported:

Recently, 7812 11th graders took a test in history and literature....Of all the answers to the 141 questions on history, only 54.5 per cent were correct. The 17-year-olds demonstrated no sense of historical chronology. Almost one-fourth thought the Civil War was waged before 1800. One-third thought Columbus had discovered the New World after 1750. Three or four could not place Lincoln within 20 years. Forty-three per cent guessed wrong on the half century that included World War I. The results in literature were even more depressing.[18]

The decline in academic achievement creates real problems for colleges. A 1997 op-ed article in the *St. Louis Post-Dispatch* carried the bold headline, "Don't Fill College Classrooms With Unprepared Students." Paul Shore, an assistant professor of education and American studies at St. Louis University, wrote:

Currently, literally millions of American high school students are not receiving adequate preparation for college level work. Not only do many of these students lack the reading and math skills needed to succeed in college, they also have not learned the habits of self-discipline or study techniques that enable college students to do well.[20]

Shore anticipated that his concerns would be shrugged off by many complacent, all-is-well readers. He added:

> Before you discount this claim as just another complaint from a cranky college professor, consider how many colleges have already instituted remedial writing programs for entering freshmen.[21]

Shore is correct. At three-quarters of American colleges, thousands upon thousands of students are struggling to master high school and sometimes middle school material in math, writing and reading. At one point in the 1980s, half of all the graduates of accredited high schools in the metropolitan St. Louis area who were enrolled in colleges in the area had to take remedial English courses. Nationwide about a third of college freshmen are enrolled in at least one remedial course.[22]

John E. Stone, an education professor at East Tennessee State University, explains the problem this way:

> Years ago it was expected that kids should be reading by the end of first grade. With the advent of "developmentally appropriate" instruction and non-graded primary classes— lumping the first three years of school together—the expectation is that they will be reading by the end of third grade.[23]

President Clinton acknowledged the seriousness of the literacy crisis. In accepting his nomination for a second term at the Democrat National Convention in August 1996, he pledged that if reelected he would work to insure that every student could read *by the time he finishes third grade!* Year after year, home schooled students and those enrolled in Christian schools which start training children with intensive systematic phonics are reading by January or February of their kindergarten year.

Professor Stone has participated in the adoption of eight or nine textbooks in his 25 years of teaching. He says:

> There's no question that every time we have to adopt a textbook the reading level of the book is lower than the last.[24]

John Agresto, president of St. John's College in Santa Fe, New Mexico, has similar concerns. He says:

> We've turned colleges into high schools. After the babysitting of high school, we've asked colleges to give students the education they should have gotten. This is disastrous for colleges. I can't teach kids physics, biology and the history of the Roman Empire if I have to teach them the difference between "their" and "there." We get students—even here— who say, "What difference does it make if I spelled it wrong? You know what I meant!"[25]

"Grade inflation" is the growing practice of making it easier to pass and even earn an "A" with little effort or ability. That's why many students with A or B high school averages have to take remedial reading, math and writing courses when they get to college.

There are tragic examples of how young people are being victimized. Walter Williams, a distinguished economics professor and syndicated columnist, wrote of such a case. His column was headlined, "Shortchanged By The School He Attended." In it he told this story of Tai Kwan Cureton:

> Tai Kwan Cureton was a student at Philadelphia's predominantly black Simon Gratz High School. An honor roll student maintaining a 3.8 (A-) grade-point average, young Mr. Cureton ranked 27th in his 308-student graduating class. He was president of the student government and the student peer mediation service. He did it all while working more than 30 hours a week in a fast food restaurant.

Williams' column, based on a January 9, 1997 story in the *Philadelphia Inquirer*, added that Cureton...

> ....was a member, and captain, of Simon Gratz's renowned track team....he was widely sought after by recruiters with scholarships in hand from top-ranking Division I colleges such as Penn State, Pitts-burgh and Boston College.

Cureton's future looked rosy until he received his Scholastic Aptitude Test (SAT) scores. For a student to be eligible to participate in freshman athletics at Division I colleges, the NCAA rules require a minimum SAT score of 700 out of a possible 1,600. Since a person gets 400 points on the SAT for simply writing his name, a minimum of 700 means the athlete must earn 300 points out of a possible 1,200. Cureton didn't make the minimum score and his dreams and hopes collapsed. The young man said:

> After I got my test scores back, they stopped recruiting me. This really hurt. It was as if my hard work, good grades and other school activities didn't count for anything.

Williams wrote:

> That's the tragedy. Mr. Cureton attended school regularly, did his school work and behaved, but his high school grades were fraudulent. He and his parents were misled into believing that Simon Gratz High School's A's and B's were equivalent to those earned elsewhere. He was academically shortchanged by his school, an outcome he did not deserve and could not have known until SAT time.

Williams concluded his column saying:

> Cureton's story should bring outrage to decent people, not against NCAA standards, but against an education system that systematically scuttles opportunities for our youths.[26]

Cureton's story was not an isolated case. In St. Louis, Anette Chancellor was proud of her frequent A's and her membership in the National Honor Society. But when she enrolled at the University of Missouri at St. Louis (UMSL), she got a rude shock. The *St. Louis Post-Dispatch* quoted her:

> In my very first semester in college I had five classes—math, English, music, biology, and law. Of those five, I failed math and English.[27]

Howard Benoist, director of UMSL's Center for Academic Development, said "close to 70% of entering freshmen need remedial math."

HOW QUALIFIED ARE THE TEACHERS?

A disturbing "alarm bell" sounded in June 1998. It may shed important light on why schools are failing to prepare students academically.

Before granting teaching certificates to new college graduates, Massachusetts decided to give 2000 of them a basic reading and writing test. When 56% flunked, the State Board of Education at first decided to grade on a curve so that only 44% would fail. Then because of public outcries it reversed itself so that all 56% or 1200 did fail.

The Associated Press reported:

> Massachusetts House Speaker Thomas Finnegan said he had seen the tests and was appalled that the applying teachers couldn't "define a noun or a verb or what democracy means or the meaning of the word *imminent.*"[28]

The Department of Education released a sample of the test which Board Chairman John Silber, the longtime president of Boston University, said seemed to be at about the eighth grade level. The samples showed that some prospective teachers, when trying to rewrite sentences, misspelled words a 9-year-old could spell—even though the words they were to use were right in front of them on the test. Some of the teachers wrote at a fifth or sixth grade level. Many wrote sen-

tences lacking both nouns and verbs. House Speaker
Finnegan bluntly called the 56% who failed the test and
those who gave them college degrees "idiots." The
Washington Times quoted him as adding:

> The teachers' colleges are conferring degrees that are as
> meaningless as a piece of used Kleenex that's been lying in
> the gutter after last week's rainstorm.

Massachusetts Governor Paul Cellucci expressed out-
rage and called for testing of all current teachers. He
was concerned that there are "perhaps thousands of
teachers who are in the classroom today who are not
meeting the standards." That prompted a reaction. The
AP reported:

> Mr. Cellucci's proposal immediately drew criticism from
> Kathy Kelley, president of the Massachusetts Federation of
> Teachers, one of the state's two major teachers unions....Ed
> Sullivan, executive director of the Massachusetts Teachers
> Association had harsh words for the Governor's proposal,
> saying, "We think it's totally unnecessary, and the teachers
> out there who have been teaching 10, 20 and 30 years find it
> insulting.

As will be shown in Chapter 11 the objection to any
testing of teacher competency is in line with resolutions
passed regularly at annual conventions of the National
Education Association (NEA). Teacher tests in other
states have shown similar failures.

> In 1983 in Houston, Texas, the school board was shocked
> when 62% of the 2,437 classroom teachers tested failed a
> standard reading skills test; 46% flunked in math, 26% in
> writing. It was also found that 763 of those tested had
> cheated.[29]

> In 1991, only 6% of the 2,603 teachers who took the exam to
> be designated as "master teachers" passed. To pass, teachers
> needed to answer 80% of the 55 multiple choice questions on
> instructional practices and score 15 out of 18 on several essay
> questions on the subject areas they teach. Jeri Stone of the

Texas Classroom Teachers Association said, "We would like to see the scoring standards revised so that teachers have a better chance of passing."[30]

In the late 1980s, most of the Texas classroom teachers required to take a competency exam ordered by a school reform commission headed by Ross Perot also failed. Very few lost their jobs, however, as they were permitted to retake tests to get passing grades.

Commenting editorially on the large numbers of teachers who fail competency tests, the *Washington Times* said:

At a minimum, current teachers—in Massachusetts and else-where—ought to be subjected to a rigorous recertification process that includes testing for basic literacy and knowledge of subject matter. And teacher education colleges that routinely graduate demonstrable "idiots" ought to be shut down.

U.S. News and World Report columnist John Leo gave some insight on why teacher education colleges "routinely graduate demonstrable idiots." In his August 3, 1998 column (which everyone concerned about education should find in a library and read), Leo listed courses given to prospective teachers at the University of Massachusetts-Amherst. The teacher preparation courses include:

"Leadership in Changing Times," four courses in "Social Diversity in Education," "Embracing Diversity," "Diversity & Change," " Oppression & Education," "Introduction to Multicultural Education," "Black Identity," "Classism," "Racism," "Sexism," "Jewish Oppression," "Lesbian/Gay/Bisexual Oppression," "Oppression of the Disabled," and "Erroneous Beliefs."

In his column, Leo said of the college graduates who failed the grade-school-level teacher test...

Apparently they went into ed school without knowing much about anything, they came out the same way. But at least they are prepared to drill children in separatism, oppression and erroneous beliefs.

Leo's column was titled, "Dumbing Down Teachers." He summed up other articles done on teacher colleges saying:

> The education schools take for granted that education must be "child centered," which means that children decide for themselves what they want to learn. Heavy emphasis is put on feelings and self. An actual curriculum, listing things students ought to know, is viewed as cramping the human spirit.

Thomas Sowell is a senior fellow at the Hoover Institute at Stanford University and a nationally syndicated columnist. In September 1996, he wrote:

> How surprised would you be to discover that another national commission has issued yet another report on the sad state of American education, along with recommendations for "reform?" There probably has not been a year in the past half century when education was not being reformed.

> Yet, when the dust finally settles, it is typically the same old story: People outside the education establishment want the schools to teach academic basics, while those inside the education establishment are looking for all sorts of "exciting" new things to do [like "new-new math" and "inventive spelling"], usually at the expense of academic skills.[31]

The newest "reform" which supposedly will cure all the academic problems previous reforms have produced is "Outcome-Based Education." (OBE and other "reforms" will be examined in depth in Chapters 6, 7, 8 and 9.)

Pennsylvania became a leader in 1992 among over 25 states in adopting "outcome based education." Thousands of parents turned out in meetings across the state and at rallies on the Capitol steps to protest the controversial "reform plan" under which Pennsylvania was to become the first state...

...to scrap traditional high school graduation requirements for a set of "student learning outcomes" that include attitudes on such issues as the environment and racial diversity, appreciating and understanding others[32] and self worth, learning independently and collaboratively, adaptability to change and ethical judgment.[33]

Public criticism caused education "reformers" to draw back in Pennsylvania and other states, but in many places the result was keeping the OBE approach *with a new name!* The "reform" proposals and the laws passed don't get to the heart of the problem. John Leo in his "Dumbing Down Teachers" column said:

> Our schools of education have been a national scandal for many years, but it's odd that they are rarely front-and-center in our endless debate about failing schools. The right talks about striving and standards, the left talks about equal funding and classroom size, but few talk much about the breeding grounds for school failure—the trendy, anti-achievement, oppression-obsessed, feel-good, esteem-ridden, content-free schools of education.

The failure of teachers' colleges to prepare future teachers to teach and the resulting "Dumbing Down" of many students rightfully get attention. However, there is another serious aspect to the agenda of the education "reformers."

In spite of all the statistics, the complaints from colleges and tragic personal stories like that of Tai Kwan Cureton and Anette Chancellor, some students do learn. They are taught to think and they do excel. The problem is that often they are taught to think and make decisions *from a faulty, humanistic, anti-traditional values foundation.* The next chapter shows how values and morals are reoriented. Chapter 10 will show how bright students are conditioned and trained to be the leaders of "a new social order"—a world with a new culture and way of life.

CHAPTER 2

WHAT ARE SCHOOLS DOING
TO OUR CHILDREN MORALLY?

To educate a person in mind and not in morals is
to educate a menace to society.
             —President Theodore Roosevelt

NOT ALL THE ALARMS and "wakeup calls" are in
the area of academics. In February 1997, for example,
parents in Northboro, Massachusetts demanded that
Douglas Matthews, a teacher, be fired. The Worcester,
Massachusetts *Telegram & Gazette* on February 18,
1997 reported that Matthews, a high school history
teacher, gave his students a list of sixteen questions
about sexuality and possible homosexual experiences.
The paper printed the questions the high school students were given. Among them were:

(1) What do you think caused your heterosexuality? (3) Is it
possible your heterosexuality is just a phase which you might
outgrow? (5) If you've never slept with a person of the same
sex and enjoyed it, is it possible that all you need is a good gay
lover? (7) Why do you as a heterosexual feel compelled to
seduce others into your lifestyle? (9) Would you want your
children to be heterosexual knowing the problems they would
face, such as unwanted pregnancy, sexually transmitted diseases, domestic violence, etc? (13) Considering the menace of
overpopulation, how would the human race survive if
everyone was a heterosexual like you? (15) How can you
become a whole person if you limit yourself to compulsive,
exclusive heterosexuality? Shouldn't you at least try to
develop your natural, healthy, homosexual potential?[11]

When parents rose up, the newspaper interviewed
school administrators. The newspaper story said:

School administrators said they believe Matthews' intent was good. Superintendent Robert Melican said he believes Matthews was trying to teach students to be sympathetic toward gay people. Matthews, the teacher, is the adviser to the school's gay-straight student alliance.

The president of the town's School Council, told the newspaper that the Council (what Massachusetts calls a school board) discussed how the questionnaire might fit into the curriculum framework, what the connection was, and how much time was spent making the connection prior to distribution of the questionnaire. Were those the questions the school board should have been asking? Parents of students who were subjected to the questionnaire didn't think so and didn't accept the "explanations" of the superintendent or the school board. Readers might say, "As uncalled for as such a questionnaire is, it was an isolated instance." However, as mentioned in the introduction, the shocking "test" questions the Illinois State School Board gave to students in 61 Illinois schools indicate traditional moral values are under attack in schools everywhere. The rest of this chapter's "horrible examples" validate that charge.

The academic problems and controversies about attacks on traditional morality in education both stem from educators shifting emphasis away from teaching traditional values and the 3R's. At the Kansas Governor's Education Summit in 1989, a leading educator told why:

> Some people say we are spending more on schools and getting less. I disagree—what we are doing is taking on more and more in schools and that will continue. We are not only feeding kids at lunch, we are feeding them in the morning also. We are supplying more psychological services. We are providing special ed services. More and more the school is the cog or center of all human resource development.[1]

To make room for the "new things" reformers have added, emphasis on the basics of the 3Rs, traditional moral values and character was downgraded in America's schools. One of the first "new" things was in-class sex education. In a 1994 column, Phyllis Schlafly gave some of the history—and the results.

> Sex education started coming into public schools about 30 years ago, and became progressively more explicit until many courses include actual demonstrations of how to use contraceptives and pornographic videos to explain the facts of life to minor children ...often without the knowledge of parents.[2]

Controversies have been ongoing ever since. Typical of the complaints was a situation which made the front page of the *Washington Times* in early 1997. Parents at Centreville Elementary School in Fairfax County (near Washington DC) were told fifth and sixth grade girls would be shown videos dealing with sexual development in girls—while boys would be shown videos appropriate for boys.

However, at the family dinner table on March 21, Mr. and Mrs. Larry Wiggins were stunned to learn that their young daughter had also been shown videos that depicted the sexual awakening of boys. The paper reported:

> Mr. Wiggins, 39, remembers his face growing red when his 11-year-old daughter talked of what she had just learned in her sex-ed class, using such words as "ejaculation," "wet dreams," and "erections."[3]

The Wiggins protested to the school. Their protests were picked up by the press. A series of follow-up stories reported "enormous confusion" as to Fairfax school policies on what videos children were to see. The paper reported:

> School administrators, parents and even school board members who voted on the policy could not agree whether girls

were supposed to see boys' videotapes and vice versa. After much discussion, it turned out the policy had been to show all sex-education material to both sexes—despite the contrary information given to parents at an orientation session.[4]

Two years of parental protests and school board "studies" resulted in the Fairfax County School Board again promising parents in December 1997 (as they had two years earlier) that fifth grade boys and girls would only see sex ed films showing sexual development pertaining to their own gender. In a lengthy editorial page letter in the December 13, 1997 *Washington Times*, a mother reviewed the controversy and said:

> In summary, the Fairfax County public school system has thwarted parents every step of the way with this film.

Children who are younger and younger get more and more sex information, including promotion of tolerance for and even encouragement of homosexual behavior. It starts in the first grade. Columnist Thomas Sowell turned the spotlight on a New York City controversy in 1992. He wrote:

> There was a recent flap in New York City over first grade textbooks titled "Daddy's Roommate" and "Heather Has Two Mommies." Both books were designed to acquaint [and condition] first-graders to the idea of homosexual parents.[5]

Widespread protests over the books being available in schools and in children's reading sections of public libraries have developed in such widely diverse places as Goldsboro, North Carolina; Roswell, New Mexico; Springfield, Oregon; and Harrisburg, Pennsylvania.

In the book, *Daddy's Roommate,* the little boy says he's "happy" about his dad's live-in partner. A *Washington Times* column by Thomas Sowell quoted from the book which has the little boy saying:

"Being gay is just one more kind of love," when he notices that his dad and the roommate Frank sleep together.[6]

Concerning the use of *Daddy's Roommate* and *Heather Has Two Mommies* books in New York city schools for little children, Sowell pointed out that, amazingly, only one local New York City school district objected. All the other districts quietly accepted this remaking of social values as a role for public schools. Even the one unwilling district objected only because it was "too early for this kind of thing." Sowell asked appropriately:

> What are American public schools doing getting into such things in the first place? Do they have time and energy to dissipate in ideological crusades to reshape the values of other people's children, when educators are failing miserably to convey the academic skills they are being paid to teach?

Sowell added:

> No small part of the reason why American school children fall so far behind their contemporaries in other countries in educational achievement is that Japanese and other young people are studying math, science and other solid subjects while our children are being brainwashed about homosexuality, environmentalism, multiculturalism or a thousand other non-academic distractions.

> Few parents or citizens realize the pervasiveness of classroom brainwashing, or the utter dishonesty with which it is smuggled into the schools under misleading labels.

> Does anyone ask himself why it should take years and years to teach schoolchildren so-called "sex education?" Obviously it does not. What takes years and years is to wear down the values they were taught at home and lead them toward wholly different attitudes and wholly different conceptions of the world. Brainwashing takes time—and it takes this time away from academic subjects.

The brainwashing can start in preschools even before children enter regular kindergarten. Family Concerns, Inc. of Atlanta, Georgia issued an alert in 1996 about a curriculum being offered in state-run four-year-old pre-kindergarten programs in Georgia. All state and private day care providers received the *Anti-Bias Curriculum* produced by the National Association for the Education of Young Children in Washington DC. One activity which teachers are instructed to use with four-year-olds says:

> Make copies of an outline of a body as drawn by a preschooler, and in small groups ask children to fill in all the body parts to show if the person is a boy or girl.[7]

What is the merit of focusing the attention of four-year- olds on the body parts of the opposite sex? At various places in the book teachers are instructed to look for opportunities to use and explain words like "penis" and "vagina" to the four year olds.

Family and church beliefs are undermined in various subtle ways. When children come to pre-school their ideas and experiences have all been derived from their families. Rather than reinforcing family values and beliefs, the national anti-bias curriculum says:

> Help children discover the contradictions between their ideas and their own experiences. Sometimes children will accept firsthand experience as truth; sometimes they will cling to social norms or their own ideas about gender behavior. Don't get discouraged when stereotypic gender play [boys playing like boys and girls like girls] and remarks continue despite a rich antisexist curriculum....The key is to provide many opportunities for new ways of thinking and reasoning. Over time, many children will integrate nonsexist attitudes into their beliefs and behavior. Children may also experience emotional conflict about acting differently than social norms, *especially when their families agree and act according to the norms* [Page 51]. (Emphasis added.)

At the time Sowell was writing about pro-homosexual brainwashing in kindergarten in New York City schools, *National Review* reported on how such pro-homosexual materials get used. The story said:

> One factor is the enlarged role homosexuals are playing in molding New York City school policy. When the Federal Government made a grant to New York's schools to support education in drug prevention, $500,000 of that money was awarded to the Gay and Lesbian Community Center....The volunteers who will staff condom distribution rooms in city high schools and who will be available to counsel children on sexuality include delegates from the Gay Men's Health Crisis and the Hetrick Martin Institute for Gay and Lesbian Youth, both of which have been designated as official resources for the New York City school system.[8]

Aroused parents led periodic fights for cleanup—but three years later the School Board hired an open homosexual from San Francisco to head the schools.[9] Some would say, "That's New York..." but the problems are showing up all over. A few examples are:

> The Provincetown, Massachusetts school board voted in August 1997 to begin teaching preschoolers about homosexual lifestyles and backed hiring preferences for "sexual minorities." School Superintendent Susan Fleming said, "The whole question is making gays and lesbians...visible." The school will have the group *Parents, Families and Friends of Lesbians and Gays* speak even in kindergarten classes.[10]

> U.S. District Judge Frank Freedman refused to order a photo exhibit of gay and lesbian households removed from elementary schools in Amherst, Massachusetts. Parents had filed suit saying the exhibit encouraged "sodomy and fornication" and was not appropriate for elementary school children.[11]

> A video designed to show teachers how to "address gay and lesbian issues with young children" is titled *It's Elementary— Talking About Gay Issues In School.* Over 1200 copies of the video have been sold to educational institutions for teacher

training. Filmed in six different eastern, midwestern and far
west schools, it shows among other things third graders debat-
ing the merits of same sex marriage. The Minnesota State
Parent-Teacher Association and the American Library Association have both endorsed the video.[12]

California state assemblywoman Sheila Kuehl, a
Democrat from Santa Monica and an open lesbian,
hosted a special screening for state education policy
makers. In 1997, Kuehl introduced AB101, a bill to
widely broaden rights on the basis of "sexual orientation." Assemblyman Steve Baldwin said full application of her bill would...

> ...require school districts to use textbooks which place gay
> lifestyle on the same moral level as a heterosexual family,
> prevent campus religious groups from refusing membership
> to practicing homosexuals, deny use of school facilities to
> groups which oppose homosexuality like churches, the Boy
> Scouts, etc.[13]

Baldwin, a Republican who has served as chairman
of the Assembly's Education Committee, compiled and
released a 58-page document which reproduced
homosexual materials used in California schools. The
exhibits printed in the report showed that much of what
AB101 would require was already being done in many
California public schools, including:

> A handout from a Union City, California Logan High School
> teacher in-service training day encouraged teachers to (1) say
> such words as lesbian, gay, bisexual often in a positive
> way....(2) identify gay, lesbian, bisexual contributors
> throughout the curriculum (in history, literature, art, science,
> religion, etc.)....and (3) to use inclusive language such as
> partner, significant other, family unit, etc. in place of
> girlfriend, boyfriend, husband, wife, etc. in the classroom,
> conversations, memos, etc. [Exhibit # 3]

> The Los Angeles Unified School District in 1994 sponsored
> the first gay and lesbian prom ever sanctioned by a public

school district. Teenagers from thirty Los Angeles High Schools packed the event at the ballroom of the Los Angeles Hilton and Towers Hotel. The L.A. School District's press release announcing the prom said that for the first time, gay students "will openly experience the magic that heterosexual students have always taken for granted. They will dance, romance, and dine without fear of exposure or rebuke." [Page 16, Baldwin Report and Exhibit #10]

California schools "diversity" classes prepared and distributed numerous flyers which claimed that a long list of historical figures were homosexual including Plato, Julius Caesar, Leonardo da Vinci, Hans Christian Anderson, Horatio Alger, Tchaikovsky, Lawrence of Arabia, etc. A full-page flyer produced by the Los Angeles Unified School District Gay and Lesbian Education Commission "documented" the homosexual involvements of Abraham Lincoln. [Exhibits #16, 23 & 24]

The California Teachers Association (CTA) policy on sex education says that "it is the responsibility of each school district to....develop a program which supports and promotes education leading to an understanding of the diversity of sexual orientation" and includes staff training in "the special needs of gay and lesbian students." The CTA Annual Calendar for 1995 promoted National Coming Out day and Gay and Lesbian Pride Month. [Exhibits 7 & 13]

Some parents got concerned. In 1992, the Second District of the California Congress of Parents, Teachers and Students issued...

> ...a three-page report documenting and protesting appearances by gays and lesbians in at least half a dozen northern California schools where the speakers gave 4th, 5th and 6th grade students detailed descriptions of sex toys and oral and anal intercourse. [Exhibit # 19]

Even with all the documentation Baldwin supplied and the work of aroused citizens, Kuehl's AB101 homosexual rights measure failed by only a 40-36 vote in June 1997. Most Democrats supported the pro-homo measure. In 1999, after the Democratic majority was increased in the 1998 elections, an even stronger version of Kuehl's bill passed the Assembly and awaits action by the California Senate as this is being written.

School districts all over California (and in major cities across America) have Gay and Lesbian Teachers Groups.

School-based clinics and sex-ed programs schools in many states became a major source for distributing condoms to students, often without parental knowledge or permission. Two years after condom distribution began in the Los Angeles Unified School District in 1992, the *Los Angeles Times* in a lengthy analysis[14] reported:

> The district's program, heavily criticized by some parents when it was adopted, is now under fire not only from those who oppose condom distribution—but from those who favor it as well.

Dr. Marvin Belzer of the L.A. County Adolescent HIV Consortium said:

> We don't feel that condoms should be given out in a vacuum. We feel there should be a program explaining how they are used and what the alternatives are....That needs to be evaluated....We know that teen-agers are extremely active sexually. People say, "Aren't you encouraging them to have sex?" The answer is if you just hand them a condom, "Maybe, maybe not."[15]

Officials at several high schools estimated that very few parents—only about five percent—returned letters asking that their children not be allowed to have condoms.

Susan Carpenter-McMillan of the Woman's Coalition, a vocal opponent of condom distribution, said the program "gives our kids a false sense of security." She added:

Fifteen-year-olds can't remember to do their homework, can't remember to put their galoshes on in the rain, and yet we expect them to remember to have a condom on when they have sex.[16]

Opponents of the condom program said abstinence is the primary message that should be conveyed—and having the schools distribute condoms doesn't reinforce that message. Syndicated columnist Maggie Gallagher points out that programs pushing abstinence are highly controversial in some places. She wrote:

Abstinence programs have been the subject of lawsuits by groups like Planned Parenthood which argue that schools invade teens' privacy if they don't unroll condoms on bananas in classrooms.[17]

Gallagher also wrote that national research supports the view that parents can exert a powerful view over the sexual behavior of their teens. A 1996 study published in *Family Planning Perspectives* showed that if parents want to help their teens postpone sex they should:

(1) Maintain a good, warm relationship with your child (children are far more likely to accept family values if they feel valued by their family). (2) Let your teens know honestly and openly that you expect them not to have sex. And (3) avoid discussing birth control.[18]

With the widely held view that all teens will have sex, the study showed some astounding results. In her column, Maggie Gallagher reported:

Separately, each factor about doubles the likelihood that a teen will choose to postpone sex. Put them together, and the power of parents multiplies: A teen who has all three things going for him—warm parents who push abstinence and who don't push contraception—is twelve times more likely to remain a virgin than a teen who has none of these things.

The study by James Jaccard, a psychology professor at the State University of New York at Albany, included 751 African-American teens and their mothers in Philadelphia.[19] His study showed that even in urban black neighborhoods strong moms can protect their teens. That strongly contradicts the philosophy underlying most school sex education programs.

Despite mandated in-school sex ed courses, the percentage of unwed teenage mothers continues to rise. Unwed teenagers accounted for 30% of teenage births in 1970. By 1990, 70% of teenage births were to unwed mothers and in some cities the figure was as high as 90%.

Educators who did their homework might have expected the failures. In 1968, a Behavioral Science Book Club monthly selection distributed to educators and school counselors advanced the idea that sex education was to be the main weapon in an ideological war against the family; its aim was divesting parents of their moral authority and the creation of revolutionary children.

The book was *The Triumph of the Therapeutic—Uses of Faith After Freud*[20] published by Harper & Row. Author Philip Rieff sets forth the vision that the "therapeutics,"—the psychiatrists, sociologists, school counselors, etc.—can use their skills and theories to remake and control society.

Rieff has impressive credentials. He taught sociology at the University of Chicago, Harvard and the University of California at Berkeley. From 1961 to 1964 he served as the chief consultant to the Planning Department of the National Council of Churches. Rieff wrote that "Christian culture has been displaced" and the book sets forth his dream for reorganizing society using the "therapeutic principles."

He has been at all the right—or "wrong" places. In the introduction to his book, Rieff quotes Bronislaw Malinowski who in his book, *Culture as a Determinant Behavior,* said:

> That we are passing through a cultural crisis of unprecedented magnitude nobody doubts...I can see only one way out...the establishment of a scientific control of human affairs.

This is a Marxist premise—the remaking of man through the application of "science" (falsely so-called).

Wilhelm Reich, on whom Rieff drew heavily, was a Bolshevik and a psychiatrist. Rieff says Reich left the organized Communist movement reluctantly, believing that by failing to convert Lenin's political revolution into the first moral revolution fought on scientific principles, the Marxists defeated themselves.

What remedy (or weapon) did Philip Rieff see for reorganizing society? Drawing on Reich, he wrote:

> Set into the context of Reich's attack on the family as the nucleus of all authoritative institutions, his repeated calls for a do-it-yourself adolescent sex education acquires political significance. Sex education becomes the main weapon in an ideological war against the family; its aim was to divest the parents of their moral authority.[21]

This is an amazing admission. It confirms the concerns and suspicions of many who have battled schoolroom sex education since the 1960s. Rieff concludes that for Reich...

> ...all hope rests with the possibility of creating revolutionary children...Because Marx theorized in terms of an adult world, for Reich, he could not possibly be subversive enough. With John Dewey, Wilhelm Reich is one of the great theorists of the child as the agent of social change...though publicly labeled an eccentric, Reich was anything but a fool.[22]

Rieff's book, promoting Reich's theories, was widely available to high school guidance counselors in 1967-

68. Those who read it should have known the far-reaching anti-family implications of the sex education programs even while they were being introduced in the 1960s.

Parents concerned about the appropriateness of school sex education have few rights as many examples show:

> In a Massachusetts case, parents sued to protest the policy of Falmouth High School, which placed condom vending machines in school restrooms. Condoms were thereby made available to students without parental consent. The U.S. Supreme Court refused to overturn a Massachusetts Supreme Court ruling which allowed the policy.[23]

In Texas, Federal District Judge Melinda Harmon, perhaps emboldened by the Supreme Court's decision, ruled that...

> ....parents give up their rights when they drop children off at public school.[24]

She made that determination after parents sued the school district when their son was questioned and made to strip naked by a female Texas Children's Protective Services worker. The CPS worker was looking for signs of paddling the boy's parents had allegedly administered.

Pennsylvania parents have also been told, "You have no rights!" As the state moved full scale into providing health services through school-based clinics, a 1996 incident (discussed fully in Chapter 9) provoked headlines nationally. Over 50 sixth grade girls at J.T. Lambert Intermediate School in East Stroudsburg, Pennsylvania were forced to disrobe and submit to genital exams. Katie Tucker, a mother, told the *Washington Times* that when the embarrassed disrobed girls learned that the doctor would force them to submit to "spread-eagled" genital exams...

...they were scared. They were crying and trying to run out the door, but one of the nurses blocked the door so they couldn't leave. My daughter told the other nurse that "My mother wouldn't like this. I want to call her." And they said, "No." My daughter said, "I don't want this test done." And the nurse said, "Too bad."

Parents are finding increasingly that they have no rights. The doctor, Ramlah Vahanvaty, when asked if some of the girls were crying said, "I don't remember." The *Pocono Record* in its report added that later the doctor said:

Even a parent doesn't have the right to say what's appropriate for a physician to do when they're doing an exam.

Pennsylvania Family Institute's research director, Tom Shaheen, commented that with President Clinton's push for national Goals 2000 standards, including increased in-school medical treatment for all children, parents in Pennsylvania and beyond might expect more incidents resembling the one at J.T. Lambert. *(Chapter 9 will examine how schools in many states have moved into providing health services in school-based clinics without legislative approval.)*

Other signs that all is not well in schools across America were spotlighted in a column by Thomas Sowell published in the *Detroit News* in 1990. Sowell is one of the few national educators and columnists who consistently speaks out on weird and tragic occurrences in schools: He wrote:

A 1990 ABC-TV program *20-20* showed, among other things, high school students being taken to a morgue to touch dead bodies. Was this just some kooky teacher's idea? Not at all. This is part of a whole nationwide movement. Your local high school may have it—even if parents don't know about it.[25]

California legislative files included reports on children in a first grade "death ed" class being required to make their own little caskets from shoe boxes. Sowell added:

> "Death education" is only the tip of the iceberg. There is a whole spectrum of courses and programs designed to brainwash children into rejecting the values, beliefs and ways of life taught them by the parents—and to accept the latest fad thinking on subjects ranging from death to sex to social philosophies in general.
>
> In innumerable ways, some very subtle, these programs undermine, ridicule or otherwise sidetrack parents as irrelevant. Sometimes children are explicitly told not to tell anyone—including their parents—what is said in the "magic circle," as these classroom brainwashing sessions are often called.[26]

The "Don't Tell" instruction is common—and frequently disturbs parents who learn of it. "Explosions" erupted in a number of communities in rural Missouri in the mid-1990s, for example, when elementary schools trained staff members, including at least one janitor, as counselors. Their mission was conducting weekly "talk sessions" with students. Three poster-type, single-page guidelines for the sessions had nice messages. Two others sparked controversy. The three "nice" pages said:

> (1) LISTEN TO ONE ANOTHER: We will pay attention to one another's words and feelings. We will give each other caring, respect and consideration. (2) NO PUT DOWNS: We will encourage and support each other. Doing this will help others feel better about themselves, and will make us feel better about ourselves. (3) RIGHT TO PASS: We want you to be comfortable discussing things with the other members. You have the right to decide if you want to join the discussion.

Those guidelines express common courtesy and kindness. Two other pages sparked the controversy. One said:

> APPRECIATE EACH OTHER: Each of us brings different things to our group. We need to let others know how much we appreciate their contributions.

That sounds nice. But what if some of the "different contributions" violate the convictions of a child and his family—basic concepts of right and wrong? Would raising questions be considered a "put down?" This part of the exercise helps advance the humanist premise that all ideas and beliefs have equal merit and should be tolerated.

The final page of "guidelines" for young people participating in these weekly "sharing" groups featured an illustration picturing a large rubber stamp. It had stamped "CONFIDENTIAL" on the paper. The message said:

> Sometimes we might discuss things that are personal and private. We will not tell others about what we hear in our meetings.

A parent who obtained a copy of the five page outline for the "meetings" objected to the paper and the instructions to children not to tell others [parents?] about what was discussed. She duplicated the guidelines and showed up with a group of parents at the school board meeting requesting that the "meetings" be halted.

Sowell concluded his column which was headlined, "Schools Brainwashing Our Children," with these words:

> Back in 1984, the U.S. Department of Education held hearings in various parts of the country on such brainwashing practices. Although the government never published these hearings, Phyllis Schlafly collected much of the testimony in a book called *Child Abuse in the Classroom*. It should be required reading for every parent.[27]

Horror stories about academic tragedies, sex education, promotion of tolerance for homosexual practices,

violation of parents' rights, undermining the authority
and values of the home, and death education rightly get
attention. They also prompt the question, "How has it
all happened in America?" The answer is, of course, "It's
all part of creating a new social order—a new way of
life in America." The next chapter looks at the words of
the people who planned it.

CHAPTER 3

USING AMERICA'S SCHOOLS
TO CREATE "A NEW SOCIAL ORDER"

*The philosophy of the classroom in this generation
will be the philosophy of politics, government and
life in the next.* —*Abraham Lincoln*

UNDERSTANDING what is happening today in
America's schools would be impossible without a
knowledge of what radical educators proposed over
sixty years ago. Without a comprehensive overview of
how they planned to change the nation's way of life and
culture, few will believe that the "horrible examples"
described and documented in this book could actually
be happening.

The goal, which the radical educators spelled out in
their writings and speeches, was using the schools to
create "a new social order." By 1934, they had enough
clout and influence to control most teacher training
institutions, the rewriting of many textbooks and the
largest organization of teachers, the National Education Association.

Implementation of their plans in the 60 years since
has dramatically changed America's culture and ways
of living and the lives of several generations of young
Americans, many of whom are not now so young.

Known as "progressivists," or "Frontier Thinkers,"
the reformers were disciples of John Dewey, head of the
prestigious Teachers College at Columbia University
in New York. He was the nation's most influential
educator in the first half of the 20th Century. By the
1950s fully 20% of all American school superintendents
and 40% of all teacher college heads had received

advanced degrees under Dewey at Columbia. As an atheist and socialist, Dewey co-authored the revolutionary, anti-God, *Humanist Manifesto I* in 1934.

In the forefront of Dewey's "Frontier Thinkers," as the group called themselves, were Dr. George Counts, professor of education at Columbia, and Dr. Harold Rugg. Dewey's theories had been concerned chiefly with teaching methods. Counts and Rugg, known as "hard progressivists" added the concept of using the schools as an instrument for "building a new social order."

Harold Rugg concentrated on training teachers and writing teaching materials and books. In his book, *The Great Technology,* written for teachers in 1933, Rugg said:

> A new public mind is to be created. How? Only by creating tens of millions of new individual minds and welding them into a new social mind. Old stereotypes must be broken up and new "climates of opinion" formed in the neighborhoods of America.[1]

Later in his book, Rugg defined how the schools were to be used to transform American political and economic institutions and create the new "public mind" which would accept complete government control of the individual:

> ...through the schools of the world we shall disseminate a new conception of government—one that will embrace all of the collective activities of men; one that will postulate the need for scientific control and operation of economic activities in the interest of all people.[2]

Note that Rugg did not say "a new type of government" but a "new conception of government." Rugg was proposing that while the outward forms of government would stay the same its functions and powers would be transformed and expanded. This could be accomplished, he said, in three ways:

> *First and foremost*, the development of a new philosophy of life and education which will be fully appropriate to the new social order; *second*, the building of an adequate plan for the production of a new race of educational workers; *third*, the making of new activities and materials for the curriculum.[3]

He cooperated with George Counts on the first and second phases of the program while he played a major role in the rewriting of textbooks and curriculum materials to produce the "new philosophy of life and education."

A CONTROLLED ECONOMY

Dr. Counts made clear that the changes he envisioned would result in:

> ... a coordinated, planned and socialized economy.[8]

Accomplishing such a drastic remaking of America would involve many changes, Counts admitted. He said:

> Changes in our economic system will, of course, require changes in our ideals.[9]

Counts saw no wrong in abandoning even the traditional concepts of morality to achieve his goals. He pointed out in his book, *The Soviet Challenge To America* that even in Russia...

> ...new principles of right and wrong are being forged.[10]

TEACHERS CHALLENGED TO SEIZE POWER

To achieve the "new social order," Counts, in 1932, called for teachers of the nation to provide the impetus. In his monograph, *Dare the School Build a New Social Order?* Counts wrote:

> That the teachers should deliberately reach for power and then make the most of their conquest is my firm conviction. To the

extent that they are permitted to fashion the curriculum and procedures of the school they will definitely and positively influence the social attitudes, ideals and behavior of the coming generation.[13]

Counts published his *Dare the School Build a New Social Order?* in 1932. Some would say, "That's an interesting bit of ancient history. We're living over 65 years later." That's true, of course, but Counts' monograph is still used in training teachers and administrators today. For example, the widely used philosophy of education text, *Philosophical Foundations Of Education*, by Howard Ozman and Samuel Craver reprints key parts of Counts' monograph including the call for teachers to reach for power quoted above.[14]

GET CONTROL OF THE NEA TEACHERS UNION

In "reaching for power" the "Frontier Thinkers" moved in two directions as Rugg and Counts advocated. They rewrote the textbooks and in his call for teachers to grab for power, Counts said:

> Through powerful organizations they might at last reach the public conscience and come to exercise a larger measure of control over the schools than hitherto.

Counts and his fellow "Frontier Thinkers" in their grab for power gained the prestige of the largest professional teachers organization. They captured the top jobs and control of the National Education Association. At the 72nd annual meeting of the NEA in Washington, D.C. in July 1934, Dr. Willard Givens, then a California school superintendent, in a report entitled, *Education for a New America*, said:

> We are convinced that we stand today at the verge of a great culture...But to achieve these things many drastic changes must be made. A dying laissez-faire must be completely

destroyed, and all of us, including the owners, must be subjected to a large degree of social control.[15]

A year after delivering this call for destruction of free
enterprise and individual freedom (laissez-faire),
Givens was named executive secretary of the NEA, a
position he held for 17 years until his retirement in
1952. As will be detailed in Chapter 11, the NEA has
become possibly the nation's most powerful lobbying
organization. It doesn't just lobby for more money for
education. In the past decade NEA conventions annually pass a host of non-education, culture-transforming
resolutions supporting abortion, homosexuality, radical feminism, nuclear disarmament, world government, etc.[16]

In the process of using America's schools to create "a
new social order," John Dewey's progressivist "Frontier
Thinkers" also significantly dumbed down the basic
education given to America's young people—the fruits
of which were seen in Chapter 1. By the late 1950s,
many voices of alarm were being heard. One of the most
influential was Admiral Hyman Rickover, the father of
the nuclear submarine and our modern nuclear Navy.
In the late 1950s, just 25 years after the Dewey's
"Frontier Thinker" disciples moved to take control of
America's schools, Rickover spoke out, saying:

> America is reaping the consequences of the destruction of
> traditional education by the Dewey-Kilpatrick experimen-
> talist philosophy...Dewey's ideas have led to elimination of
> many academic subjects on the ground that they would not be
> useful in life...The student thus receives neither intellectual
> training nor the factual knowledge which will help him under-
> stand the world he lives in, or to make well-reasoned decisions
> in his private life or as a responsible citizen.[17]

WHAT DID JOHN DEWEY REALLY BELIEVE?

Who was this man, Dewey, who is so roundly criticized by the renowned Hyman Rickover, the "father" of the nuclear submarine? Dewey was identified briefly in the introduction to this chapter. The detrimental impact he had on American education warrants a further examination of the man and his philosophies.

John Dewey was an educational philosopher. His experimental philosophies of education were first tried in a model school at the University of Chicago before 1900. They were dismal failures. Children learned nothing. Undismayed, Dewey left Chicago in 1904 and went to Teachers College, Columbia University, where with the support of major "charitable foundations," he became the dominant figure and the most influential man in American education.

Dewey's disciples, under the pretext of improving teaching *methods*, changed *what was taught* to American children.

A CONFIRMED ATHEIST AND SOCIALIST

What did Dewey believe? As an atheist and a socialist, Dewey co-authored the revolutionary *Humanist Manifesto I* in 1934. Key points included:

> Religious humanists regard the universe as self-existing and not created....Humanism believes that man is a part of nature and that he has emerged as a result of a continuous [evolutionary] process....We are convinced that the time has passed for theism, deism, modernism, and the several varieties of "new thought"....It follows that there will be no uniquely religious emotions and attitudes of the kind hitherto associated with belief in the supernatural.[18]

Implementing the anti-God principles of humanism in his writing and teaching, Dewey rejected fixed moral laws and eternal truths and principles. He adopted pragmatic, evolutionist, relativistic concepts as his guiding philosophy. Dewey believed that because man's environment is constantly changing, man also changes constantly. Therefore, Dewey concluded, teaching children any of the absolutes of morals, government, or ethics was a waste of time.

He saw the destruction of a child's individualistic traits as the primary goal of education. Once this was accomplished the youngster would conform or adjust to whatever society in which he found himself. Ability to "get along with the group" became the prime measuring stick of a child's educational "progress."[20] Dewey summarized his theories, saying:

> Education, therefore, is a process for living and not a preparation for future living.[21]

THE END OF TRADITIONAL EDUCATION

Dewey laid the foundation for the future "destruction of traditional education" decried by Admiral Rickover when he said:

> We violate the child's nature and render difficult the best ethical results by introducing the child too abruptly to a number of special studies, of reading, writing, geography, etc. out of relation to his social life...the true center of correlation of the school subjects is not science, nor literature, nor history, nor geography, but the child's own social activities.[22]

INTO THE TEXTBOOKS

The introduction of a 1960s first grade "social studies" curriculum guide prepared by the Contra Costa County, California schools shows how Dewey's theories were implemented. It told teachers:

> No longer can history, geography and civics, taught separately as in the recent past, be considered adequate preparation for effective citizenship.[23]

Some would ask, "Why not?"

LEVELING DOWN TO THE GROUP'S LEVEL

The *group* is the nucleus of the progressive system. The long-established Washington newsletter, *Human Events,* revealed that to elevate and promote the "group," Dewey had to destroy individualism and the thinking which encourages it. The publication quoted Dewey as saying:

> Children who know how to think for themselves spoil the harmony of the collective society which is coming, where everyone is interdependent.[25]

No child is permitted to forge ahead of another. This would hurt the *group.* Automatic "social promotions" become the norm. Nobody is left behind because of poor work. This would disrupt the *group.* Grading and graded report cards showing actual percentages earned are frowned upon. Grading promotes competition. Competition breeds rivalry and encourages students to excel and rise above the *group.*

In the 1990s, Dewey's emphasis on the group has resulted in schools adopting the practice of "cooperative learning."

Rosalie Gordon wrote *What's Happened to Our Schools?* It was widely circulated in the early 1960s and said of Dewey's progressive education:

> The progressive system has reached all the way down to the lowest grades to prepare the children of America for their role as the collectivists of the future...The group—not the individual child—is the quintessence of progressivism. The child must always be made to feel part of the group. He must indulge in group thinking, in group activity.[26]

She explains Dewey's obsession with the group and group activity by saying:

> You can't make socialists out of individualists.[27]

Dewey was a socialist.[28] At the climax of his career in 1950, he became honorary national chairman of the League for Industrial Democracy, the American counterpart of the socialist British Fabian Society.[29] Fabians believed socialism could be achieved by a process of gradualism rather than Karl Marx's call for a violent revolution.

CUTTING A CULTURE'S TIES TO THE PAST

Dewey and his disciples wanted to create "a new social order." The first step in doing so was rewriting textbooks to prevent an upcoming generation from learning of the traditions, values, heroes and glorious accomplishments of their nation. The next chapter shows how it has been done.

It was in the area of new materials, textbooks, and teaching aids, that Dewey disciple Harold Rugg achieved greatest influence. He concentrated on the job of indoctrinating teachers and preparing teaching materials designed to "influence the social attitudes, ideals, and behavior of coming generations."

Completely new textbooks were needed. Rugg wrote them. They were called "social studies." All traditional presentations of subject matter was scrapped, and a variety of economic, political, historical, sociological, and geographical data was lumped into one textbook. With such a conglomeration of material in one book, the deletion or slanted presentation of key events, basic truths, facts and theories was not so evident.

MILLIONS DEPRIVED OF THEIR HERITAGE

Five million school children "learned" American political and economic history and structure in the 1930s from 14 social studies textbooks Rugg authored.[30] He also produced the corresponding

teachers' guides, course outlines, and student
workbooks.

So blatant was the downgrading of American heroes
and the U.S. Constitution, so pronounced was the anti-
religious bias, so open was the propaganda for socialistic control of men's lives in Rugg's textbooks that the
public rebelled.[31]

Rugg's textbooks went too far, too fast for complete
public acceptance. Thus, in 1940, the National Education Association began promoting a set of "social
studies" texts known as the *Building America* series.[33]
They were replacements for the discredited Rugg
series. They were widely adopted but a few years later
the Senate Investigating Committee on Education of
the California legislature condemned the NEA-spon-
sored series for subtly playing up Marxism and destroy-
ing American traditions.[34] The Senate committee
report...

> ...found among other things that 113 Communist-front or-
> ganizations had to do with some of the material in the books
> and that 50 Communist-front authors were connected with it.
> Among the authors are Beatrice and Sidney Webb, identified
> with the Fabian Socialist movement in Great Britain.[35]

Rugg's efforts and the efforts of others who followed
his lead had an effect. A dozen years later young
Americans went to Korea to fight. They had grown up
on the books produced by Rugg and others with similar
goals. Thousands of them became POW's. Unlike wars
before or since, nearly one-third collaborated with the
communist enemy. In their early months of captivity
nearly four out of every ten died from a new disease
Army psychiatrists called, "Give-Up-Itis."

A very unflattering professional evaluation of the
typical American was written by the Chief of the
Chinese Peoples Volunteer Army during the Korean

War. Prepared for his superior in Beijing, it fell into American hands. It said:

> The American soldier has weak loyalty to his family, his community, his country, his religion, and to his fellow soldier. His concepts of right and wrong are hazy and ill-formed. Opportunism is easy for him. By himself he feels frightened and insecure. He underestimates his own worth, his own strength, and his ability to survive.

> There is little understanding of American political history and philosophy, the federal, state, and community organizations, state and civil rights, freedom safeguards, checks and balances and how these things allegedly operate within his own system.

> He fails to appreciate the meaning of and the necessity for military or any other form of organization.[36]

It would be easy and reassuring to pass this capsule indictment off as Communist propaganda. However, without use of physical torture, drugs, intensive psychological treatment, coercion, or any of the other tactics usually associated with brainwashing, the Chinese Communists made collaborators of one-third of all American POW's who fell into their hands during the Korean War.[37]

This shocking record so astonished and concerned military authorities that a full-scale inquiry was conducted. The report of the Presidential Commission which made the study said pointedly:

> The uninformed POW's were up against it. They couldn't answer arguments in favor of communism with arguments in favor of Americanism because they knew so little about America.

Fifteen years after Korea many from another generation of poorly schooled young Americans, including a future President of the United States, ran off to Canada or used other methods for avoiding service in the U.S.

Armed Forces. They refused to fight communism in Viet Nam.

A NEW GENERATION WORKS IN EVERY AREA

Dewey, Counts, Rugg and most of the other "progressivist" culture-changers are long gone. But now, 65 years later, students shaped and influenced by the "new education" of Dewey and his "progressivists" control most of the basic culture-shaping institutions in our society. The press, the radio and TV and the entertainment industry and the government and its bureaucracy with trillion dollar budgets no longer promote and uphold traditional American values. Even many mainline churches, which should be defending traditional Bible-based values, have broken their ties to an authoritative Bible and support abortion, radical feminism, ordination of homosexuals, world government, etc.

Dewey is history, but a new generation of "reformers" is carrying on the war for a new society—a new way of life. (Their identity, words, and work will be discussed in Chapters 6-9.) These so-called "reformers" are using Goals 2000, School-to-Work and Outcome-Based Education to create a new way of living—a new culture for the upcoming generation. They are building on the "new foundations" Dewey and his followers laid as they used schools and textbooks to destroy the solid foundations on which America grew great. The next chapter documents how Dewey and his followers used the schools and textbooks in the transforming of America— in the creation of "a new social order."

CHAPTER 4

TEXTBOOKS DESTROY FOUNDATIONS OF AMERICA'S WAY OF LIFE

The fear of the Lord is the beginning of wisdom; and the knowledge of the holy is understanding.
—Proverbs 9:10

HENRY STEELE COMMAGER JR. was a Columbia University historian, educator and scholar. He also taught at Harvard and the University of Chicago. In the early 1960s he wrote the introduction for a paperback reissue of *McGuffey's Fifth Reader*. In his introduction he said:

> What is most impressive in the McGuffey readers is the morality. From the First Reader through the Sixth, the morality is pervasive and insistent, there is rarely a page but addresses itself to some moral problem, points up some moral lesson— industry, sobriety, thrift, propriety, modesty, punctuality— these were essential virtues and those who practiced them were sure of success....The world of the McGuffeys was a world where no one questioned the truths of the Bible, or their relevance to everyday conduct.

This renowned historian's evaluation of the McGuffey readers confirms that America and its schools once had a Biblical foundation which shaped the nation's culture and way of life. The books and the schools in which they were used for much of the 19th Century promoted character, responsibility and achievement. That's the culture and way of life "reformers" in the 1930s set out to replace with "a new social order." After acknowledging the thrust of the McGuffeys, Commager concludes with both a sneering attitude and troubled question. He wrote:

> That our children, today, are better taught than were their
> luckless predecessors is generally conceded, though we are
> sometimes puzzled that we have not produced a generation of
> statesmen as distinguished as the founding fathers.

Commager's pronouncement that "our children,
today, are better taught than were their luckless
predecessors..." is open to serious question and skep-
ticism. However, most would agree with Commager
that it would be hard to find men with the wisdom,
courage, ethics and selflessness of George Washington,
Thomas Jefferson, Benjamin Franklin or Abraham
Lincoln among the political leaders of today.

As Commager indicated, America was once a society
which had its roots in the Bible. The founding fathers
were the product of western civilization. That civilization developed over several centuries after Gutenberg
invented the printing press and published the Bible. In
a Bible-based society, America grew great on a foundation of twelve very basic concepts. They were
proclaimed in the nation's churches and taught in the
nation's homes and schools.

Before the "reformers" could establish their "new
social order" in America, the twelve foundational concepts which   shaped the nation, its people, its culture
and its leaders had to be destroyed. The foundational
concepts are:

(1) The Sanctity of Marriage and the Family
(2) No Sex Outside Marriage
(3) The Sanctity of Life
(4) The Sanctity of Private Property
(5) If You Are Able and Don't Work, You Don't Eat
(6) There are Absolutes of Right and Wrong
(7) The Sanctity of Written and Spoken Contracts
(8) National Independence and Sovereignty

(9) *Man's rights come, not from the government or a Constitution but from God (as the Declaration of Independence declares)*

(10) *Order Is Maintained in Society Through a System of Accountability to God's Authorities in the Family, Church and State*

(11) *The possibility that I'll have to answer later even if I get away with it now*

(12) *There is a God, that He is the Creator, that He revealed Himself through the Old and New Testaments, that He is Sovereign over the earth and that therefore man is responsible to Him for every action and decision*

For more than half a century, textbooks and other curriculum materials produced under humanist control have attacked and undermined these twelve foundational concepts, setting the stage for creation of "a new social order."

Foundational Concept #1.
MARRIAGE, FAMILY AND HOME
Have ye not read, that he which made them at the beginning made them male and female, And said, For this cause shall a man leave father and mother, and shall cleave to his wife: and they shall be one flesh? What therefore God hath joined together, let not man put asunder. —*Matthew 19:4-6*

NEW FAMILIES traditionally have been established by the marriage of one man and one woman. That was the standard in America's beginning. *The 1828 Webster's Dictionary* defined marriage in that century as:

> The act of uniting a man and woman for life; the legal union of a man and woman for life. Marriage is a contract both civil and religious, by which the parties engage to live together in

> mutual affection and fidelity, till death shall separate them. Marriage was instituted by God himself for the purpose of preventing the promiscuous intercourse of the sexes, for promoting domestic felicity, and for securing the maintenance and education of children.[3]

For over thirty years textbooks and other curriculum materials, personality tests, etc. have exhibited anti-family bias and a different view of marriage. *Land of the Free, A History of the United States* by Caughey, Franklin and May, a high school history book published by Benziger Brothers in 1966, ignored love and presented the Marxist view that men established families only to gain economic advantage. The book says that in the Colonial period:

> The family was the most important social unit....With labor so much needed, a wife and children were important to any young man who wanted to get ahead....Children were under the complete control of their father until they were grown. If a father wanted to send a child away to learn a trade, the child was expected to go. If he stayed at home, he would have to work as the father ordered, and he would be punished for any disobedience. (Page 106)

DIVORCE IS ACCEPTABLE

The Goodheart-Wilcox *Homemaking Skills For Everyday Living* takes a neutral position on the permanency of marriage. After acknowledging that some people believe marriage is forever, the book tells girls in sixth through eighth grades:

> Others have a "till love do us part" attitude toward marriage. They see marriage as a short term goal. They seem to expect that someday their love will come to an end. They plan to end their marriage at that time....Divorce is considered an acceptable way of solving the problem. (Pages 102, 107)

The undermining of families can start in kindergarten or first grade. A first grade "social studies" curriculum guide prepared years ago by the Contra Costa County, California schools says correctly that "every child of this age needs to feel that his family is adequate and competent to take care of his needs." However, a theme which then runs through the book undermines a first grader's attitude toward his father. Teachers are to focus on such problems as "Parents who commute to work have little time to spend with children in the evening" and "Fathers who travel have time with their children only on certain days." Children then memorize this poem titled "Newspaper" by Aileen Fisher:

I always hope father is going to play, with the paper in front of his face that way.

I think he might look from the edge and wink or peekaboo me, but what do you think?

He reads all the pages from A to Z and never once thinks of being Daddy to me.[4]

The child who has memorized that poem gets the message "Daddy doesn't care for me" whenever father reads the paper (as Dads ought to do to stay informed).

NEW READING METHOD CHANGES VALUES

Words in Color, a new method for teaching reading, was also a "vehicle" for transmitting changed values and ideas. Published by the Encyclopedia Britannica Press in the late 1960s, it was later distributed by the Xerox Corporation. In attempting to help students learn to read, words with different vowel sounds were printed in different colors.

An Ohio mother became concerned when halfway through the sermon in church she saw that her first grade daughter was writing "Sam is a filthy rat...Mom is a filthy rat...Dad is a filthy rat." A picture was drawn on the paper of a woman's body with a rat's head. It was labeled, "Mom."

Horrified, the mother asked, "Brenda, where did you learn anything like that?" The little girl replied, "In school, Momma." The mother visited the school and found a number of papers Brenda had written which said:

> Sam is a nut....tim is a nut....tom is a nut....pam is a nut....tim is filthy....mom is filthy....daddy is filthy....mom is a pest....dad is a pest.

On several papers the teacher had written "Good!"

The *Words in Color* workbook gives the first grader words such as "mom...pop...filthy...pest...rat...dad...sam... tim" and an "is." Then the child is instructed to "make sentences using words you now know." There are just so many ideas which can be expressed with those words.

A conservative congressman from Ohio, John Ashbrook, saw Brenda's papers and wrote:

> I'm 500 miles away in Washington but seeing this stuff makes my blood boil.

Eroding the student's view of the family shows up indirectly in every curriculum area. For example, the Scott Foresman Seventh Grade *Guide To Modern English* does an excellent job of teaching students to write. However, almost all of the examples used in illustrating writing techniques and in making writing assignments focus on family problems and unhappy circumstances. For example, as background in giving students a writing assignment, the text pictures a totally unhappy family, saying:

> Pat, a seventh grade student, has been told to write a theme about a family problem. The following is a stream of thoughts which went through Pat's mind soon after the assignment was given. "I guess my main family problem is that Mom and Dad just don't realize that I am growing up...Here I am almost thirteen years old and in seventh grade, but I have to get home

within fifteen minutes after school lets out, or phone to say where I am [this is unreasonable?]...And I have to be in bed by nine every night, even on weekends...I sure did want to stay up last Saturday and watch *The Big Suspense Hour*...I'm sorry I argued about it, though, because Dad got awfully sore...He said he was tired of the whole subject of TV....That was probably because Denny and Lois and I had argued so hard earlier in the day, about whether to watch cartoons or the two-hour movie...There sure is too much wrangling about TV in our house...Like yesterday, when Denny insisted on watching that program for high school kids, when I was dying to see the bowling matches...That reminds me of last week when.... [the illustration then details two additional family squabbles].[5]

After reading Pat's "thoughts," the student is asked to write a summarizing paragraph. In doing so, he is to (1) read and reread all the unhappy happenings in the family, (2) analyze, sort out and write the details presented, (3) write the paragraph and then (4) proofread it. In the process, the impression that the family is an unhappy place is made four times. Such exercises through the book reinforce the negative ideas about families.

The "generation gap" is fostered—if not caused—by instructional materials. For example:

The Family You Belong To from the Turner-Livingston Reading Series was used in Missouri schools and elsewhere in eighth grade family living classes. After reading numerous brief stories about families in constant turmoil, students are asked to "list things your family fights about most." Another lesson in the same book tells students that "ideas like things are bound to become outmoded and change from generation to generation." The student is then asked to list six old-fashioned things in his own home and six old-fashioned ideas his parents have. The unit on family living contains half a dozen similar units.

An occasional negative reference in a textbook or test won't destroy a good parent-child relationship. How-

ever, when the negative is emphasized continually, it
has an impact. Years ago, for example, Congressman
John Ashbrook (R-OH) introduced a bill to ban
psychological testing of students without advance permission from parents. To support his contention that
many tests were designed not to measure attitudes but
to implant them in the minds of students, Ashbrook
entered widely used personality tests into the *Congressional Record.* One of them, the Science Research Associates *SRA Youth Inventory* was given to secondary
school students throughout the nation. The test had
eight sections with 298 questions about attitudes
toward school, life, boy meets girl, home and family, etc.
Almost all of the questions conveyed totally negative
attitudes and the student was asked to answer "yes" or
"no." The home and family section has 52 questions of
which these were typical:

> There is constant bickering and quarreling in my home...I feel
> there's a barrier between me and my parents...I can't discuss
> personal things with my parents...My parents play
> favorites...My parents are too strict about letting me use the
> family car...I am ashamed of my father's job...My parents
> often pry into my private affairs...My father is a tyrant....I am
> ashamed of my parents' dress and manners.[6]

Including 52 such "questions" which convey negative
attitudes toward the family and parents could lead a
student to conclude, "My parents are just awful."

Attacks on marriage and the family continue today.
The New York-based Institute for American Values
evaluated how twenty social studies textbooks published between 1992 and 1996 treat marriage. The books
are being used in over 8000 college courses across
America. The September 1997 report concluded that
the books regard marriage as a relic with no place in a
street-smart society. It said:

These textbooks repeatedly suggest that marriage is more a problem than a solution....The potential costs of marriage to adults, particularly women, often receive exaggerated treatment, while the benefits of marriage, both to individuals and society, are frequently downplayed or ignored.[7]

If classroom and textbook attacks were the only influence undermining children's attitudes toward the family, many would survive. However, what children receive in school is reinforced by messages from the TV and entertainment media and all of the culture shaping institutions. Even national leaders get involved. For example, Hillary Clinton delivered a Mother's Day commencement address at George Washington University. Speaking of the American family, she said:

If it ever did, it no longer does consist of two parents, two children, a dog, a house with a white picket fence, and a station wagon in the driveway. Instead of families looking like the Cleavers on "Leave It To Beaver," we have families that include test tube babies and surrogate moms. Instead of Sunday night family dinners, we now have cross-country telephone conference calls. Instead of aunts and uncles and grandmas and grandpas, we have nannies and daycare centers.[8]

Dr. James Dobson, whose family-oriented *Focus on the Family* program broadcasts on over 2500 radio stations, supports traditional family values. He said:

Mrs. Clinton's remarks that day conveyed another message— that the traditional family is ineffectual and no longer viable. She expressed no regret over the social and governmental forces that have assaulted the institutions of marriage and parenthood. She did not urge graduates to preserve and support the traditional family unit. Nor did she speak of its vital role in the culture. Rather, Mrs. Clinton began with the supposition that families as we have known them are gone forever, and then suggested ways of replacing them.[9]

The attacks on marriage and family which start in textbooks have even affected the dictionaries. The 1951 *American College Dictionary* defined "family" as:

Parents and their children, whether dwelling together or not.

The 1995 *Webster's New American Dictionary* defines "family" differently. It says a family is:

A group of individuals living under one roof and under one head.

Governments use the new definition. In Ohio, the *Family and Children First Council* was created in 1992 by Governor Voinovich's Executive Order 92-212V. The Council's *Briefing Book* defines a family as...

...a group of people, related by blood or circumstances, who may rely on one another for sustenance, support, security, socialization and/or stimulation.

Such influences in schools and government are producing tragic results in society. In 1900, only one marriage out of 100 ended in divorce. By 1960, three out of ten went to court. By the 1990s, half of all new marriages were ending in divorce. And—those statistics don't give the entire grim picture. Because many young people don't get married before living together, when they "split" it doesn't show up statistically.

Foundational Concept #2
NO SEX OUTSIDE MARRIAGE

Be not deceived: neither fornicators, nor idolaters, nor adulterers, nor effeminate, nor abusers of themselves with mankind...shall inherit the kingdom of God. —*I Corinthians 6:9-10*

A "FOUNDATIONAL CONCEPT" which has protected the family (and society) down through the ages is: No sex before or outside of marriage. Therefore for most of America's history, laws against adultery, fornication, sodomy and sex with children were the basis for a stable and civilized society. If the traditional definition of marriage is held to, the concept of "no sex outside marriage" bans homosexual perversions which have destroyed every great society where they became accepted, including Sodom and Gomorrah, Greece and Rome. The "No sex outside marriage" concept is under attack today by the TV and entertainment media, in government and also in schools. Here are five examples of what textbooks have been exposing young people to in the last twenty years:

> Adolescent petting is an important opportunity to learn about sexual responses and to gratify sexual and emotional desires without a more serious commitment. (Picture caption, page 161, *Life and Health*, Random House, 1980, Grades 9-10.)
>
> Rarely is any harm done to the child by child molesters and exhibitionists...Oral-genital sex happens when one partner uses the mouth to stimulate the sex organs of the other....a large percentage of partners experiment with oral-genital sex. Many continue to practice it on a regular basis....a person with variant sexual interests is not necessarily bad, sick or mentally ill. (Pages 234, 59, 209, and 218, *Finding My Way*, Bennett, 1979, Grades 6-12.) The Teacher Guide for the book instructs the teacher to have the students "write a one sentence statement on "Why sex can be fun for an adolescent." (Page 10)

Delbert and Sally are living together while they are in college. They do not expect to marry...they feel that living together provides each with love, affection and support. (Page 278, *Person To Person,* Bennett, 1981, HS Homemaking.)

The place, the opportunity, and their bodies all say, "Go!" How far this couple goes must be their decision. (Picture caption, page 21, *Masculinity and Femininity,* Houghton-Mifflin, 1976, Grades 7-12 Sex Education.)

Everyone must develop his own set of principles to govern his own sexual behavior. (Page 189, *Psychology For Living,* McGraw-Hill, Webster Division, 1971.)

These texts and a host of others and the curriculum guides developed for sex ed classes basically follow guidelines for sex education classes developed and promulgated by the Sex Information and Education Council of the United States (SIECUS). SIECUS is the foremost proponent of "comprehensive sex education" and condom-based HIV/AIDS education. Excerpts from the guidelines SIECUS publishes[10] and promotes to schools are reproduced here word for word with great reluctance. Parents must see what children are being taught:

AGES 5-8: Both girls and boys have body parts that feel good when touched (p. 11); Sexual intercourse occurs when a man and a woman place the penis inside the vagina (p. 12); Some men and women are homosexual, which means they will be attracted to and fall in love with someone of the same gender (p. 15); Touching and rubbing one's own genitals is called masturbation (p. 32).

AGES 9-12: Sexual intercourse provides pleasure (p. 12); There are ways to have genital intercourse without causing pregnancy (p. 12); Homosexual love relationships can be as fulfilling as heterosexual relationships (p. 15); Members of the same family may have different values (p. 25); Masturbation is often the first way a person experiences sexual pleasure (p. 32); Many boys and girls begin to masturbate for sexual pleasure during puberty (p. 32); Masturbation does not cause physical or mental harm (p. 32).

AGES 12-15: Some of the reproductive organs provide pleasure as well as reproductive capability (p. 12); Some young people have brief sexual experiences with the other gender but mainly feel attracted to their own gender (p. 15); It is common for people to feel some attraction to men and women (p. 15); Sexual orientation cannot be changed by therapy or medicine (p. 15); Gay men, lesbian women, and bisexuals can lead fulfilling lives (p. 15) Masturbation, either alone or with a partner, is one way a person can enjoy and express sexuality without risking pregnancy or an STD/HIV (p. 33).

AGES 15-18: Teenagers who have questions about their sexual orientation should consult a trusted and knowledgeable adult (p. 16); The telephone number of the gay and lesbian switchboard is 1-212-...-.... (p. 16); For most people, sharing a sexual experience with a partner is the most satisfying way to express sexuality (p. 33); Some common sexual behaviors shared by partners include kissing, touching, caressing, massage, sharing explicit literature or art, bathing/showering together, and oral, vaginal, or anal intercourse (p. 33); Individuals are responsible for their own sexual pleasure (p. 33).

That SIECUS "guidelines" are a full implementation of the concepts on sexuality set forth in *Humanist Manifesto II* is not surprising. SIECUS founder Lester Kirkendall was a manifesto signer, as was Planned Parenthood President Alan Guttmacher. The *Humanist Manifesto II* states:

In the area of sexuality, we believe that intolerant attitudes, often cultivated by orthodox religions and puritanical cultures, unduly repress sexual conduct....While we do not approve of exploitive, denigrating forms of sexual expression, neither do we wish to prohibit, by law or social sanction, sexual behavior between consenting adults. The many varieties of sexual exploration should not in themselves be considered "evil"....individuals should be permitted to express their sexual proclivities and pursue their life-styles as they desire.[11]

On reading the SIECUS "guidelines" the most common reaction would be, "No school would teach such stuff!" Most schools will deny using SIECUS guidelines or materials. They claim to have developed their own sex-ed program using "community-based standards." However, recalling or rereading the excerpts presented from textbooks shows SIECUS philosophy is being implemented.

It's being done officially. In March 1994, the U.S. Center for Disease Control (CDC) made a five-year agreement with SIECUS "to promote comprehensive sexuality and HIV/AIDS education in America's schools." Included in SIECUS responsibilities under the CDC cooperative agreement is surveying and evaluating...

> ...each state program...addressing both the HIV/AIDS prevention and the sexuality curricula/guidelines, as well as the state infrastructure to support these programs...highlighting both the strengths and weaknesses of the existing programs, and offering specific recommendations and strategies for improvement. In addition, SIECUS will develop guidelines for states in the curricular areas that are most frequently omitted.[12]

That the federal CDC/SIECUS alliance is having an impact in the states was shown at the 16th annual Minnesota School Health Education Conference. It was held February 5-6, 1996 in Brooklyn Park, Minnesota, co-sponsored by Bethel College and Bemidji State University. A report prepared by Taxpayers For Excellence in Education said:

> Ruth Ellen Luehr, an official from the Minnesota Department of Children, Families and Learning, announced that the SIECUS guidelines are the framework for teachers to use in the public schools for K-12 sexuality education. She also

stated that the full sexual continuum—heterosexuality, bisexuality and homosexuality—is healthy and normal.[13]

That the problem is widespread was shown by a test the Illinois State Board of Education gave to 11th graders in 61 high schools during May 1998. The test included "health questions" that described various sexual acts in explicit terms. The program got widespread media attention and sparked responses from conservative groups. Giving the test was part of developing and testing a new "Illinois Goal Assessment Program" slated to debut in the spring of 1999.

Four of the questions given to high school juniors and seniors in 61 Illinois high schools were:

38. Which of these activities is least likely to expose a person to HIV?
    a. *Engaging in French kissing.*
    b. *Sharing IV drug needles.*
    c. *Having unprotected sexual intercourse.*
    d. *Receiving a blood transfusion.*

41. Which of these choices is the most effective way to avoid getting a sexually transmitted disease (STD)?
    a. *Having sexual intercourse only with people you know.*
    b. *Limiting the frequency of sexual intercourse.*
    c. *Always using a latex condom and foam during sexual intercourse.*
    d. *Having only oral sex with your partner.*

43. Of the following sexual behaviors, which would put a person at the greatest risk of getting the human immunodeficiency virus (HIV)?
    a. *Giving hand-genital stimulation without a latex condom.*
    b. *Receiving oral-genital stimulation without a latex condom.*
    c. *Masturbating.*
    d. *Vaginal intercourse without a latex condom.*

44. Of the following sexual behaviors, which would put a person at the least risk of getting the human immunodeficiency virus (HIV)?
    a. Engaging in open-mouthed kissing.
    b. Receiving hand-genital stimulation without a latex condom.
    c. Having anal intercourse with a latex condom.
    d. Giving oral-genital stimulation with a latex condom.

That students should be subjected to such questions and forced to make such "choices" is despicable. A Copley News Service story[14] by John O'Connor pointed out that the multiple choice answers gave students *no opportunity* to indicate that abstinence was the best way to avoid sexually transmitted diseases and HIV.

As the outcries and public shock grew, State School Superintendent Joseph Spagnolo issued a public apology[15] —but children in 61 Illinois high schools were exposed to the sexually-explicit descriptions and were forced to make the outrageous choices the test gave them. The State Board had actually instructed 63 schools to give the test. Just two of the 63 schools had the values or the courage to refuse after checking the questions.

Some readers may say, "I'm glad I don't live in Illinois!" Anyone with that response should know that Illinois got the questions from the Council of Chief State School Officers. Illinois officials said the questions received "pilot use" in other states also.

America's culture-shaping institutions have been influenced and are undermining the foundational concept of "No sex outside marriage." Schools are no exception.

THE SANCTITY OF LIFE

Who knoweth not in all these that the hand of the Lord hath wrought this? In whose hand is the soul of every living thing, and the breath of all mankind....Thou shalt not kill.

— *Job 12:9-10, Exodus 20:13*

THE MARRIAGE RELATIONSHIP normally produces children, creating a family. The unborn, the limited and infirm and the aged have all, traditionally, had the protection of laws which were supported by the teaching of schools and churches. That's no longer true. The Sanctity of Life is being assaulted. Rinehart & Winston's Biology II text, *Biology*, for example, tells students:

> Since the dawn of history, human beings and other (particularly social) animals have regulated their reproduction....Thus valuable energy has not been spent on offspring that are not likely to survive....Induced abortion is probably the oldest human birth control method known. Abortion was accepted, and fairly common, in the United States and Europe until the early nineteenth century....Religious and ethical opposition did not develop until some time later. (Pages 578-79)

Promoting acceptability of abortion is an implementation of the affirmations of *Humanist Manifesto II* which states:

> The right to birth control, abortion and divorce should be recognized. (Page 18)

School-based clinics in many states can dispense condoms and refer children to an abortion provider without parental permission or notification.

"Death education" in "health" and other books may be a factor in increased teenage suicide. A typical passage is:

> THE EXPERIENCE OF DYING...the individual experiences a cosmic consciousness, characterized by a sense of unity with other people, nature, and the universe, a feeling of being outside time and space; and extraordinary feelings of contentment and ecstasy. (Page 530 *Life and Health*, Random House, 1980, Grades 9-10 Health.)

How does the author know this? Might this promote suicide? A Ginn & Company 10th grade "literature" book, *New Voices*, included this "poem" discussing ways of suicide:

> Razors pain you.   Gas smells awful;
> Rivers are damp;   You might as well live.
> Acids stain you; and   Yeah, you might as well live.
> drugs cause cramp.   Suicide is a bit grim.
> Guns aren't lawful;   Now if only I could think
> Nooses give;   of a better way

During the 1992-93 school year 6th and 7th grade students in Palm Desert, California, were shown a video titled, *CARL*. Sequences in the film showed a boy being teased and praying to God for help. Then the hymn "Amazing Grace" played as the video showed the silhouette of the boy's body hanging in his room. The funeral message was:

> We are here to celebrate the death of Carl, for he is now experiencing happiness that eluded him in life....From this day on he will find a better life.

This video was written and produced by a Waseca, Minnesota firm and was marketed to schools across America. Might its message push an unhappy teenager to end it all?

In 1962, before schools started "death education" 550 teenagers killed themselves.[16] By 1987, teen suicides were approaching 6000 annually. Could "death ed" classes and use of films like *CARL* be stimulating students to consider ending it all? Some authorities believe there could be a correlation. On September 10, 1991 *USA TODAY* reported that schools claim that...

> ...they have suicide-prevention programs, but an article in the *Journal of the American Medical Association* last December indicates various of these programs seem actually to be stimulating students to consider suicide. (Page A10)

Such "death education" programs stem from the *Humanist Manifesto II's* seventh affirmation which states:

> To enhance freedom and dignity the individual must experience a full range of *civil liberties* in all societies. This includes...a recognition of an individual's right to die with dignity, euthanasia, and the right to suicide.

Foundational Concept #4

THE SANCTITY OF PRIVATE PROPERTY

Thou shalt not steal....Thou shalt not covet thy neighbor's house...nor his ox, nor his ass, nor anything that is thy neighbor's. —*Exodus 20:15,17*

THE RIGHT OF OWNERSHIP of property is derived directly from the sanctity of life. To acquire property an individual has to invest some part of his life. (Teen-agers, for example, need to understand that if they burn the tires off their father's car, they are stealing part of his life—the hours he invested working to get the tires.)

With humanist rejection of "the right to life" and their socialist orientation, they also reject the sanctity of private property. In *Humanist Manifesto I*, John Dewey and his fellow humanists stated:

> The humanists are firmly convinced that existing acquisitive
> and profit-motivated society has shown itself to be inadequate
> and that a radical change in methods, controls, and motives
> must be instituted.

Once America was relatively free of class hatred. The
progressivists realized that it would be impossible to
pit one class against another for political gain, if such
classes did not exist, or were without basic antagonism.
Dr. George Counts proposed that the schools should
disrupt this stabilizing influence in America. In the
magazine, *The Social Frontier,* he wrote:

> In view of the absence of a class mentality among workers, it
> would be reasonable to assume that it is the problem of
> education to induce such a mentality rather than to take an
> existing mentality and base a course of action upon it.[17]

This cruel and cynical admonition to the educators of
America to purposefully promote class strife and bitter-
ness against property owners and the profit motive was
an open acceptance of Lenin's strategy of "incite one
against another." In the 50 years since, many textbook
authors have been carefully following the Counts advice. Class hatred is induced in students by presenting
American history as a prolonged class struggle between
those who have property and those who don't, as these
examples show. In describing the American Revolution, Craven and Johnson in their textbook, *The United
States: Experiment in Democracy,*[18] tell the student:

> The *upper class*, numerically weak, consisted of those who
> owned so much wealth that they did not have to engage in
> manual labor....they joined in the American cause, but with
> the full intention of checking later the aspirations of the
> *average citizen* for a more democratic way of life. (pages 60,
> 103)

This is the Marxist view of American history, first
propagated early in this century by Charles Beard in

An Economic Interpretation of the Constitution. It has been followed blindly by many textbook writers, even though Beard later repudiated his interpretation as faulty.

Faulkner, Kepner and Merrill in *History of the American Way*,[19] use the same theme to describe the Constitutional Convention:

> ...the delegates were *conservative* or slow to change. And that is easy to understand. They were the *property holding class*. (Page. 71)

The delegates were "conservative" in that they drew upon the accumulated wisdom and experience of the past in framing the Constitution of the new nation. To describe them "as slow to change" is absurd.They instigated, financed, and fought the American Revolution. The authors also fail to tell the student that when the Constitution was written, over 90% of *all* Americans were property holders.

With the foundation for the class struggle firmly laid, business, free enterprise, and profits are painted as the source of all evil, just as Counts, Rugg, and other "Frontier Thinkers" recommended. Gavian and Hamm in *The American Story*[20] defame business and stir class hatred by quoting Mary Lease, an English socialist, who said:

> Wall Street owns the country. It is no longer a government of the people, by the people, and for the people, but a government of Wall Street, by Wall Street, and for Wall Street. The parties lie to us...the people are at bay; let the bloodhounds of money who have dogged us thus far beware! (Page 401)

Gavian and Hamm do not counterbalance this quotation by pointing out that nearly every American family has a stake in Wall Street. Over 25% of American families own stock in industry directly. Almost all others share in some way through insurance policies, company pension plans, or union welfare programs whose assets are invested in Wall Street. All Americans have a stake in protecting the right of ownership and use of private property.

Even so, student discussions and role playing are used to undermine property rights. For example, the Scott Foresman HS Geography text, *Land and People,* gave these instructions:

> Develop a skit based upon the need to redistribute land. The main characters should be wealthy landowners, landless farmers, and government officials. Let each explain how the redistribution would affect them, and have each suggest possibilities of solving the problem so all would benefit.[21]

Textbook attacks on private ownership of property, on business and profits continues today. (To acquire property individuals must make a "profit"—they must live on less than they earn with the excess being the "profit" which they can invest in acquiring property.) Radical environmentalism undermines business and industry and the rights of owners to use their property. The attacks in school start early and very subtly. For example, the 1989 second grade Scott Foresman text, *Discover Science,* focuses repeatedly and to a degree correctly, on the harmful effects of "pollution." Automobiles and factories were cited repeatedly as two major sources of pollution. By page 171, the students are asked to match three pictures with descriptive words. The three words were "ground water," "dam" and "polluted." The "matching pictures" showed a dam, an old-fashioned hand pump, and a factory. When a second grader was asked on the same page to define a factory he wrote, "a place that pollutes." His mother, upset when she checked his work, pointed out that it was in a factory that his father worked to support the family. On page 270, the book's glossary used words from the book in sentences. For "factory" the illustrating sentence said: "Smoke from a factory can pollute the air."

Foundational Concept #5
IF YOU DON'T WORK, YOU DON'T EAT

For even when we were with you, this we commanded you, that if any would not work, neither should he eat. — *II Thessalonians 3:10*

THE CLASS STRUGGLE THEME is the vehicle used in numerous texts to openly advocate cradle-to-grave welfare. F. A. Magruder's *American Government* (1952) equates opposition to the welfare state with selfishness of the few. In a section blatantly entitled, "Welfare of the People from the Cradle to the Grave," Magruder says:

> The United States has increasingly *curbed the selfish* and provided for the *welfare of the many*. The Government has established the Children's Bureau to look after the welfare of *every* child born in America. (Page 15)

Magruder's text, *American Government*, is a study in propaganda techniques in itself. The class struggle idea is reinforced in this passage which uses a false premise to discourage thrift, saving, and family responsibility and justify welfare payments for all:

> Because of sickness, accidents, and occasional unemployment, it is *difficult or impossible* for a laborer who has reared a family to save from his meager wages. And it is more just to place all the burden of supporting those who have been unfortunate, *or even shiftless,* upon everybody instead of upon some dutiful son or daughter who is not responsible for the condition. (Page 339)

A 1983 Allyn & Bacon text, *Civics, Government and Citizenship*, gave eighth graders this class assignment:

DISCUSS: Some people feel that the government should pay every family in the United States a minimum amount every year if they do not earn that amount by working. Would you support such an idea? If so, how much should the amount be? If not, why not? (Page 407)

Ideas taught in class do have consequences. Within a few years, such a program was instituted under the so-called "Earned Income Credit." The idea had its source originally in *Humanist Manifesto II* which says...

> ...society should provide means to satisfy basic economic, health, and cultural needs including...a minimum guaranteed annual income [apparently whether they work or not].

Indoctrination in the availability and "rightness" of the "free" handout is not limited to older students. The attack on the Biblical concept, "If you are able and don't work, you don't eat," starts in the first grade. Recall the Biblically-based story about the wise, hard-working little squirrel who gathered and stored nuts for the winter. It was once taught to first graders and had a moral: Work hard and save for uncertain days ahead.

That story has been rewritten. The new version is entitled, "Ask for It." In it, a little squirrel named, Bobby, ate nuts from a tree during the summer. Other squirrels suggested that Bobby put some nuts away for winter. As Bobby Squirrel didn't like to work, he ignored the advice. Here's what happened:

> Winter came and one morning Bobby awakened to find the world covered with snow——and all the nuts were gone from the tree. He got awfully hungry but remembered that a boy who lived in a *white house* had taken some of the nuts from *his* tree during the summer. Bobby went to the *white house* and gave a squirrel call. A door opened and a "fine brown nut" rolled out.

Bobby Squirrel learned his lesson. The story concluded:

> Well! thought Bobby, I know how to get my dinner. All I have to do is ask for it.

This story was in the widely used first grade reader, *Our New Friends*, published by Scott Foresman and Company in 1956.

With the school children of America having been educated in this philosophy for over 50 years, is it any wonder that total government expenditures for welfare have risen from less than $5-billion annually during the depths of the Great Depression in the 1930s to where "Entitlement Payments" were approaching a trillion dollars annually by 1997.

Foundational Concept #6
RIGHT AND WRONG ARE ABSOLUTES

For ever, O Lord, thy word is settled in heaven....Heaven and earth shall pass away but my words shall not pass away....the word of the Lord endureth for ever.
>   —Psalm 119:89, Matthew 24:35, I Peter 1:25

THE STABILITY OF ANY SOCIETY and the relationships of people and organizations within the society must be based on trust and shared understandings. Being able to trust in the basic honesty and the words and promises of others in the family, the workplace, the church, the school and government is foundational. That foundation must stem from the concept that there are certain unchanging absolutes of right and wrong. Concepts of right and wrong set forth and supported in the McGuffey readers of a century ago have been undermined for the young people of recent generations by revisionist textbooks and curriculum materials. In Allyn & Bacon's 1978 high school psychology book, *Inquiries In Sociology*,[22] students read:

> There are exceptions to almost all moral laws, depending on the situation. What is wrong in one instance may be right in another. Most children learn that it is wrong to lie. But later they may learn that it's tactless, if not actually wrong, not to lie under certain circumstances. (Page 45)

The Teacher's Edition of the 1980 Houghton-Mifflin sixth grade social studies text, *Around Our World*[23] tells teachers:

> Stress that whether a specific action is right or wrong depends on the meaning that a given group attaches to the action. (Page 70)

Such textbook teaching has its source in the *Humanist Manifesto II* which states:

> We affirm that moral values derive their source from human experience. Ethics is *autonomous* and *situational,* needing no theological or ideological sanction. (Page 17)

A commonly used manual for teachers in Pennsylvania schools dealing with Junior High students reads:

> The development of values must be seen as a lifelong process which recognizes changing circumstances rather than a fixed set of unyielding principles. Rather than reacting to a predetermined, fixed moral code, youngsters must be encouraged to develop a self-determined value system which reflects respect for self, others, and things.

In a Pennsylvania House of Representatives speech in 1997, Rep. Sam Rohrer said of this teachers' manual:

> Do you understand what's being said here? By rejecting a fixed moral code, children are taught that there is no such thing as absolute truth. They are told that there is nothing always wrong or right. Therefore, by natural deduction, the rules of their parents are not right and they should question them, doubt them, and frankly reject them. The even larger concept being

taught is that by logical extension, the entire basis for our Constitution, American law and justice, and ultimately God and His moral law don't apply.[24]

In Silver Burdett's Grade 5 social studies book *Man and Society*,[25] the student is told in pages 10 and 11 that "It is important to work hard," "You should tell the truth" and "Stealing is bad." A parent examining the child's text would see these good values. However, in instructing the teacher on how to present this lesson, the Teacher's Edition on page 11 says:

> Let each pupil decide for himself how he feels about each. Emphasize that this is not a test, and there are no "right" or "wrong" answers.

Field's High School history book, *Perspectives In United States History*, tells students that the value system based on absolutes of right and wrong has passed away and, in effect, situational ethics is OK. The book says:

> The moralistic value system remained firm in rural areas and small towns of America until World War II...since World War II, rural and small town America began to pass into history. Today urban America, with a changing set of values, is taking over....Protestant evangelists continue to crisscross the land, attempting to revitalize the old religion, the old culture....They preach the old values, the old standards, the "old-time religion"...But now they represent a waning culture. (Page 514)

For several generations schools and even churches have promoted "situational ethics" rather than the concept that there are absolutes of right and wrong that do not change. As a result, research, by George Barna and Associates in 1994-95, found that 71% of Americans surveyed reject the concept of absolute truth. Even more disturbing, 61% of those who claimed to be born-again Christians concluded that "there is no such thing as absolute truth."[26]

How has it happened? How and why have schools and textbooks (and much of society and life) moved away from the foundational concept that there are absolutes of right and wrong?

Chuck Colson has an answer. Colson became a Christian after his "wheeling and dealing days" as a White House attorney and confidante of Richard Nixon during Watergate. As to why society has moved away from moral absolutes, Colson in the *Breakpoint* radio commentaries on 350 stations in early 1998, said:

> It's the logical outgrowth of the denial of God in science classes.

He explained:

> Darwinism [evolution] is not just about fossils and mutations. It also entails a complete worldview—called naturalism—that allows for nothing but nature and natural causes and denies any transcendent purpose to life....From elementary school on, Americans are taught that the universe needs no God to explain it, that Darwinian evolution is enough to explain where we came from.

There are logical consequences from teaching such a theory, starting in the earliest grades. Colson said:

> If there is no God, then obviously we have to throw out the idea that God has revealed absolute, universal truths, valid for all people to live by. Without divine revelation, each person is locked into the limited perspective of their own race, gender or ethnic group.

The rejection by textbooks, and by much of society, of the foundational concept that there are absolutes of right and wrong is a logical outgrowth of the evolutionary teachings of science that eliminate God and His law. As a result, every student does that which is right in his own eyes.

SANCTITY OF CONTRACTS

The Lord Jesus said: But let your communication be Yea, yea; Nay, nay; for whatsoever is more than these cometh of evil. —*Matthew 5:37*

AS "SITUATIONAL ETHICS" have replaced the concept that there are unchanging absolutes of right and wrong, agreements or contracts made between people in spoken or written form lose their value, depending on the *situation*. Examples are:

In 1994, major league baseball players signed multi-million dollar contracts to play 162 baseball games. When August came, they either found a "loop-hole" in their contracts, or ignored them, and the rest of the season and the World Series were canceled.

A major factor in George Bush's election in 1988 was his pledge to the Republican convention and the American people that year in which he said: "Read My Lips—No New Taxes!" Breaking that promise—that *contract*—with the American people after he won the White House was a major factor contributing to his defeat by Mr. Clinton in 1992.

Court dockets are clogged with cases which stem from people looking for loopholes to escape from even their written agreements and contracts.

The million-plus divorces each year result when husbands and wives ignore pledges (contracts) made to stay together "from this day forward, for richer for poorer, in sickness and in health, to love and to cherish, till death do us part."

The United States Constitution, as written, was a contract between the states and the new federal government. Its purpose was to limit the areas in which the federal government could operate. Article 1, Section 8 spelled out specifically the only areas in which Con-

gress was to have the power to legislate. Much of the
rest of the Constitution sets forth "thou shalt nots"
which apply to the federal or state governments. The
10th Amendment went a step further. It limited the
federal government to those things it was specifically
permitted to do by the Constitution. It reads:

> The powers not delegated to the United States by the Constitu-
> tion, nor prohibited by it to the states, are reserved to the States
> respectively, or to the people.

These limitations on the powers of the federal government were written by men who knew the sinful nature
of man. They knew from history that governments
always restrict man's freedom by controlling or taking
the fruits of his labor.

If the Constitution (a contract) were to be applied
today as it was written, there would be no $5-trillion
federal debt. There would be no need for a federal
income tax. The federal government would not have a
million bureaucrats and 60,000 armed agents from
dozens of agencies involving themselves in every area
of a citizen's life, business, farming, transportation,
education, etc. (Read Article 1, Section 8 of the Constitution to see in how many of these areas the federal
government is authorized to operate.)

As spelled out previously in the section on the sanctity
of private property, textbook authors Todd and Curti
and others, in writing of America's history, laid the
foundations for undermining the Constitution (a contract). They presented American history as a class
struggle. They pictured the founding fathers as greedy
men looking to protect their property and hold down
the "poor." This handling of the U.S. Constitution by
textbook writers demonstrates a commonly used
propaganda technique. Instead of directly attacking

the provisions of the Constitution, they impugn the motives of the men who wrote it.

F. A. Magruder, in his *American Government,* uses a different technique. Instead of smearing the men who wrote the Constitution as some textbooks do, he openly admits that important Constitutional safeguards are being by-passed today—breaking the contract. The student is given the impression that such infringement on constitutional guarantees against an all-powerful government is "sophisticated and progressive." Magruder says:

> The principle of checks and balances in government is not held in such esteem today as it was a century ago. The people no longer fear the officers whom they elect every few years. (Page 73)

The people of Germany elected Hitler in 1933. Because they didn't "fear" him they ignored the checks and balances of the German constitution. They allowed him to assume more and more power. As a result they never had an opportunity to vote him out. Students don't learn that from Magruder—or other textbook writers.

Once students have accepted "situational ethics," guided class discussions can be used cleverly to bring them to believe the Constitution is outmoded. The teacher's manual for the McGraw-Hill/Webster Division 1980 high school text, *American Government* tells teachers to start a discussion of "OUR LIVING CONSTITUTION" this way:

> ...ask students whether they would consider going to a dentist...[or] use a doctor who practiced medicine as it was practiced in the thirteen colonies?...ask them how they manage to live under a United States Constitution that is 200 years old. Is that Constitution as out of date as the dental and medical techniques of 200 years ago? (Page 75)

Such "guided" discussions condition students to see the "wisdom" of ignoring or reinterpreting much of the "outmoded" Constitution. The Constitution is pictured as "a living document" which is being "evolved" by today's wise men to meet today's problems. That's a far cry from what our founders envisioned. Even so, the author of the 1991 Houghton-Mifflin eighth grade social studies text, *A More Perfect Union* tells students:

> The Constitution is not a rigid document. Because of imprecise language in some sections, it is <u>open to interpretation.</u> Most historians feel that this is more of a strength than a weakness. A level of interpretation is ensured, while another level can be <u>reinterpreted by successive generations.</u> ...By <u>unofficial [change] method</u> is meant...<u>the Supreme Court's interpretation</u>...which <u>differs sometimes depending on the views of new justices.</u> (Emphasis added.)

An educational researcher Michael J. Chapman did an exhaustive review of the book. He concluded:

> Children are being taught that moral-relativism is a virtue built into our Constitution. Without accountability to absolute law, legislation is vaguely written and then left up to the courts to define "depending on the views of new justices."[27]

Thomas Jefferson foresaw this possibility and warned future justices about the danger. On June 12, 1823 he wrote to Justice William Johnson:

> On every question of construction, carry yourselves back to the time when the Constitution was adopted, recollect the spirit manifested in the debates, and instead of trying what meaning may be squeezed out of the text, or invented against it, conform to the probable one in which it was passed.

In his Farewell Address, George Washington gave a similar warning. He called upon future Americans to be vigilant and "resist with care the spirit of innovation" which would alter constitutional principles "to undermine what cannot be directly overthrown."

If freedom is to be maintained, contracts, whether written or spoken by men, by businesses, or by governments must mean what they say. That was the message young people learned from the McGuffey Readers a century ago—a message missing in most textbooks today.

Foundational Concept #8

PROTECTING NATIONAL SOVEREIGNTY

Blessed is the nation whose God is the Lord; and the people whom he hath chosen for his own inheritance. —Psalm 33:12

NATIONAL SOVEREIGNTY—keeping the United States as a free and independent nation—is vital to maintaining the culture and way of life traditionally regarded as being "American."

Here's why: Under faulty Supreme Court interpretations of Article Six of the U.S. Constitution, if America should lose its sovereignty to the United Nations, the UN Charter and its policies and programs would supersede the Constitution and become the "law of the land."

What would that mean? Consider that the UN has population control policies similar to those of Red China. In China when any woman gets pregnant a second time, the baby is aborted forcibly. So, even if the U.S. Constitution should be amended to protect the life of the unborn, it would be meaningless if national sovereignty is lost. Likewise, freedom of speech and religion, the right to keep and bear arms, etc. would all be in jeopardy. Those rights, seemingly granted by the UN Charter, are limited by the words: <u>unless they conflict with government policies.</u> That's significantly different from our Bill of Rights which forbids government to interfere with the exercise of our rights!

Since World War II, propaganda for world government under the United Nations has been added to textbook promotion of a collectivist society envisioned by Counts and Rugg. Replacing national sovereignty was called for by the *Humanist Manifesto II* which said:

> We deplore the division of humankind on nationalist grounds. We have reached a turning point in human history where the best option is to transcend the limits of national sovereignty and to move toward the building of a world community.

The drive to transcend national sovereignty was spearheaded in America by the National Education Association. The NEA effort is part of a world-wide movement by UNESCO, the United Nations Educational, Scientific, and Cultural Organization. President Truman's Commission on Higher Education in 1947 gave its official blessing to the drive. Its report had these recommendations:

> The role [to transcend national sovereignty] which education will play officially must be conditioned essentially by policies established in the State Department in this country, and by ministries of foreign affairs in other countries. Higher education must play a very important part in carrying out in this country the program developed by UNESCO...The United States Office of Education must be prepared to work with the State Department and with UNESCO.[28]

What was the UNESCO program which the Presidential Commission recommended American schools should implement? The nine-volume 1947 UNESCO study, *Towards World Understanding*, has been the blueprint for conditioning American children for the day when their first loyalty will be to a socialistic one-world government under the United Nations.

The work of Counts and Rugg laid the foundation for the eventual destruction of the U.S. Constitution and our free market system so that America could be easily merged into a socialistic world federation under UN-ESCO guidelines. UNESCO's Director General, under whom the plan was prepared, was Julian Huxley. He was an atheistic philosopher, a British socialist and a signer of *Humanist Manifesto II.*

The goal of UNESCO was stated plainly in the study's first volume. It recommended that children should be educated in...

> ...those qualities of citizenship which provide the foundation upon which international government must be based if it is to succeed.[29]

Under Huxley, UNESCO envisioned that destruction of children's love of country and patriotism was the first step towards education for world citizenship. The report said on the opening page of Volume V, *In the Classroom with Children Under Thirteen Years of Age*:

> Before the child enters school his mind has already been profoundly marked, and often injuriously, by earlier influences...first gained, however dimly, in the home.

The attack on home and parents continues. On page 9 of Volume V of the UNESCO report, the teacher is told:

> The kindergarten or infant school has a significant part to play in the child's education. Not only can it correct many of the errors of home training but it can also prepare the child for membership, at about age seven, in a group of his own age and habits—the first of many such social identifications that he must achieve on his way to membership in the world society.

Note the UNESCO attitude toward the family, the sanctity of which is the very first of the foundational concepts for America's culture and traditional way of life. Within 25 years, the UNESCO attitudes were being openly advocated in education circles. At the Childhood International Education Seminar in Denver

in 1973, Chester M. Pierce, M.D., a professor of education and psychiatry at Harvard, told educators at the
meeting:

> Every child in America entering school at the age of 5 is
> mentally ill because he comes to school with certain allegian-
> ces to our founding fathers, toward our elected officials,
> toward his parents, toward a belief in a supernatural being, and
> toward the sovereignty of this nation as a separate entity. It's
> up to you as teachers to make all these sick children well—by
> creating the international child of the future.[30]

After guarded references to the "injurious influence"
of the family on the young child, the UNESCO study
makes it plain that the errors of home training include
parental encouragement of patriotism. On page 58, the
guidebook for teachers says:

> As we have pointed out, it is frequently the family that infects
> the child with extreme nationalism. The school should there-
> fore use the means described earlier to combat family at-
> titudes.

Among the "means described earlier" are the suppres-
sion of American history and geography which might
enhance pro-American sentiments of the children. UN-
ESCO gives specific suggestions in Volume V, page 11,
on how this can be done:

> In our view, history and geography should be taught at this
> stage as universal history and geography. Of the two, only
> geography lends itself well to study during the years
> prescribed by the present survey (3-13 years). The study of
> history, on the other hand, raises problems of value which are
> better postponed until the pupil is freed from the nationalist
> prejudices which at present surround the teaching of history.

Translated, this means that if the grade school student is taught American history early and objectively,
he is likely to realize that America's government,

economics, and social values outstrip those found anywhere else in the world.

Twenty years later, the U.S. Undersecretary of Education Gary Bauer in 1986 told textbook publishers that their books were...

> ...hypercritical of American institutions while glossing over the faults of the Soviet Union and other totalitarian governments.[31]

He added that textbooks "should not be written as if they were written by neutrals in the struggle between freedom and slavery."

After recommending that American students be denied full knowledge of the greatness of their nation, UNESCO admits that detailed study of foreign countries will lead the student to the conclusion that America is a better place to live. This problem was solved by recommending that teachers obscure the truth from their pupils in this way:

> Certain delicate problems, however, will arise in these studies and explorations. Not everything in foreign ways of living can be presented to children in an attractive light. At this stage, though, the systematic examination of other countries and manners can be postponed, and the teacher need seek only to insure that his children appreciate, through abundant and judicious examples, that foreign countries, too, possess things of beauty, and that many of them resemble the beauty and interest of his own country. A child taught thus about the different countries of the world will gradually lose those habits of prejudice and contempt which are an impediment to world-mindedness.

Thus, UNESCO recommends the deliberate "under education" of children. The student who does not know or understand the accomplishments of America and the shortcomings of the rest of the world is more likely to accept a "world government." Recommended 50 years ago, the UNESCO program is being implemented in schools today. It's a program for "globalism" and it is called "multi-culturalism." The student who knows nothing of the horrors of the communist system in Russia and the failures of socialism everywhere it has been tried, might well agree to a communist-influenced socialistic one-world government.

Because the United Nations has no real successes of its own to point to, textbooks have frequently given the UN credit for winning World War II. *History of America* by Southworth was widely used in the 1950s as an eighth grade history text. The text incorrectly tells how when a great invasion force was assembled in England to assault Hitler's Europe...

> General Dwight Eisenhower of the United States Army came from the Italian front to command this mighty new United Nations force. (Page 769)

Captions on the photographs show "United Nations troops going ashore on D-Day" and "The United Nations beachhead on the French coast." There is only one thing wrong with the story. D-Day, when Allied forces landed on the French coast, was June 6, 1944. The United Nations was founded in San Francisco at a conference which opened on April 25, 1945—ten months *after D-Day*.

The war in the Pacific was pictured similarly. The student who has been taught that the United Nations protected America from Nazism and Mussolini's Fascism, would see nothing wrong with looking to the U.N. to maintain world peace and freedom. The Southworth text was not an isolated example. Almost fifteen years later, in the mid-1960s, the Prentice-Hall text, *Our Nation from Its Creation,* by Nathaniel Platt and Muriel Jean Drummond and a companion 10th grade world history text by the same authors, used the same approach. In a review the Richmond, Virginia *News Leader* said of the book:

> In its discussion of the campaigns of World War II, it uses terminology that will come as a great surprise to many of the men who fought in those campaigns.

> Throughout the text, in both headlines and narrative, the authors refer to Allied campaigns as having been waged by the "United Nations"....The text is absurd with casual references made to "Commander Eisenhower and his United Nations advisers planning D-Day events" and "United nations troops entering Rome in 1944."[32]

Of course, the UN was not formed until almost a year later.

UNESCO's recommendations appeared to have been implemented rather fully in the three-volume report of the National History Standards Project released in 1994. The UCLA National Center for History in the Schools received $2-million in federal tax money to produce standards on how to teach American and world history in K-12. The standards provoked much controversy.

The *Reader's Digest* published "Hijacking America's History" by Lynne V. Cheney. As chairwoman of the National Endowment for the Humanities during the Bush Administration, she had launched the project. She was outraged at what was produced and said:

> Imagine a version of American history in which George Washington makes only a fleeting appearance and is never described as our first President. Or in which the foundings of the Sierra Club and the National Organization for Women are considered noteworthy events, but the first gathering of the U.S. Congress is not.

> The Great Depression is addressed in three sections, yet not a single one directly mentions the U.S. Constitution except to tell students to "ponder the paradox that the Constitution

sidetracked the movement to abolish slavery that had taken rise in the revolutionary area."

Students were instructed to conduct a trial of the famous 19th Century entrepreneur, John D. Rockefeller, on charges that he used "unethical and amoral business practices...in direct violation of common welfare."[33]

Mrs. Cheney said that counting how often subjects and people were mentioned "yields telling results." She wrote:

Senator Joseph McCarthy and McCarthyism get a total of 19 references, and the Ku Klux Klan gets 17. A declaration of independence for women, signed in Seneca Falls, N.Y. in 1848 is cited nine times. Lincoln's "Gettysburg Address" gets one mention. As for individuals, Harriet Tubman, an African-American who helped rescue slaves via the Underground Railroad is mentioned six times. Civil War General and U.S. President Ulysses S. Grant gets one mention; Robert E. Lee gets none.

The famous midnight ride of Paul Revere is ignored—as are Alexander Graham Bell, Thomas Edison, Albert Einstein, Jonas Salk, and the Wright Brothers. One of the few Congressional leaders actually quoted is Tip O'Neill, who was quoted calling Ronald Reagan "a cheerleader for selfishness."[34]

After the U.S. Senate condemned the standards, Professor Joy Appleby, the president-elect of the American Historical Association, said, "You couldn't name more than five historians who would criticize them."[36]

John Patrick Diggins, in a fall 1996 issue of *American Scholar,* told why the standards went wrong. He wrote:

To today's academic historians, the American story is the history of misguided white men, noble Indians, class struggle, and McCarthyism.[37]

Some 32,000 teachers across the country received the original standards, complete with classroom exercises.

Later because of the controversy, the same "historians" who produced them issued revisions. However, the Richmond, Virginia *Times-Dispatch* columnist Robert Holland called the revisions "a public relations coup," writing:

> The bottom line is that the vaunted revisions...are cosmetic. That's the assessment of no less an authority than the Standards' principal author, Gary Nash, director of UCLA's National Center for History in the Schools, recipient of the standards-writing federal grant. On April 3, Mr. Nash told *USA Today* that "cosmetic changes were necessary" for clarification.

Historian Elizabeth Fox-Genovese is professor of humanities at Emory University and a member of the National Council for History Standards. She summed up the real tragedy of the history standards saying:

> Nowhere in those standards will you find any mention of the fact that it was the Western tradition that first produced the idea of individual freedom. Nowhere will you find that it was in Christianity that the concept of individual freedom originated. That slavery is evil is a western ideal. Because the bias of the standards is so weighted against the United States and the West, you will find no acknowledgement of the fact that we have produced what no other country and tradition has.[38]

The National History Standards were not breaking new ground for the teaching of what they call "American History." They were just codifying and formalizing what was already being taught (or not taught) in America's schools.

That was shown in a public hearing before the Texas State Board of Education on November 9, 1989. Veteran textbook evaluators Mel and Norma Gabler dropped a bombshell. Besides bias, they documented how professional educators missed 195 blatant factual errors in eight "classroom-ready" world history textbooks recommended for Texas adoption. Two years later, Gabler research devastated textbook publishers again. After five opportunities to correct ten American history books being considered for Texas grade school and high school adoption, the books still contained blatant errors. The stories in major Texas newspapers had headlines saying:

> State Panel Re-endorses Flawed Texts....Textbook Errors Show Sad State of Public Schools....More Errors Turn Up In Proposed Textbooks....Textbooks Covering U.S. History Contain A Multitude of Errors....Textbook Critics Gain Creditability With Discovery of Errors...State Approves Texts Despite Warnings of More Errors.[39]

The *Wall Street Journal* covered the fiasco. A front page headline in its second section on February 12, 1992, read:

> Readers of Latest U.S. History Textbooks Discover a Storehouse of Misinformation.

The *Houston Chronicle* had the headline, "New History: Amount of factual errors in textbooks is appalling." The article's first paragraph read:

> The mistakes discovered so far are outrageous. For example, one textbook said the United States had settled the Korea war by "using the bomb." Other textbook inaccuracies declare that Martin Luther King Jr. and Robert Kennedy were assassinated while Richard Nixon was president. Lyndon Johnson was actually in office at the time. They also claim that George Bush defeated Massachusetts Gov. Dukakis for the presidency in 1989 rather than 1988.[40]

Those were a few of 7,000 errors, many of them "outrageous," the Gablers found in ten U.S. History textbooks.

Deliberate "under education" is a theme which runs through the entire UNESCO program. Karl W. Bigelow, a professor at Columbia, and a UNESCO board member, directed a seminar on Volume II of the *Towards World Understanding* series. The UNESCO seminar report, *The Education and Training of Teachers*, recommended:

> Therefore, we regard it as a matter of first importance for social and international living that educators should be more concerned with the child, and the healthy development of his body and mind, than with content of the various subjects which go to make a school curriculum...Because of failure to adopt a wise approach to child growth and development, the primary school still tends to function as if it were an institution *for the abolition of illiteracy.*

Bigelow's scorn for the idea that schools should be institutions for "the abolition of illiteracy" (held by other reformers also) has produced tragic results. Today, government studies and employer experience indicate that 40% of younger Americans are functionally illiterate. By contrast, *School and Society* in its January 30, 1915 issue reported that a study done by the U.S. Bureau of Education found that only 22 out of 1000 children between the ages of 10 and 14—slightly over two percent—were illiterate. Things have changed! Replacing intensive phonics with "look say" and "whole language" has produced the change for which Bigelow called.

"Graduates" produced by such "education" do not have the *basic* knowledge on which to make sound judgments. If they do not understand the source of America's strength, they cannot see the fallacies of a world collectivist order. In short, UNESCO recommended that schools be converted into indoctrination centers for the production of emotionally conditioned children who react like Pavlov's dogs rather than reason and think logically.

Professional education journals and faculty members at Teachers College, Columbia University started agitating for mandatory revision of textbooks to conform to UNESCO standards, even before the standards were publicly announced. In the April 1946 *NEA Journal* Isaac Leon Kandel of Teachers College, Columbia University wrote:

> Nations that become members of UNESCO accordingly assume an obligation to revise textbooks used in their schools...unilateral efforts to revise the materials of instruction are futile. The poison of aggressive nationalism injected into children's minds is as dangerous for world stability as the manufacture of armaments. In both, supervision by some kind of international agency is urgent.

Patriotic impulses are generally belittled and equated with extremism, in line with UNESCO proposals for overcoming "injurious parental influences." *The United States: Experiment in Democracy*, by Craven and Johnson, says:

> In the 1920s, many Americans were *excessively nationalistic and tolerantly patriotic*...The official (Ku Klux) Klan literature reflected the average middle class in its assertions of "100 per cent Americanism." (Page 662)

Note the linking of the "middle class" and patriotism with the Ku Klux Klan. Scott Foresman's five volume *Promise of America* series implied that decent Americans who held to traditional American values were the racist, hooded cross-burners. Eighth grade students were told that the KKK members in the 1920s were...

> ...for the most part, honest, hard-working and God-fearing. They had been educated to respect George Washington, the Constitution and the Flag.[41]

Belittling references to patriotism in textbooks are not the only methods used for downgrading love of country. Display of the American flag in the classroom is neglected in many areas. The pledge of allegiance was once a standard exercise for opening the school day. This practice was discarded to such a degree that in 1961 members of the California State Legislature felt compelled to pass a law requiring that the pledge or the singing of the "Star Spangled Banner" be used daily. The bill passed—*but by only one vote*. A similar bill was passed in Illinois in 1963—but was vetoed by the governor. A Missouri state senator introduced a bill in 1998 which required that all schools recite the pledge at least once a week. It didn't get out of committee.

The downgrading of American heroes contributes to national disillusionment. Todd and Curti in their *America's History*, have this to say about George Washington:

> Outwardly, Washington seemed to most people somewhat cold and over dignified. After his death *American patriots developed a myth of his godlike qualities*...(Page 184)

After 15 or more years of such anti-patriotic propaganda in the schools, the FBI Director J. Edgar Hoover spoke out. At Valley Forge on February 22, 1962, he said:

> Too often in recent years, patriotic symbols have been shunted aside. Our national heroes have been maligned, our history distorted. Has it become a disgrace to pledge allegiance to our flag—or to sign a loyalty oath, or pay tribute to our national anthem? Is it shameful to encourage our children to memorize the stirring words of '76? Is it becoming opprobrious to state "In God We Trust" when proclaiming our love of country?

> What we desperately need today is patriotism founded on a real understanding of the American ideal—a dedicated belief in our principles of freedom and a determination to perpetuate America's heritage.[42]

Today, nearly one-third of the "developing" nations of the world have no traditional concepts of law; some have not completely rejected cannibalism. Only a handful of United Nations members have concepts of private property and freedom similar to those which made America strong. Racial and religious differences further complicate the problem, making hopes for unity with freedom unrealistic.

Ignoring these facts, Magruder, in his *American Government*, sets forth some illogical reasoning on page 14 of his text, writing:

> We have peace in the United States because we have agreed to federal laws and have an army to enforce them.
>
> When we have definite international laws and an army to enforce them, we shall have international peace. When atomic bombs are made only by a world government and used only by a world army, who could resist?

Who could resist? Certainly not the United States if the "neutralist" Afro-Asian-Muslim block united, as usual, with Red China and the "former" communist countries in the Soviet-bloc and voted *democratically* to tax all Americans. Would it be wrong? Perhaps. But it would be democratic.

Yet throughout the book, the student is conditioned to accept world government, without discussing whether it would be good or bad.

In May 1992 Mikhail Gorbachev spelled out the blueprint for the New World Order in a speech at Fulton, Missouri. Gorbachev said:

> This is a turning point on a historic and worldwide scale and signifies the incipient substitution of one paradigm of civilization for another...An awareness of the need for some kind of global government is gaining ground, one in which all the members of the world community would take part.[43]

Gorbachev recognized that there were roadblocks on the road to world government. He said:

> Even now at a time of sharply increased interdependence in the world, many countries are morbidly jealous of their sovereignty, and many peoples of their national independence and identity. This is one of the newest Global contradictions, one which must be overcome.[44]

Several generations of Americans have been made ready to accept steps toward world government.

Not all those who support and promote world government are communists. Those who write such textbooks, put them into school systems, and vehemently defend them when they are exposed, are for the most part misguided idealists. They are consumed with the idea of solving world problems through a one-world government (which would be socialistic). They believe that, if all human differences (economic, religious, political, etc.) can be eliminated (or ignored), mankind's problems will disappear. In striving for this idealistic goal, they emotionally banish all fact and reason.

Foundation Concept #9
INDIVIDUAL RIGHTS COME FROM GOD

Every good gift, and every perfect gift is from above, and cometh down from the Father of lights, with whom is no variableness, neither shadow of turning.
—James 1:17

AMERICA WAS ESTABLISHED on a concept that was, and is, different from that of any other nation on earth.

Our founding fathers didn't give us our rights and our freedoms. We did not get them through our Bill of Rights or our Constitution. Many nations have had—and lost—freedoms granted by a ruler or a constitution.

What makes America different is that our founding fathers discovered and set forth the truth that the rights of the individual come, not from a king, a government, a Constitution or a Bill of Rights, but from God. Our governmental documents acknowledge this truth and restrict government from interfering with man's God-given rights. The *Declaration of Independence* affirms:

> We hold these truths to be self-evident, that all men are created equal, *that they are endowed by their Creator with certain unalienable rights*, that among these are Life, Liberty and the pursuit of Happiness.—That to secure these rights, Governments are instituted among Men, deriving their just powers from the consent of the governed. [Emphasis added]

If God gives men their rights then government can't tamper with them. That, of course, is the concept which underlies the Constitution's Bill of Rights.

Some textbooks publish the text of the Declaration of Independence (or have an unreadable picture of it). However, an exhaustive search has failed to find any public school history or government text published in the last sixty years that spells out clearly the truth set forth in the Declaration of Independence. Textbook authors ignore the vitally important foundational truth that an individual's rights come from God rather than government. It is this truth which makes America different from any other nation in history.

Since humanists deny God they must ignore Him and the *Declaration of Independence* which sets forth the truth that rights come from Him. Their Manifesto says:

> To enhance freedom and dignity the individual must experience a full range of civil liberties in all societies....We would safeguard, extend, and implement the principles of human freedom evolved from the *Magna Charta* to the *Bill of Rights*, the *Rights of Man*, and the *Universal Declaration of Human Rights*.

Note that because humanists reject God, they have omitted the *Declaration of Independence* from the list of documents from which they say "the principles of human freedom have *evolved.*"[45]

The 1991 Houghton-Mifflin eighth grade social studies text *A More Perfect Union* edits its presentation of the Declaration to conform to humanist views which deny God—and Supreme Court decisions which ban Him from public schools. On page 66, the text "quotes" the Declaration this way:

All men are created equal...with certain unalienable rights.

The three dots in the center of the "quote" replace the seven critical words "...that they are endowed by their Creator..." Of course, it is difficult to acknowledge the Creator in history or government class when He is denied in science classes which are completely evolution-based.

The *Elementary Textbook Evaluation Guide* published in 1961 by the Textbook Study League Inc. of San Gabriel, California, warned of the ultimate result of ignoring God as the source of an individual's rights. It said:

Withhold from the children for one generation the truth of "rights endowed by the Creator" and our Constitution could be altered and our freedom could be voted away without citizens ever knowing the cause of their slavery.

Those words are basically a paraphrase of the words of Thomas Jefferson, the author of the Declaration, who said:

God who gave us life gave us liberty. Can the liberties of a nation be secure when we have removed a conviction that these liberties are the gift of God? Indeed I tremble for my country when I reflect that God is just, that His justice cannot sleep forever.

DELEGATED AUTHORITY

Let every soul be subject unto the higher powers. For there is no power but of God; the powers that be are ordained of God. Whosoever therefore resisteth the power, resisteth the ordinance of God: and they that resist shall receive to themselves damnation.
—Romans 13:1

THE DECLARATION OF INDEPENDENCE was correct in stating that all rights come from God. Therefore, man is accountable to God for how he uses his rights. To maintain order and accountability in society, God, in His Bible, establishes a "chain of command" through which He administers the world. He established three primary institutions through which He works. They are the family, the church and the state. Into each of these institutions He has placed authorities who are responsible for teaching His ways and administering His temporal justice. In I Timothy 2:1-2, God commands His people to pray for all those in authority "that we may lead quiet and peaceable lives." He also makes everyone responsible for obeying those in authority. In Romans 13:1. God's Word commands:

Let every soul be subject unto the higher powers. For there is no power but of God: the powers that be are ordained of God. Whosoever therefore resisteth the power, resisteth the ordinance of God: and they that resist shall receive to themselves damnation.

In the family, children first develop concepts of obedience to authority. This establishes the foundation for obeying school, church, work and governmental authorities through life. Textbooks, in undermining parental authority, set the stage for a life of rebellion.

However, undermining the authority of the family starts even before children read textbooks. By the 1990s, the *Anti-Bias Curriculum* of the National Association for the Education of Young Children was encouraging overcoming family values, even though it was doing it subtly. It said:

> Help children discover the contradictions between their ideas and their own experiences. Sometimes children will accept firsthand experience as truth; sometimes they will cling to social norms or their own ideas about gender behavior. Don't get discouraged when stereotypic gender play [boys playing like boys and girls like girls] and remarks continue despite a rich antisexist curriculum....The key is to provide many opportunities for new ways of thinking and believing. Over time, many children will integrate nonsexist attitudes into their beliefs and behavior. Children may also experience emotional conflict about acting differently than social norms, *especially when their families agree and act according to the norms. (Page 51) [Emphasis added.]*

When children can read for themselves textbook undermining of authority includes:

> It is not always wrong to challenge rules. Questioning, and even rebelling against some rules, is part of growing up. (Page 56) *Health And Safety For You*, McGraw Hill/Webster Division, 1980.

> Everyone must develop his own set of principles to govern his own sexual behavior. (Page 189 *Psychology For Living*, McGraw-Hill, Webster Division, 1971.)

> Your decision about using marijuana is important to you. You should be the one to make it. (Page 178 *Good Health For You!* Laidlaw, 1983, Grade 5 Health.)

These textbook examples of the promotion of the individual as the ultimate authority have their roots in *Humanist Manifesto II* which says:

> We believe in maximum individual autonomy consistent with social responsibility....All persons should have a voice in

developing the values and goals that determine their lives....in the economy, the school, the family, the workplace and voluntary associations.[46]

Since the 1950s, the authority and influence of parents and family has been undermined particularly in books for middle schools. The Science Research Associates text, *A Guide To Successful Fatherhood* used in 7th and 8th grade "family living" classes undermines God's authority structure telling students:

> A few generations ago, Father usually was the undisputed head of the household....Things have changed a great deal since those days. In the ideal modern household no one is "boss."

If no one is "boss," kids take control. A Ginn & Company Basal Reader, *Rebels,* tells eighth graders:

> Think of a situation that would probably result in a difference of opinion between yourself and your parents. How would you defend your position? With what arguments would your parents counter? Write a dialogue between your parents and yourself. (Page 85)

On page 41 of the Teacher's Manual for MacMillan's *Gateway English,* teachers are told to ask students:

> From whom might you resent getting some unasked for advice about how to dress, how to wear makeup or how to behave? Why? (From some teachers, from "old-fashioned parents," from bossy older brothers and sisters, etc.")

Textbooks are not the only school attack on the family's authority. School officials, and apparently school counselors also believe they know better than parents what children need. In November 3 and December 4, 1997 letters to the Pennsylvania State House of Representatives Education Committee with copies sent to all members of the legislature, Dr. Robert B. Cormany, Executive Director of the Pennsylvania School Counselors Association, wrote:

Counselors, teachers and administrators are...professionals who are able to take the needs of our students into account in a somewhat more objective manner than can parents. The idea that parents know what is best for their children is a flawed concept at best....A parent is much too close to the child and has seen them in far too different a set of circumstances to always be objective to their needs....The issue of parents' rights is to a large extent an emotional rather than a logical one.

It's not likely that a counselor with such an attitude would give a child advice supporting Scripture which says:

Children, obey your parents in the Lord: for this is right. Honour thy father and mother; which is the first commandment with promise: that it may be well with thee, and that thou mayest live long on the earth. (Ephesians 6:1-3)

Foundational Concept #11
THE CERTAINTY OF ANSWERING TO GOD

For we must all appear before the judgment seat of Christ; that every one may receive the things done in his body, according to that he hath done, whether it be good or bad. —II Corinthians 5:10

IT IS IMPOSSIBLE to maintain law and order with freedom unless there is a widespread acceptance of the possibility that even though an individual might get away with it in this life, he might have to answer to God later. Acceptance of that truth puts restraint on the desires of the sinful nature that all men are born with. Because God and His morality are ignored in modern textbooks, the concept of a coming judgment is impossible to find. It's all in line with the false humanist teaching which says:

Promises of immortal salvation or fear of eternal damnation are both illusory and harmful....There is no credible evidence that life survives the death of the body.[47]

Sinful man might hope the humanist teaching is true, but the Bible says otherwise. Hebrews 9:27 says:

...it is appointed unto men once to die, but after this the judgment.

The concept is taught repeatedly in Scripture. Romans 14:11 and II Corinthians 5:10 warn:

As I live, sayeth the Lord, every knee shall bow to me, and every tongue shall confess to God....For we must all appear before the judgment seat of Christ; that everyone, may receive the things done in his body, according to that he hath done, whether it be good or bad.

Textbooks which implement the humanist teaching totally ignore the concept of life after death and any possibility of a coming judgment. As the concept of future accountability is eroded, society is suffering.

Foundational Concept #12
GOD'S EXISTENCE IS FOUNDATIONAL

Because that which may be known of God is manifest in them; for God hath shewed it unto them. For the invisible things of him from the creation of the world are clearly seen, being understood by the things that are made, even his eternal power and Godhead; so that they are without excuse....The fool hath said in his heart, There is no God.
—Romans 1:19-20, Psalm 14:1

MUCH OF AMERICA'S MONEY carries the national motto, "In God We Trust." In the Pledge of Allegiance Americans affirm this nation to be "under God." Henry Steele Commager's introduction for the reissue of the 19th Century McGuffey readers concludes that...

...the world of the McGuffeys was a world in which no one questioned the truths of the Bible, or their relevance to everyday conduct.

The eleven concepts shown thus far to be foundational to America's traditional way of life and culture are all based on the presupposition that God exists. That presupposition is at odds with the statement the secular humanists expressed in their *Humanist Manifesto I*, and restated in *Humanist Manifesto II* when they said:

> As in 1933, humanists still believe that traditional theism, especially faith in the prayer-hearing God, assumed to love and care for persons, to hear and understand their prayers, and to be able to do something about them, is an unproved and outmoded faith....traditional dogmatic or authoritarian religions...do a disservice to the human species.....No deity will save us, we must save ourselves.[2]

Because of the influence and work of Dewey's humanist disciples, school textbooks virtually ignore God's place in American history—and in life today. In 1983, a government- funded study found that to be true. The U.S. Department of Education's National Institute of Education funded a two-year study by New York University professor Paul Vitz. He was to evaluate how traditional American values were treated in public school textbooks. He and his team studied over 60 social studies texts and 640 stories in elementary reading books. When the study was released in 1985, it attracted significant media attention—but after a brief flurry of concern nothing changed. Vitz's study found:

> Among 40 social studies textbooks for grades 1-4 not one had one word of text that referred to any religious activity representative of contemporary life....The importance of religion in America's past was grossly under represented. In many cases there was almost no reference to what had happened of a

religious nature in this country, particularly in the last 100 years.[48]

In several sixth grade world history or world culture texts, Mohammed's life gets more coverage than that of Jesus.[49]

....books [studied] included not a single reference to television evangelists, born-again Christians or the Moral Majority organization.[50]

Many texts mention the first Pilgrim Thanksgiving but never acknowledge that they were giving thanks, not to Indians for saving them from starvation as some now seem to believe, but to God.[51]

The Vitz study showed that the failing of text books generally was not in denying God's existence but rather ignoring Him and the influence of His people on society.

Nowhere is this more evident than in a widely used teacher training text. For over twenty years *Philosophical Foundations of Education* by Howard Ozmon and Samuel Craver has been the basic text in philosophy of education courses in many teacher training institutions. The book has an introduction and ten chapters. In the introduction, the authors say:

The book is organized in a way that enables students to develop a coherent grasp of various philosophies of education. Each of the first nine chapters gives the historical development of a given philosophy, its current status, how it has influenced education, and a critique of its leading ideas. Taken together, these chapters provide a chronological development of the philosophy of education.[52]

As the authors set forth in that introduction, they purport to examine each of the nine philosophies of education or schools of thought down through history which together have shaped or influenced today's schools. The chapter titles covering the nine philosophies are:

1. Idealism and Education
2. Realism and Education
3. Eastern Philosophy and Education
4. Pragmatism and Education
5. Reconstructionism and Education
6. Behaviorism and Education
7. Existentialism, Phenomenology and Education
8. Analytic Philosophy and Education
9. Marxism and Education.

The tenth chapter attempts to pull it all together and relates philosophy to educational practice.

Look at those nine chapter titles. This book supposedly explains and evaluates for future teachers how the "contributions" of nine different philosophies have shaped education today. What's missing? The authors look at Plato, Aristotle, Dewey, Skinner, Counts, Marx and some other heathen pagans and their philosophies. Christianity is ignored except for a brief mention that Augustine (5th Century), Thomas Aquinas (13th Century) and Martin Luther (16th Century) were leaders of Christianity. Christianity is labeled as an "Eastern religion or philosophy" along with Buddhism, Zen, Islam, Confucianism, Taoism, etc. The authors claim Augustine, Aquinas and Luther were influenced by Plato and Aristotle. But otherwise in their 400 pages, the authors completely ignore Jesus Christ, the Bible and Christianity's contributions to shaping western civilization and its schools. They do not, for example, tell future teachers that Luther said:

> I am much afraid that schools will prove to be great gates of hell unless they diligently labor in explaining the Holy Scriptures, engraving them in the hearts of youth. I advise no one to place his child where the scriptures are not paramount. Every institution in which men are not increasingly occupied with the Word of God must become corrupt.[53]

In examining various philosophies which have influenced the development of education, how can such a statement by Luther be ignored? In fact, how can a philosophy of education textbook totally ignore the Christian foundations of American education—those foundations which the liberal historian Henry Steele Commager Jr. acknowledged in his introduction to the reissue of the McGuffey reader. For almost 200 years the church, or pastors who were "moonlighting" in the town's school, provided the education children received. Future teachers and administrators learn none of this in a textbook which supposedly surveys the philosophies which have influenced America's schools.

After doing his exhaustive survey of textbooks in the 1980s, Paul Vitz concluded that for the most part God, Christians and the influence of their heritage on America and its institutions are ignored in teacher training materials and students' textbooks.

Today "politically correct" scholars on university campuses are eliminating the "B.C." and "A.D." method for designating dates in history. Textbooks are being effected. For example, the 1997-released Sixth Edition of Prentice Hall's *Sociology* by John Macionis informs the student:

> Throughout this text, the abbreviation B.C.E. designates "before the common era." We use this terminology in place of the traditional B.C. ("before Christ") in recognition of the religious plurality of our society. Similarly, in place of the traditional A.D. (anno Domini, or "in the year of our Lord"), we employ the abbreviation C.E. ("common era").[54]

Model social studies curricula in Ohio and some other states use the B.C.E. dating.

Sometimes God is not ignored. For example, Scott Foresman's *Promise of America* series presents a last letter supposedly written to a priest by a young German soldier at Stalingrad during World War II. Titled "I Have Searched for God," it describes all the desolation and death he faced. In the letter, he repeatedly says that God never showed himself "even though my heart cried for Him." His "letter" concludes:

> No...there is no God...And if there should be a God, He is only with you in the hymnals and the prayers and the pious sayings of the priests and pastors, in the ringing of bells and the fragrance of incense but not in Stalingrad.[55]

After the sad depiction of faith in Christ as an exercise in hopelessness, another text in the *Promise of America* series conveys a sneering attitude towards the Christian faith. A story titled, "I am the New Black," equates love for Jesus Christ with a culture in which eating with your fingers is acceptable. The story quotes a young black student as supposedly saying:

> I am the New Black. I will neither babble about how much I love Jesus, nor entertain you with sparkling racial comedy. I will not eat with my fingers nor go out of my way to sit down at a dining hall table with you.[56]

Vitz showed that not only was religion largely discounted—but other Bible-based foundational concepts didn't get fair coverage either. He said:

> It was not just religion that received short shrift. Traditional family values were almost totally unrepresented. For example, in the social studies texts, which are supposed to introduce the child to contemporary American life, not one book mentioned that marriage is the foundation of a family and of family life. In fact, the word "marriage" and the word "wedding" did not occur in any of these books, nor did "husband," "wife," "homemaker" or "housewife."

Vitz was quoted in the *New York Times* as charging that the bias resulted because...

...secular humanists have been able to dominate and control education. Those who write and publish the textbooks are of a relatively homogeneous, secular and anti-religious mentality. Individual principals or superintendents who select textbooks are of the same attitude.[57]

What does eliminating God's place in the world mean for education? Chuck Colson, in his *Breakpoint* radio commentaries[58] said:

It means schools should not train children in any particular character traits, like courage or honesty. Instead schools should maximize a child's ability to choose for himself, after critical consideration of competing alternatives.

This explains modern sex education, for example, where students are not taught to restrain their sexual impulses until marriage. Instead they're taught a wide range of sexual practices, with the message that "Only you can judge what's right for you." [The DARE anti-drug program uses much the same approach.]

Colson pointed up the contradictions in such school teachings based on the concept that there are no absolute truths based on God's law. He said:

Ironically, if you walk down the hall to the science classroom, you'll find educators employing the opposite method. There they have no qualms about teaching that there is one and only one right way to think—namely, to embrace Darwinism. Evolution is not open to question, nor are students invited to judge for themselves whether it is true or not.

Colson asks, "Why such a sharp discrepancy in teaching styles?" The answer he said is...

...that science is taught in absolute terms because it is regarded as giving the *truth* about what "really exists." And what "really exists" is nature alone. There is no God. Naturalism in science then becomes the basis for liberalism in morality: If there is no God, then kids should be taught to make up their own minds about moral questions. Is it any surprise that some of them make up their minds to cheat and fight? No wonder schools are becoming battlegrounds.

Colson concluded:

If God is kicked out of science courses, eventually His commandments will be taken off classroom walls—and out of students' hearts.

Those are thoughts a nation troubled by recurring in-school murders of students and teachers by other students must face. The nation also needs to know of Colson's encounter with a newspaper editor who boasted of his efforts to remove the Ten Commandments from the walls of local classrooms. The editor was proud of his success in promoting a more "liberal" education. Yet, moments later, Colson said...

...he was bemoaning crime in the schools—the epidemic of cheating and fighting. "Perhaps," I suggested, "you ought to put a sign on the wall...telling kids not to steal." The editor stared at me and then turned away without uttering a word. For, of course, he had worked hard to remove just such a sign—one that said "Thou shalt not steal"—along with the rest of the Ten Commandments.

Colson added:

What this editor failed to see is that the liberal approach to education is closely linked to increasing crime and disorder. As Philip Johnson explains in his book, *Reason In The Balance*, liberal education is based on the philosophy of naturalism: that there is no God. The implication is that morality is based not on God's commandments but on individual choices. Every person's goals in life are intrinsically as good as every other person's, and no one has a right to "impose" morality on anyone else—not even on his or her own children.

Colson pointed out how removing God from science class has impacted on the nation's legal system. He said:

...law schools today teach a view heavily influenced by former Supreme Court Justice Oliver Wendell Holmes. Holmes was a convinced Darwinist, who believed that Darwinism is not just about biology but also entails a complete naturalistic worldview: that there is no God—that nature is all that exists.

If there is no God, then obviously a nation's laws cannot be based on divine decrees. Darwinism implies that justice and morality are merely ideas that the human mind invents when it has evolved to a certain level. Laws are then based on the "moral" ideas of whoever has the most power.

That is how the U.S. Supreme Court decided that killing unborn infants in their mothers' wombs is legal. Ideas do have consequences!

God has been effectively removed from the nation's schools as the two-year Paul Vitz survey of public school textbooks revealed. Vitz summarized his findings in the *Wall Street Journal*. He wrote:

> Taken all together, these results make it clear that public school textbooks commonly exclude the history, heritage, beliefs and values of millions of Americans. Those who believe in free enterprise are not represented, those who believe in the traditional family are not represented, and those who are committed to their religious traditions—at the very least as part of the historical record—are not represented.

Without the knowledge of their history, heritage or values based on God's laws which schools once imparted, too many young Americans have become a part of "a new social order." That was the goal of John Dewey and his educational "reformers."

CHAPTER 5

THE REVOLUTION WE'VE LIVED THROUGH

For over one hundred years Americans have been running a gigantic experiment in government schools, trying to find out what a society looks like without God. Now we know.
— *Douglas Wilson*

HUMANIST REFORMERS took control of America's schools in the 1930s with a goal of using them to create "a new social order." It was to be a society in which God and His foundational concepts would either be ignored or denied. They stated their goals plainly in their books and speeches—but they didn't proclaim them openly in the newspapers or meetings of the PTA. Therefore few parents knew what was being planned for their children.

By 1960 more than a generation of students trained in the "new" schools were parents rearing their own children. They were sending them off to schools largely staffed with teachers, administrators and school board members who were themselves also products of the "new" education. Of course, not all graduates became teachers. Others moved into key positions in culture-shaping institutions—the law, the press, the TV and entertainment media, government and the churches.

Since then the United States has lived through a "revolution" that has touched every area of American life and culture. It has drastically changed how children are trained at home and in school—and the other influences to which they are subjected. The "revolution" has transformed America, producing a people in rebellion against traditional values and the foundational concepts on which America's greatness was built.

People under 50 have a hard time comprehending the changes. They haven't known any America other than today's violent, sex crazy, drug dependent world. Because many of the changes have happened little by little, even older Americans who lived through them didn't notice what was happening. The Revolution has produced a different America than that which existed before 1960.

Commander Jeremiah Denton was a man who saw the change. Denton was a Navy pilot. He was shot down over North Vietnam on July 18, 1965—during the first days of America's open participation in the Vietnam War. He spent seven years, five months and 25 days in the Communist prison camp known as the "Hanoi Hilton."

He was tortured and forced to go before Communist propaganda TV cameras. He was forced to tell how well the Communists treated the prisoners. He condemned America's involvement in the Vietnam war. Jerry Denton spoke the words the Communists wanted. But even as he was reciting the words the Communists forced him to say, his eyes squinted and blinked—seemingly blinded by the bright TV lights.

When the Communist propaganda films were shown on the world's TV screens, Jerry Denton's message got through. The blinking was not caused by the TV lights. Denton was blinking his eyes to spell the Morse Code message: T-O-R-T-U-R-E.

When, as a full-fledged hero, he came home in February 1973 he found a different America than the one he left seven-and-a-half years before. In his book,

When Hell Was In Session, Jerry Denton told of the shock he experienced:

> In the first weeks...I saw the evidences of the new permissiveness, group sex, massage parlors, X-rated movies, the drug culture, that represented to me an alien element. I also noted a mood of national political disunity which has damaged the foundations of the most powerful but compassionate nation on earth.

> When I returned from Vietnam, I was shocked at the deterioration in our society. It quickly became obvious that the basic problem was a deterioration in our national attitude towards the family and family life....individual responsibilities, accomplishments, and vocations.

> The consequences are manifest in our inability to respond effectively to all the major challenges of our society, our economy and even our national defense.[1]

In his book, *Character Is The Issue,*[2] published in 1997, Arkansas Governor Mike Huckabee commented on the transformation of America during the time Jerry Denton was in a communist prison in Vietnam. Huckabee said:

> I became a teenager in 1968, a year I have always considered a watershed date in American history. That year marked the death of innocence: the assassinations of Robert Kennedy and Martin Luther King Jr., the Chicago riots, and the horror of Vietnam. The world didn't change completely in a single year, but in 1968 the shift in our society became too apparent to miss. People were angry. Student protests and the hippie movement were at a fever pitch. The Black Panthers came into their own. There was a total loss not just of innocence, but a sense of community and wholesomeness. It really did mark a turning point. From that year onward, we have lived in the age of the birth control pill, free love, gay sex, the drug culture, and reckless disregard for standards (Page 127).

Huckabee added:

People felt free to do whatever they wanted. No longer did we live by the standards of God; it became, "You define your standard, I'll define mine, and everybody will be happy. Nobody can tell me what is right and wrong. I have to make those decisions for myself." It was the beginning of the Me Generation, which mushroomed in the seventies. By the time of Watergate, morality had become a joke. (Page 170)

The internal demoralization that Jerry Denton and Mike Huckabee saw continues. It could destroy America. Lenin, the man who brought communism to Russia, said that America would some day become so rotten from within that she would fall like "an overripe fruit" into Communist hands. The "overripe fruit" produced by the revolution America has lived through can destroy America even if there were no communist threat.

In 1962, three years before Jerry Denton went to Vietnam, the U.S. Supreme Court banned Bible reading and a 22-word prayer recited in the schools of New York. The prayer the Supreme Court declared "unconstitutional" said:

Almighty God, we acknowledge our dependence upon Thee, and we beg They blessings upon us, our parents, our teachers and our Country.[3]

If the schools of America had not already eroded the Bible-based foundational concepts on which the nation grew great, there would have been a massive uprising of the American people. They would have never accepted the Supreme Court's striking down, by reinterpretation, what had been fully constitutional for 175 years. However, in that most Americans had already given up on prayer and Bible reading in their own homes, little but talk resulted.

Once prayer and Bible reading in schools were banned, the decay which resulted from the "reforms" educators planned and started thirty years before accelerated. In 1960 there were...

...no legalized abortions in America...no X-rated, R-rated or PG movies...no co-ed dorms on college campuses...there was no "gay rights" movement and there was no AIDS or HIV...a radio or TV station was in danger of losing its operating license from the Federal Communications Commission if it permitted the words "Hell" or "Damn" to go out over the air waves.

Since then...

The divorce rate doubled...single parent families jumped 250%...incidence of adultery and unfaithfulness in marriages tripled...pregnancies of girls in the 15-19 age bracket increased 550%...pregnancies of girls under 15 went up 400%...sexually transmitted diseases increased 350% between 1963 and 1975...suicides doubled in the 15-24 age bracket.[4]

By 1985, educators ranked drug abuse, pregnancies, rape, robbery, assault, absenteeism, vandalism, arson, etc. as the major school discipline problems. Violence and corruption were not just in schools. Between 1960 and today...

...the rate of violent crimes (rape, murder, assault, etc.) has increased 422%...burglary, robbery, etc. increased 11 times faster than growth in population...prosecution of government officials for corruption increased five fold...per capita alcohol consumption jumped 29%...the number of high school seniors who had tried marijuana increased 15 fold in the 20 years between 1962 and 1982...child abuse and neglect cases tripled and reported cases of sexual abuse of children increased ten fold.[5]

America has lived through a revolution. The revolution has transformed the culture and way of life of millions of Americans. That the transformation has largely happened since 1960 was demonstrated by two big power blackouts which darkened New York City. The first was in 1965. The other came twelve years later. Both affected basically the same areas and involved the same segments of the population. What happened during the blackouts was dramatically different. In 1965 when the lights went out in New York, a few stores were broken into. There were a few isolated instances of looting. It was far different when the power went off in 1977. The *United Press* reported:[6]

> An army of night stalkers preyed on the blacked out neighborhoods of the city through the night of the power failure. An orgy of looting and vandalism resulted in more than 3000 arrests and about 900 fires—55 of which were considered major blazes—at a cost of billions to small businessmen....In contrast during the northeast power blackout in 1965, fewer than 100 persons were arrested.

A detective assigned to the blighted Bedford-Stuyvesant section during the blackout gave this personal evaluation:

> In 1965 you were dealing with human beings. Now you are dealing with animals. This is an absolute disgrace.

Americans have become accustomed to the "disgrace." It happens whenever some segment of the population becomes irate—whether it is a riot over a Rodney King verdict, a shooting of a hoodlum by a policeman or people trampled to death in a stampede when rock concert doors are not opened as quickly as the mob demands.

For over twenty years, America's schools have been plagued by growing violence. America's teachers and their students daily face threats. In early 1992, syndicated columnist Clarence Page delivered a speech in Norfolk, Virginia.[7] As he finished, a local schoolteacher asked a question which Page said, "Stopped me cold." The question was:

> How can we stop our students from killing each other?

Challenged by the teacher's question, Page wrote:

It was a sobering question. The nation's schools are turning into war zones, the problem is spreading to middle-size cities...

Page recounted events which few Americans face— until it happens in their school or their neighborhood. Among the facts he stated were:

> Gunshots had claimed two teenage Norfolk boys in the week before my speech....A young black doctor told me he hadn't seen anything like the violence since his residency at Chicago's Cook County Hospital, where gunshot wounds in some hot summer nights gave the place a striking resemblance to a M.A.S.H. unit....The federal Centers for Disease Control says one student in five carries a weapon of some sort and one in 20 carries a gun....A fourth of the nation's school systems use metal detectors....Most big city schools have armed security guards to keep order.

It's not just inner-city or metropolitan areas that are plagued. The nation was shocked when a 14-year-old boy sprayed bullets into a before-school prayer meeting in West Paducah, Kentucky just before Christmas in 1997. Half-a-dozen students were wounded. Three were killed. Within six months there were five other in-school killings of students by students. The nation was shocked when in March 1998, two boys, 11 and 13-years-old, pulled the fire alarm at Westside Middle School in Jonesboro, Arkansas and gunned down students and teachers as they came from the building. They killed four fellow students and a teacher and wounded about a dozen others.[8]

Over 20 years ago Indiana Senator Birch Bayh headed a committee which studied the impact of violence in schools. He concluded:

> In terms of levels of school related crime, there is abundant evidence that a significant and growing number of schools in urban, suburban and rural areas are confronting serious levels of violence and vandalism. Vandalism costs schools over $600-million annually.[9]

Bayh based his speech to educators on information developed in Senate hearings and said:

> When teachers testify that they are afraid to walk the halls of their school; when a superintendent attributes the high truancy rate in his school to a fear of gangs operating in the school; when students describe a large variety of weapons in schools, from knives and karate sticks to an occasional Saturday Night Special gun; when students are victimized by organized extortion operations demanding lunch money; and when illegal drugs can be easily obtained in school hallways and playgrounds, then there can be no question that the already challenging task of education becomes almost impossible to carry out.[10]

Shortly after Bayh spoke...

> Leaders of two St. Louis teacher organizations said that educators must stop "covering up" incidents of beatings, extortion and robbery that have become everyday events in many city and suburban schools. "No one likes to admit that these things happen in schools," said Tom Downey, president of the 1,000-member St. Louis Teachers Association. Mike Bingman of the St. Louis Suburban Teachers Association said such problems exist "even in some of your so-called finer schools."[11]

A National Education Association study showed:

> Over 100 murders were committed on school grounds the previous year by students. At the elementary and secondary level, students committed 9,000 rapes, 12,000 armed robberies, 204,000 aggravated assaults against teachers and each other, 270,000 school burglaries—and vandalized well over $600-million in school property.[12]

For twenty years the press has turned the spotlight on school violence periodically. Headlines in St.Louis area newspapers collected over the years read:

> Murder and Mayhem in Public Schools....Cover-up of School Violence Charged By Teachers' Group....It's "Blackboard Jungle" On Some City Schools Buses, Drivers Say.... "It's The

Strong Against The Weak," Area Student Says....School Violence, Congress Is Moving To Intervene

Violence makes headlines but this isn't the only problem. Even the "nice" kids have been affected. In October 1995, a *Reader's Digest* article was headlined, "Cheating In Our Schools: A National Scandal." The story reported that 34 percent of high school students admitted using "cheat sheets" on tests in 1969. By 1989 the figure had doubled. Even the highest achieving students routinely cut ethical corners. The *Reader's Digest* reported:

> In a survey of 3100 top high school juniors and seniors that was conducted for *Who's Who Among American High School Students,* 78 percent said they had cheated. And 89 percent said cheating was common at their schools.[13]

Stephen F. David, professor of psychology at Emporia State University in Kansas, said:

> The numbers alone are disturbing but even more alarming is the attitude. There's no remorse. For students, cheating is a way of life.[14]

Jay Mulkey of the Character Education Institute in San Antonio, Texas, said of the danger to society:

> Cheating is habit forming. Students who cheat in class may well cheat in their jobs or on their spouses. When you have a country that doesn't value honesty and thinks character is unimportant, what kind of society do you have?[15]

The *Reader's Digest* indicated that even when schools try to deal with cheating, they face confrontations with parents. The same thing happens when schools try to deal with even simple discipline problems. Why? The parents (and many grandparents) of today's students are themselves products of the education for "a new social order."

In the introduction to a revision of his best-selling book, *Baby and Child Care,* Dr. Benjamin Spock wrote:

> The rearing of children is more and more puzzling for parents in the twentieth century because we've lost a lot of our old-fashioned convictions about what kind of morals and ambitions and characters we want them to have. We've even lost our convictions about the purpose of human existence.[16]

The "new" education imposed on America's schools in the last sixty years has had an impact on those who are today's parents and grandparents. If you are not aware that a revolution has so drastically changed our society and the way we raise our children, you are typical of so many parents today. Dr. Spock explained why when he wrote:

> You may not be conscious of these changes—because you are so much a part of these times.[17]

Spock didn't say it but the biggest single cause of the "changes" which have transformed America is the "new education" imposed on America and its children over several generations. It's an "education" which has eroded and destroyed the twelve foundational concepts on which a stable society must rest. The question which must be asked is: "Why would any group of educators develop a system of education which produces crime and corruption, violence and vandalism, drug abuse, changing moral standards and the selfishness which destroys marriages?"

Alexis de Tocqueville, a French political philosopher, wrote his classic, *Democracy In America,*[18] 160 years ago. In it, he provided an answer, saying.

> ...if a despotism should be established among the democratic nations of our day, it would probably have a different character. It would be more widespread and milder; it would *degrade* men rather than torment them....I do not expect their leaders

to be tyrants, *but rather their schoolmasters. (Page 691)*
(Emphasis added.)

De Tocqueville visited the United States to learn what
"magic quality" enabled a handful of people to defeat
the mighty British Empire twice in 35 years. He looked
for the greatness of America in her harbors and rivers,
her fertile fields and boundless forests, mines and other
natural resources. He studied America's schools, her
Congress and her matchless Constitution without comprehending America's power. Not, he said, until he
went into the churches of America and heard pulpits
"aflame with righteousness" did he understand the
secret of her genius and strength. De Tocqueville
returned to France and wrote:

America is great because America is good, and if America ever
ceases to be good, America will cease to be great.[20]

In his book de Tocqueville explores and examines all
facets of American life and government.Near the end
of the book in a chapter titled, "What Sort of Despotism
Democratic Nations Have To Fear," he expressed concerns for America's future. In doing so he almost
seemed endued with prophetic wisdom. He reviewed
the absolute despots who ruled empires in the past. He
commented that although in the past the whole government of an empire was concentrated in the hands of the
emperor alone and he could decide everything...

...yet the details of social life and personal everyday existence
normally escaped his control. (Page 690)

In contrast, de Tocqueville feared a "despotism" even
ancient emperors did not envision. It would provide
what is called "cradle-to-grave care." It would
"degrade" men and keep its citizens wrapped up in
"enjoyments" to stop their thinking. He wrote:

Over this kind of [degraded] men stands an immense, protective power which is alone responsible for securing their enjoyment and watching over their fate. That power is absolute, thoughtful of detail, orderly, provident and gentle. It would resemble parental authority if, fatherlike, it tried to prepare its charges for a man's life, but on the contrary, it only tries to keep them in perpetual childhood. It likes to see the citizens enjoy themselves, provided they think of nothing but enjoyment. (Page 692)

De Tocqueville was almost looking ahead to see the "new social order" envisioned by the education "reformers." It is about to be achieved by the new generation of reformers. Of this despotism, he wrote:

It gladly works for their happiness but wants to be the sole agent and judge of it. It provides for their security, foresees and supplies their necessities, facilitates their pleasures, manages their principal concerns, directs their industry, makes rules for their testaments, and divides their inheritances. Why should it not entirely relieve them of the trouble of thinking and all the cares of living? (Page 692)

De Tocqueville's genius was in his ability to foresee what people would accept. He continued:

Having thus taken each citizen in turn in its powerful grasp and shaped him to its will, government then extends its embrace to include the whole of society. It covers the whole of social life with a network of petty, complicated rules that are both minute and uniform....It does not break men's will, but softens, bends, and guides it; it seldom enjoins, but often inhibits, action; it does not destroy anything, but prevents much being born; it is not at all tyrannical, but it hinders, restrains, enervates, stifles, and stultifies so much that in the end each nation is no more than a flock of timid and hardworking animals with the government as its shepherd. (Page 692)

Concerning elections under such a *despotic* system, de Tocqueville wrote:

Under this system, the citizens quit their state of dependence just long enough to choose their masters and then fall back into it. (Page 693)

He adds:

It is difficult to imagine how people who have entirely given up managing their own affairs could make a wise choice of those who are to do that for them. (Page 695)

De Tocqueville summed up his concerns with a certain scorn saying:

The citizens are led insensibly, and perhaps against their will, daily to give up fresh portions of their individual independence to the government, and those same men who from time to time have upset a throne and trampled kings beneath their feet bend without resistance to the slightest wishes of some [government] clerk. (Page 688)

In his "far-fetched" fictional look at the future, *Brave New World*, written in 1934, Aldous Huxley wrote:

A really efficient totalitarian state would be one in which the all-powerful executive of political bosses and their army of managers control a population of slaves who do not have to be coerced, because they love their servitude. To make them love it is the task assigned, in present-day totalitarian states, to the ministries of propaganda, newspaper editors and school teachers.[21]

The next chapter turns the spotlight on the new generation of "educational reformers" and government bureaucrats. They are moving America into the final phase of the despotism or tyranny which de Tocqueville and Huxley in their writings feared would destroy the nation.

CHAPTER 6

THE NEW GENERATION OF REFORMERS

*We no longer see the teaching of facts and informa-
tion as the primary function of education...building
a new kind of people must be a part of education.*
—1989 Kansas Governor's Education Summit

DR. SHIRLEY McCUNE, a key education
bureaucrat, provided a confirmation that education
reformers are planning even further changes in
schools. On November 2, 1989, she addressed a high
level Kansas Education "summit" called by Kansas
Governor Mike Hayden. For an assembly of governors,
former U.S. cabinet officers and local education officials, Dr. McCune outlined the plan for using schools
to restructure society. She said:

> It seems to me far too much of our effort has been focussed on
> the issue of let's find a short term fix for the schools...rather
> than the issue of understanding that what we are into is a total
> restructuring of society. What is happening in America
> today—what we are facing is a total restructuring of our
> society....but I am not sure we have really begun to com-
> prehend or to act on sufficiently the incredible amount of
> organizational restructuring and human development restruc-
> turing...[needed] to produce human capital.[1]

In addition to confirming that the goal of school
reform is "restructuring society," McCune told how it
would be done:

> We no longer see the teaching of facts and information as the
> primary function of education....Building a new kind of people
> must be a part of the curriculum.....more and more schools are
> the center of all human resource development....The earlier we
> can intervene in the lives of people the more effective we can
> be.[2]

McCune is typical of the new generation of school "reformers" and "planners." She led the way in bringing key educators to see boys and girls as "human capital"—raw material to be shaped and molded into the bricks and mortar for building a new world order. At the time she was the director of the Mid-Continent Regional Laboratory, one of twelve federal education "think tanks." She has also served with the U.S. Department of Education, the National Education Association, the Association of State Chief School Officers and other key education bureaucracies.

Lamar Alexander, president of the University of Tennessee and a former governor of that state, told the conference how McCune's vision was to be imposed on America's children. To achieve the restructuring of society, Alexander challenged the governors and top educators who were present to create what he called "brand new American schools." He described what he meant, saying:

> I would think the brand new American school would be open year round—open from 6 a.m. until 6 p.m. A second characterization might be that these schools would serve children from age three months to eighteen years of age. A shocking thought to you—but if you were to do an inventory of every baby in your community and think about the needs of those babies for the next four or five years, you might see that those needs might not be served in any other way—they have to be served in some way—and maybe around the school. Or if you study a little more, you might go back to think the school might need to serve the pregnant mother of the baby in terms of prenatal care.[3]

After making the speech, Alexander was named U.S. Secretary of Education by President George Bush. Since then new federal and state laws have moved schools toward being centers for meeting (and shaping) all human needs as McCune and Alexander envisioned.

In 1998, for example, Missouri's legislature authorized spending over $50-million to provide year-round 6 a.m. to 6 p.m. child care for children from birth on with "voluntary" kindergarten on the same schedule for 3- and 4-year olds. Stay-at-home moms could also get assistance *if* they enrolled in state-provided parenting programs like Parents As Teachers. In state after state, legislators are considering similar proposals. It's all "encouraged" by President Clinton's $20-billion child care program which the Republican Congress authorized in 1998.

In her speech at the Kansas education summit Shirley McCune said schools were moving toward becoming the "Community Centers" for meeting all human needs. She said:

> Some people say we are spending more on schools and getting less. I disagree—what we are doing is taking on more and more in schools and that will continue. We are not only feeding kids at lunch, we are feeding them in the morning also. We are supplying more psychological services. We are providing special ed services. More and more the school is the cog or center of all human resource development.[4]

What McCune and Alexander outlined at the Kansas summit was largely based on the "consensus" which came out of the National Governors' Education Summit held a few weeks earlier at the call of President George Bush. Key leaders of that 1989 landmark education summit were four men: Lamar Alexander, former governor of Tennessee who later served as President Bush's Secretary of Education; Richard Riley, then governor of South Carolina, who became President Clinton's Secretary of Education; Clinton himself who was then governor of Arkansas and John Ashcroft, then governor of Missouri who now serves in the United States Senate. (Since Ashcroft was elected to the

Senate he shows signs of awakening to the dangers in
some of the programs which developed from the Summit in which he played a key role.)

From that 1989 education summit came federal laws:
Goals 2000, School-to-Work, the New American
Schools Act and the re-enactment and expansion of the
Elementary and Secondary Education Act of 1965. Related "school reform" programs at the state and local
levels implement the blueprint. When fully implemented, these "reforms" will deeply involve schools in
society, health care, job training and employment. The
combined impact will create a nation which will be
drastically different from that in which most
Americans have grown up.

Robert Holland, who reports on education for the
Richmond, Virginia *Times-Dispatch*, revealed that
President Clinton was not alone in promoting "a new
social order." He quotes Clinton's wife Hillary as aspir-
ing to lead...

> ...a remaking of the American way of politics, government,
> and indeed life.[5]

Until she and her husband moved into the White
House, Mrs. Clinton, along with David Rockefeller and
Ira Magaziner (author of the controversial Clinton
health plan), was a key board member of the National
Center on Education and the Economy.[6] NCEE,
headed by Marc Tucker, in 1992 prepared the State of
Washington's proposal to the New American Schools
Development Corporation. The proposal was seeking
grants for reforming schools in Washington as a model
for the nation. The 50-page plan presented an idealistic
vision for "new" schools. The concluding section was
titled, "How We Plan To Do It." That's where the real
goal came to light. Transmitted on a letterhead with

Hillary Clinton's name, it acknowledged the necessity of creating "a new culture," saying:

> Our objective is to make schools of the kind we have described the norm, not the exception, first in cities and states which are Alliance members, and later elsewhere. Getting there will require more than new policies and different practices. It will require a change in the prevailing culture—the attitudes, values, norms and accepted ways of doing things....The question is how to bring about this kind of cultural transformation on the scale we have in mind....and to organize in such a way that the growth of the new culture is geometric.[7]

Arkansas, Kentucky, New York, Vermont and individual school districts in California, Pennsylvania and New York joined in the proposal.[8] More than twenty states are among the targeted members of the "Alliance" formed by NCEE. They pay $100,000 to $500,000 annually in dues or "fees" depending on their population. (Hillary Clinton collected $100,000 personally in consultant or legal fees in one year from the Alliance.)

The Tucker/Rockefeller/Clinton proposal for Washington went far beyond school reform. It proposed making schools the suppliers of all family services. They wrote:

> The design problem here is to improve the planning, financing and delivery of health and human services so they will more effectively support student learning. Specifically, we aim to produce a design that will assure that all children will enter school ready to learn [by taking control of them at three months as Lamar Alexander proposed?] and that none will fail to learn because of health, family or other problems that effective human services could have prevented. This means assuring the availability of integrated, comprehensive services, beginning with prenatal care, and including continuing health care, family support services, child care and preschool education. It will also mean assuring that teachers will be able to mobilize services and supports for the child and family

when they spot a child who needs help. And it means that the
supports—before and after school care, safe recreational opportunities and strong links between school and home—are in
place. We are assembling a team to address these issues.[9]

Accomplishing the entire restructuring which the
50-page document envisions would result in the total
control of society and its families, its health care and
justice systems.

Eight months after the radical proposal was
presented with Hillary Clinton's name on the letterhead, William J. Clinton was elected President of the
United States. A few days after the election, Marc
Tucker of the National Center for Education and the
Economy wrote an 18-page "Dear Hillary" letter outlin-
ing how the radical proposals in the Washington state
plan (and more) could be implemented nationally. It
was sent to her at the Arkansas Governor's Mansion in
Little Rock. The letter (which will be analyzed in detail)
contained the blueprint for a complete restructuring of
education, job training and "labor market policies" in
America.

Tucker's proposals drastically curtail individual
freedom and opportunity. As will be spelled out in the
next chapter on School-to-Work, the plan Tucker outlined in his letter to Hillary Clinton creates a system
for changing the schools of America from agencies for
teaching basic academic skills into workforce development institutions. Full implementation, scheduled for
2001 will produce a top-to-bottom transformation of
American society.

Tucker is not some freelance visionary. His letter
undoubtedly received Mrs. Clinton's close attention.
She was a key member of the board of Tucker's National Center on Education and the Economy before her
husband became President. Her name was on the

letterhead of his "Dear Hillary" letter. Other members of Tucker's high-powered board included David Rockefeller, Apple computer founder John Scully, New York Governor Mario Cuomo and Ira Magaziner, the architect of the Clinton socialized medicine health reform package.

In the introduction of the 18-page November 11, 1992 after-the-election letter,[11] Tucker wrote:

Dear Hillary:

I still cannot believe you won. But utter delight that you did pervades all the circles in which I move. I met last Wednesday [the day after the election] in David Rockefeller's office with him, John Scully, Dave Barram, and David Heselkorn. It was a great celebration. Both John and David R. were more expansive than I have ever seen them—literally radiating happiness...(Page 1)

The subject we were discussing was what you and Bill should do about education, training, and labor market policy....We think the great opportunity you have is to remold the entire American system of human resources development....interwoven with a new approach to governing. (Page 1)

What is essential is that we create a seamless web of opportunities, to develop one's skills that literally extends from cradle to grave and is the same system for everyone— young and old, poor and rich, worker and full-time student....guided by clear standards that define the stages of the system for people who progress through it, and regulated on the basis of outcomes...(Page 2) (Emphasis added.)

Tucker called what he described, "a vision for a kind of national human resources development system." His 18-page letter spelled out the details. Tucker's choice of words fits closely into the vision for producing "human capital" Shirley McCune presented at the Kansas Governor's Conference three years earlier.

Under Tucker's comprehensive plan, all students are trained to meet certain national and international standards. At certain stages "certificates" rather than diplomas are awarded. The type of certificate awarded would determine whether the student goes on into higher education or a specified type of vocational training. Tucker told Hillary there should be...

> ...national standards and exams for no more than 20 broad occupational areas, each of which can lead to many occupations in a number of related industries. Students who qualify in any one of these areas have the broad skills required by a whole family of occupations. (Page 5)

Individuals who did not meet the standards at certain stages or who dropped out would be denied further education or opportunities to enter the workplace of their choice.

As the next chapter on School-to-Work shows, "assessments" channel young people at an early age into one of the 20 life occupational areas. The plan will result ultimately in a total top-to-bottom transformation of American education and national employment practices and governance.

Could it happen? Most Americans—including perhaps many who have read thus far in this book would say, "Never!" However, the authorizing legislation to implement the Tucker plan was passed by Congress during Mr. Clinton's first three years in the White House. Congressman Henry Hyde, chairman of the House of Representatives Judiciary Committee, sees how all the various pieces of education reform legislation fit together. He wrote a three-page "Dear Colleague" letter[12] to all members of Congress in March 1996, saying:

> President Clinton's plan for a national workforce of skilled laborers is being achieved through the Goals 2000 Educate

America Act (HR1804), School to Work Opportunities Act (HR 2884), and Improving America's Schools Act (HR 6), all of which were passed and signed into law by President Clinton in 1994.

Hyde called for repeal of all three laws. He explained:

The plan for Goals 2000 was developed by Bill Clinton, Hillary Clinton, Ira Magaziner, and Marc Tucker, President of the National Center on Education and the Economy (funded by the Carnegie Foundation), prior to Clinton's election. It is a concept for dumbing down our schools and changing the character of the nation through behavior modification (a vital part of this plan). It moves away from an academically intensive curriculum to one that is integrated with vocational training, producing skilled manpower for the labor market. The economy will be controlled by the federal government by controlling our workforce and our schools.

Our children are the guinea pigs who will become the human resources needed for the global labor market. Working adults will be included later.

Hyde enclosed a copy of the 18-page "Dear Hillary" letter in the package he sent to the other members of Congress. Examination of the "Dear Hillary" letter shows that the charges made by Congressman Hyde are correct.

Because the Tucker blueprint seems to provide possible solutions to real problems it has a surface appeal. That's probably why Congress has passed most of the implementing legislation. Some of it won't be mandatory until 2001 after Mr. Clinton leaves office.

Almost everyone recognizes that schools are not turning out students with the basic skills and know-how needed to go into the workplace. Major industries spend millions trying to give new employees basic reading, writing and math skills they should have gotten in school. However, behind all the high sounding visionary concepts and proposals, Tucker's plan will place

America's children, their schools and their future workplaces under total control of unelected but appointed people, boards and committees. It will all be done while paying lip service to state and local autonomy.

Marc Tucker's "Dear Hillary" letter sees America's transformed schools as the foundation for the entire program. On pages 15 and 16, he wrote:

> ...with respect to elementary and secondary education...a new vision and a whole new structure is required....a comprehensive program to support systemic change in public education.

Although the specific term "Outcome-Based Education" is never used in the Tucker letter, the word "outcomes" appears frequently and his proposals are pure OBE [See Chapter 8].

Tucker's letter to Hillary also advocated first steps towards implementing the Lamar Alexander/Shirley McCune proposals for taking control of children at a very early age. He told Hillary:

> Early childhood education should be combined with quality day care to provide wrap-around programs that enable working parents to drop off their children at the beginning of the workday and pick them up at the end. (Page 16)

In Representative Henry Hyde's letter to members of Congress, he provided this evaluation of Tucker's plan for restructuring as it is now being implemented through federal and state legislation. Hyde wrote:

> Dumbing-down education is a prime component in creating a willing workforce. Higher education is not conducive to accepting [by the student] skilled labor training for a career that fits into the federal government's planned labor force. Goals 2000 abandons the American competitive tracking system. It is replaced by new national achievement standards which assess students' behavior and attitude.

Behavior modification is a significant part of restructuring our schools. School children will be trained to be "politically correct," to be unbiased, to understand diversity, to accept alternative lifestyles, to contribute to the community through mandatory community service...

Chapters 1, 2, and 4 which detail what is happening to America's children academically and morally show that Hyde's concerns are valid. Hyde also dealt with widely used school programs called "cooperative learning" and their relationship to the "dumbing down" he discussed earlier. He wrote:

Students are not allowed to excel independently. They must achieve higher levels as groups/units. The brighter students will tutor slower students until the entire unit can move to a higher level. In order not to harm any student's self-esteem, no one fails and no one excels. Everyone receives "satisfactory" when their assignments are completed (at their own pace.)

Near the close of his letter Hyde added a comment showing the far reaching impact of federal and state laws on school reform. Under the new laws schools can use resources for all sorts of supplemental training and social services at the expense of teaching the 3R's. Hyde said:

Preschool, health clinics, daily meals, and parental assistance (they have the gall to instruct parents on how to rear their children, including how students' free time should be spent), are all in this all-inclusive "cradle-to-grave" plan to control our children's minds and careers.

Hyde called for repeal of Goals 2000 and School-to-Work which Congress passed and Clinton signed in 1994. He closed his appeal to the other members of Congress saying:

I ask you to please investigate Goals 2000 yourself. I think you will come to the same conclusion that I have. Goals 2000 must be rejected, and the sooner the better—for our children's sake.

The sad fact is that Goals 2000 is in place. President Clinton would veto any repeal effort and it would take a 2/3 vote of Congress to overturn his veto. There is a way to halt federal involvement, but Congress never appears to have the courage to do it. Every year Congress has the opportunity to cut off all the funding for bad programs. Refusing to pass the budgets for an unconstitutional agency like the Department of Education or the National Endowment for the Arts which has financed blasphemous and pornographic "art" would close them down. It's that simple. However, Congress never does it—and in fact has annually been appropriating more money for "education" than even Clinton asks for.

Hyde's letter to Congress dealt primarily with the impact of Goals 2000 and School-to-Work on schools and children, but employers will be affected too. Under the subtitle "Labor Market Systems," the Tucker/David Rockefeller/Carnegie plan as outlined in the "Dear Hillary" letter said:

> The Employment Service is greatly upgraded and separated from the Unemployment Insurance Fund. All available front-line jobs —whether public or private — must be listed in it by law....So it is no longer a system just for the poor and unskilled, but for everyone. (Emphasis added.) (Page 7)

Note that the Tucker/Rockefeller/Carnegie plan requires that all jobs, public and private, "must be listed" with the new Employment Service.

That the blueprint forcibly encompasses everyone rather than just those with special needs is presented again in sugarcoated language. Tucker makes forcing everyone into the system appear to be a desirable goal

to protect those who are limited. Tucker said of the
Employment Service proposals:

> We would sweep away means-tested programs, because they
> stigmatize their recipients and alienate the public, <u>replacing</u>
> <u>them with programs that are for everyone,</u> but also work for
> the disadvantaged. (Emphasis added.) (Page 7)

To oversee and control the entire education-labor
market structure, the Tucker/Rockefeller/Carnegie
plan called for establishing a National Board for Professional and Technical Standards, a private, not-for-
profit, unelected group funded by Congress and
foundations. However, neither Congress nor the executive branch of government could interfere with the
standards set by the board. His letter to Hillary explains:

> The object is to create a single comprehensive system for
> professional and technical education that meets the require-
> ments of everyone from high school students to skilled-dislo-
> cated workers, from the hard-core unemployed to employed
> adults who want to improve their prospects. (Page 8)

Tucker acknowledges that creating a system which
would encompass the education, training and job place-
ment *of everyone* would produce public outcries and
opposition. To Hillary he wrote:

> Focus groups conducted by JFF and others show that parents
> everywhere want their kids to go to college, not to be shunted
> aside into a non-college apprenticeship "vocational" pro-
> gram....The question is how to get from where we are to where
> we want to be. Trying to ram it down everyone's throat would
> engender overwhelming opposition. (Page 9)

Tucker anticipated the opposition of parents who
would resent having it determined at age 16 that their
children could or could not go to college. He also expected opposition from trade unions to government
assignment to and conduct of apprenticeship programs.

To overcome both parental and union opposition, Tucker proposed having the vocational apprenticeship programs conducted by junior colleges. President Clinton's call for everyone to have "two years of college" fits Tucker's blueprint in that Clinton's two years of college would, for most, not be conventional academic training but rather vocational training conducted by the junior colleges. Tucker's letter to Hillary said:

> All students <u>who meet the new national standards</u> for general education are entitled to the equivalent of three more years of free additional education....So a student who meets the standard at 16 would be entitled to two free years of high school and one of college....Eighty percent or more of American high school graduates will be expected to get some form of college degree, though, most of them less than a baccalaureate. These new professional and technical certificates and degrees typically are won within three years of acquiring the general education certificate [at age 16]. (Page 4)

Tucker also included specific ideas for getting Congressional approval for some parts of the program—and for by-passing Congress on other more controversial aspects. Tucker also deceptively "sugarcoats" proposals to keep parents from realizing that their late-blooming children could be denied college training and be forced into one of twenty job training tracks.

What about the cost? Tucker first said it would be free. But then he added:

> Everyone who meets the general education standard will be able to go to "some form of college," being able to borrow all the money they need to do so, beyond the first free year....Loan defaults will be reduced to a level close to zero. (Page 6)

Tucker then makes what could be a controversial and revolutionary proposal for reducing student loan defaults to "a level close to zero." He wrote:

140 *NONE DARE CALL IT EDUCATION*

...the new postsecondary loan system uses the IRS to collect what is owed from salaries and wages as they are earned. (Page 6)

Tucker's letter to Hillary concluded with these words:

Radical changes in attitudes, values and beliefs are required to move any combination of these agendas....That's it. None of us have any doubt that you have thought long and hard about many of these things and have probably gone way beyond what we have laid out in many areas. But we hope that there is something here that you can use.

Very best wishes from all of us to you and Bill,

Marc Tucker

By 1994 the framework for much of what Tucker proposed was included in the Goals 2000 and School-to-Work laws passed by Congress during President Clinton's first term. Deadlines for putting all the pieces into place are set for the year 2000 and beyond. Nearly all states are already implementing those laws, including the use of school-based clinics to deliver health services to ever growing numbers of America's middle-class families.

CHAPTER 7

HOW WILL SCHOOL-TO-WORK

TRANSFORM AMERICA'S FUTURE?

Dear Hillary: I still cannot believe you won. The subject we were discussing was what you and Bill should do now about education, training and labor market policy. ——*Marc Tucker*

MARC TUCKER'S letter to Hillary was the outline for merging education, job-training, and employment. It did not have the force of law. However, as Congressman Henry Hyde wrote:

> President Clinton's plan for a national workforce of skilled labors is being achieved through the Goals 2000 Educate America Act (HR1804), School-to-Work Opportunities Act (HR2884), and Improving America's School Act (HR6), all of which passed and were signed into law by President Clinton in 1994.

The three laws encompass several thousand pages. What do those laws say—and what will they do?

All three laws presented idealistic, high sounding goals with which almost anyone could agree. However, when their provisions are dovetailed together the net effect is a massive transfer of power. During a five-year period ending in 2001, control over education and employment practices will move from individuals, families, local and state school systems, state legislatures and employers to the unelected National Skills Standards Board and State Workforce Development Boards. Washington's power (and money) will by then have transformed local schools, shifting the purpose of education from creating thinkers to training workers.

Although the School-to-Work process won't be in place fully everywhere until the year 2001, Robert Holland, an editor and columnist for the Richmond, Virginia *Times-Dispatch,* shared "horror stories" of what has resulted already at a high-level Goals 2000 Conference in Washington, D.C. hosted by Congressman Henry Hyde. Holland's stories show what happens as STW is implemented. He reported:

> In Las Vegas, Nevada young Ashley Jensen, who has a 4.0 GPA, dreams of one day going to work for NASA. However, her middle-school career assessment says that her choices ought to be between sanitation worker and interior decorator. Another Nevada student aspires to be a veterinarian, but was told by her counselor that she ought to become a bartender. Her Christian parents understandably felt that their rights had been trampled; they would not want their daughter to become a server of alcoholic drinks.[1]

How could this happen? Under the School-to-Work system, students are matched to what bureaucrats in Workforce Development Boards believe will be the future employment needs in the region. Obviously Las Vegas has more future needs for bartenders than for veterinarians. Holland's examples continued:

> In Dresden, Ohio, high school students can use two class periods a day to learn basketweaving on the job at a local manufacturing company. The students receive academic credit. The company gets to sell the baskets at a profit.

> Before entering Milwaukee's Hamilton High School, students in eighth grade must choose the "career cluster" they will pursue. A student in the Health and Human Services Cluster, for example, studies such profound subjects as food service, fashion and fabrics, parent-hood education, and human diversity—while not being required to take any foreign language. Core subjects like English are integrated into the vocational training.[2]

As part of what School-to-Work calls the "assessment process," the company which markets the ACT college entrance exams now offers a 10-hour series of tests called "Work Keys." Some schools administer the $39 test as a graduation prerequisite. A 16-year-old Wichita, Kansas junior, Jenny Potochnik, took the tests. She then described them as "a waste of time" in a letter to the *Wichita Eagle*.[3] She wrote: "As a junior at Heights High School, I took the Work Keys last week. It costs the school district $39 per student for this test and it takes 10 hours out of valuable classroom time." She continued, "Here are examples of test questions, as well as my editorial comments:"

> An audio tape was played for us and we were to take down the message in detail. Taking phone messages—now that's a good thing to test high school students on! Everyone I talked to thought it was stupid.

> A video tape was played showing us how to transfer a phone call. We were instructed to press flash, the extension number and then flash again. The multiple choice question was: After pressing flash and the extension number, what button do you press? At that point I was beginning to wonder exactly why I had gotten out of bed. I could have taken this assessment in my sleep!

> Then came the floor mopping question. We were instructed by video on how to mop a floor. Then we were given a scenario in which the person mopping did something wrong. We were supposed to say what went wrong.

She commented: "No, I'm NOT kidding!" Her letter continued, "The math portion of the test was 32 questions of simple arithmetic with a few questions about area and volume. No algebra required. The reading assessment was also very simple. It consisted mainly of short memos that we were given to read with very short basic questions to answer."

She added, "The only part of Work Keys I was uncertain of was the technology assessment." She described several questions, saying:

> We were given a diagram of a golf course and its sprinkler system. We were asked which valves to shut off on which greens to maximize water pressure and so on. There were also questions about refrigerator repair, the installation of electrical outlets, and the inner workings of a vacuum cleaner.

She said, "I am a high school student—not an appliance repairman or electrician!" She concluded saying, "A recent article in the Heights newspaper said that we are now spending 19.1 days taking some kind of assessments. This is over ten percent of the school year. Is this overkill?[4]

Jenny addressed her letter to Denny Clements, the editor of the *Wichita Eagle*. She felt he had editorially ridiculed citizens and parents for finding "subversion" in School-to-Work and education "reform." She asked:

> Mr. Clements, are you really so certain that what is being done to reform our schools, right now, will result in greater student learning? Ask my teachers. They are the experts and they will tell you no.

> Jenny Potochnik

The *Work Keys* assessments Jenny described are being used in most states.

Robert Holland commented on Jenny's letter in his Richmond, Virginia *Times-Dispatch* column. He wrote:

> Ah, yes, Jenny, but the point of STW is to redefine education radically so that it is systematically about work, with academics no longer existing apart from "work-based learning."

Holland added:

> Assessments also drive the curriculum. If phone skills and office cooperation are what's being tested, that's what will be

taught. Do we really want education to be more about transferring phone calls than transferring the core knowledge about our heritage and literature from one generation to the next?

Donna Hearne is an author and educational researcher who had three high-level Presidential appointments in the U.S. Department of Education during the Reagan years. She posed these questions about School-to-Work:

Should America's schools teach the next generation the core knowledge and information necessary to produce free, moral, intelligent and independent thinkers? Or should our resources and efforts be directed to creating a compliant, narrowly task-trained workforce with politically correct beliefs and behavior?[5]

Just two weeks before he was killed in a tragic skiing accident during the 1997 Christmas holiday, California Congressman Sonny Bono wrote this letter to a constituent concerning full implementation of School-to-Work:

Under the national School-to-Work system, children's careers will be chosen for them by Workforce Development Boards and federal agencies. Our schools will be restructured to teach labor skills and to focus on changing attitudes and social behavior. The new skill standards replace higher academic standards and emphasize teaching vocational skills as well as social engineering. The School-to-Work system requires all students to receive at least three years of vocational training, two in high school and one in a community college in order to qualify for work certificates....The state of education in America today is tragic.[6]

This is all part of the Human Resources Development Plan devised by Marc Tucker and promoted by the National Center on Education and the Economy in the late 1980s. In 1988, while with the Carnegie Task Force on Teaching, Tucker issued *A Nation Prepared*. After the National Center on Education and the Economy

(funded initially by the Carnegie Foundation) was established, it published Tucker's *America's Choice: High Skills or Low Wages*. His efforts laid the foundation for the Department of Labor's 1991 SCANS Commission report which spelled out the skills schools should teach. (SCANS is the acronym for the *Secretary's Commission on Achieving Necessary Skills*.) The Commissions' *Skills and Tasks For Jobs* was issued in 1992 by Republican Secretary of Labor Lynne Martin's department "for use by curriculum developers, job counselors and training directors." The report showed what it wanted schools to teach by describing 35 jobs broken down by "tasks." To become a "farm worker," for example, the student must be taught and be made willing to "Participate as a Member of a Team." According to the federal job description he would then learn how to:

> Handle manure (e.g., cleaning the barn and spreading manure on fields.)[7]

The student's federal job training description says:

> To perform this task, one farmer sets the spreader in place (farmhand A). The other farmer, using a tractor with loader, fills the spreader (farmhand B). Then the first farmer spreads the manure on the field. Once the manure is spread, both farmers use hand scrapers and shovels to clean areas missed by the tractor.[8]

That is all word-for-word from the federal *Skills and Tasks For Jobs*. The "task" of spreading manure is given the federal identifying number ID#8091631.

A critical aspect of Tucker's plan is replacing traditional diplomas with *Certificates of Initial Mastery (CIM)* and *Certificates of Advanced Mastery*. These are the "work certificates" Congressman Bono's letter mentioned. The "certificates" would be issued at certain ages and stages of school development, i.e. job training. They determine whether a student will go on to college, vocational training—or a job in the workplace. The "certificates" would not be issued to a student on the basis of traditional grades. Instead they are issued based on subjective "assessments" made of his work, whether his attitudes are politically correct, his willingness to be part of a team, etc. Results of the "assessments," including personality and attitude evaluations, etc. are, or will be, included in the learner's "portfolio" which follows him through life.

Tucker's plan is now being imposed on the entire nation through the three bills Congress passed and Clinton signed in 1994. Virginia Miller, a nationally recognized education consultant and research analyst, spoke at the February 1997 Goals 2000 conference hosted by Congressman Henry Hyde. Of Tucker's plan she said:

> It will elevate tasks over knowledge. It will elevate government bureaucrats over the economic freedoms of individuals. It will change the way America educates its children and the way America does business....It will emphasize the acquisition of skills over the acquisition of knowledge.

> This plan is destructive to American liberty because it shifts the purpose of education from creating thinkers to training workers. Projections [about possibly needed types of workers] will become the basis for vocational technical education that is integrated into the curricula of our schools, thereby erecting a mechanism by which the government can centrally plan the labor force.[9]

Goals 2000 and the Improving America's Schools Acts are the foundation on which Marc Tucker's School-to-Work plan is being built nationally. President Clinton signed the third "leg of the stool" or piece in the puzzle, the School-to-Work (HR2884-S1361) bill into law early in May 1994.

In a *New York Times* op-ed article on February 3, 1998, Lynne Cheney who headed the National Endowment for the Humanities in the late 1980s and early 1990s summed up how it has been put into practice. She wrote:

> A central thesis of School-to-Work plans, for example, is that eighth graders should choose careers. To help them along, schools administer interest and personality assessments that direct students toward specific occupations, often ones that seem to have little to do with their ambitions.
>
> School-to-Work programs don't just direct job choices. They also seek to inculcate attitudes. The Federal School-to-Work Opportunities Act of 1994, which prescribes much of what is going on in the state, requires that young women be encouraged to consider "nontraditional employment."
>
> School-to-Work materials frequently insist that all courses, even those in elementary school, relate to the world of work. In Salida, Colorado the entire curriculum from kindergarten through fifth grade—reading, writing, arithmetic and social studies included—recently focussed for a year on careers in health care.

It's all in accordance with the law. The purpose of School-to-Work as set forth in the 1994 federal legislation is...

> ...to establish an educational framework that prepares students for work.[10]

To some people that might sound reasonable. However, educational researchers Ray Ryan and Susan Imel in 1996 produced "School-to-Work Transition: Genuine Reform or the Latest Fad?" Their article was published in ERIC REVIEW, an official publication of the U.S. Department of Education. They charged that in practice...

> ...School-to-Work changes the purpose of education from intellectual development to vocational preparation.[11]

Many Americans would say, "It might be happening somewhere, but not in my state!" However, the 1997 Report to Congress on Implementation of the School-to-Work Opportunities Act by the Secretary of Education Richard Riley and Secretary of Labor Alexis Herman said:

> Our assessment continues to be that the School-to-Work effort shows promising signs of achieving the Congress's objectives. To date, 37 states and more than 1000 communities have been funded for implementation and are putting in place the school and work-based components of School-to-Work....all 50 states have applied for and received planning grants....As of June 1996, 23 percent of the roughly 111,500 elementary and secondary schools in America were engaged in STW.[12]

To properly evaluate the degree to which the STW initiative has penetrated America's schools it is necessary to realize that the 1994 School-to-Work Opportunities Act initiated a system for getting all schools in America involved during the seven-year period ending in 2001.

The 1997 report of the Secretaries of Education and Labor to the Congress spelled out the progress made thus far—and what is still to be accomplished. Their report said:

> The Congress provided seven years for the Federal "seed" money to allow states to design and implement comprehensive STW opportunities systems. Eight states are ready to start the fourth year of their Federal funding, 19 others are starting their third year, and 10 states are in their second year.[13]

The National Governors' Association is pushing STW aggressively. It reported this "progress" at the end of 1996:

> 41 of 50 states had developed skill standards...29 of 50 states had developed assessment tools...39 of 50 states had developed STW curriculum...36 of 50 states had developed "outcome standards"...34 of 50 states had developed career

majors...41 of 50 states had integrated skills standards into
curriculum...and 41 of 50 states were requiring community
service for students...17 of 50 were requiring work experience
in high schools.[14]

So, if STW isn't *fully* in place in a local school district
or state yet, just wait. It is coming. Phyllis Schlafly
addressed the 1996 National Conference of State Legislators meeting in Philadelphia,[15] speaking on "What's
Wrong With School-to-Work?" Rather than "telling"
legislators, she said:

> Let's read directly from the School-to-Work law which was
> passed by Congress in 1994 and signed by President Clinton.
> It states very clearly what this initiative is about.
>
> The purposes of School-to-Work, as spelled out in the law,
> define the new mission of the schools as a transition to the
> workplace. We all thought the mission of the school was to
> educate the child to achieve his potential, but the mission is
> now to transition the student to the workplace.
>
> The whole tenor of the bill is extremely mandatory, compul-
> sory, high-handed. Section 213 requires states to have a com-
> prehensive statewide School-to-Work plan that meets federal
> requirements. No two ways about it, states must conform. The
> state plan must designate labor market development areas to
> be served by Workforce Development Boards. These are
> boards whose members sit around a table and decide what jobs
> the local area is going to need in the next five to ten years....and
> then structuring the public school curriculum to serve the
> employer needs. That is what we call National Economic
> Planning.

Phyllis Schlafly concluded by saying, "All these mandates are laid out in law....and the law repeatedly uses
the words *all students*. This does not mean all public
school students. It does not mean all students who
choose School-to-Work. It means *all* students and that
is made very clear in the law....And it repeats over and
over that career awareness must begin at the earliest

possible age, but no later than seventh grade." She then asked the legislators...

Can you see now why parents don't like School-to-Work?

The more fully School-to-Work is implemented, the more parents don't like it. A review of STW in a publication of the U.S. Department of Education's Office of Educational Research and Improvement warns that parental attitudes about their children's future poses a serious threat to STW. The study said:

> Parents' attitudes about what they want for their children represent one of the greatest barriers to successful implementation of School-to-Work.[16]

Research conducted by the influential Education Commission of the States indicates that most parents think the changes being introduced to schools are "on the wrong track."[17] Research conducted by Public Agenda indicates that rather than vocational job-oriented training that...

> ...parents want schools to increase the focus on academics, teach traditional (subject-specific) knowledge and skills (i.e. math facts, mental computation, phonics, grammar and spelling), increase the rigor of educational standards, base promotion on standardized tests, group students homogeneously (by grade ability) and prepare students for college.[18]

As Marc Tucker anticipated in his letter to Hillary, labor unions don't like it. The Texas AFL-CIO has sued the Texas Workforce Commission which is the oversight agency for School-to-Work implementation in the state. All five labor representatives in the agency had been fired. In filing the suit, Texas AFL-CIO President Joe D. Gunn said:

> From its inception the Texas Workforce Commission has focused solely on what is good for employers, not the

workforce...the No. 1 workforce priority is cheap, compliant labor.[19]

State legislators don't like the Goals 2000 and School-to-Work agenda either. Legislators in Michigan, North Carolina, Oregon, Pennsylvania, Tennessee and numerous other states have spoken out against the bypassing of legislators and their legislative control over education, health care, etc. Federal laws coupled with executive orders at the federal and state levels bypass elected state legislators to institute the STW system.

Oregon was a pioneer state in instituting school "reform" and STW. In 1998, the sponsor of a bill in the Missouri legislature on workforce development said his bill was based on the "Oregon Model." In a February 12, 1998 letter to Missouri legislators, Representative Ron Sunseri, chairman of the Oregon House Education Committee, said:

> It is my hope that Missouri legislators will view this new model of education with great caution. It is clear now that many of our legislators in 1991 did not understand the scope nor the nature of our reform. Many members have acknowledged that had they understood what this reform was to become, they would never have voted to do this to Oregon citizens.
>
> The bill called for academic excellence, intellectual rigor, and the best educated kids in the nation by the year 2000. That was the rhetoric. The reality was that by 1994 one of our pilot school districts went down 17 points in math and 36 points in verbal skills. One entire school (Humboldt Elementary) was shut down because none of the students could read even near level. This past week, one model School-to-Work high school released an independent report showing sixty percent of the student body had a D or less average. The report was covered up for 8 months. Parents are, of course, outraged.

The Oregon legislator's letter continued:

> If Missouri adopts education legislation that parallels what Oregon has done, you, too, will be shifting from effective education (reading, writing and arithmetic) to affective education where the emphasis is on attitudes, behaviors, and socialization. Academic subjects become secondary. We were continually assured that these things would never happen...That was the rhetoric and now we must live with the reality. Please do not be deceived or falsely persuaded.

A year earlier, over 75 Missouri legislators had signed a joint letter to members of Missouri's congressional delegation asking them to "Revise federal education laws by repealing Goals 2000." They spelled out their concerns about the process initiated by Goals 2000 and STW which...

> ...centralize unprecedented powers at the federal level....superseding state laws and took us, the local elected officials of the people of this state, OUT of the process of education....In Missouri, the Democrat governor instructed his bureaucrats to make application for Goals 2000 monies by defining a whole system of laws and procedures that we would put in place in order to get the money. Most legislators are only now, for the first time, even seeing what he is binding us and our children to....This practice of avoiding the legislature is unacceptable.[20]

The decision to implement STW is generally made by a governor and state agencies. Texas offers a characteristic example. On August 18, 1996, the Republican Governor George W. Bush submitted an application for a STW implementation grant. This application committed Texas to meet the federal requirements for obtaining STW funding without the approval of the state legislature or the State Board of Education. The state education laws had not been amended to legislate the specific requirements for STW. After the deal was done the legislature was urged to "review" school reforms initiated by state agencies to meet requirements that "emanate from federal legislation."[21]

How do these programs get adopted and then imposed on local school districts? Bob Offutt is a member of the Texas State Board of Education. He says:

> School-to-Work came to Texas like a thief in the night. One morning parents will wake up to learn that the American Dream has been stolen from their children...unlimited educational opportunity has been replaced by limited job training options determined by regional workforce needs. The state Board of Education didn't approve this radical transformation of the public education system, and we are powerless to change it.[22]

Offutt didn't say it, but some students will prosper. Those with intelligence who absorb and demonstrate the politically correct agenda and attitudes will be taught to think and reason—but from a humanistic foundation. They will be trained to be the leaders of the "new social order" the early reformers set out to establish over 65 years ago.

Offutt wasn't alone among state boards of education members in his concerns about School-to-Work and the way it is being imposed on America. Diana Fessler is an elected member of the Ohio State Board of Education. In early 1997 she prepared a detailed 72-page, carefully referenced report on STW for the Ohio State Board of Education.[23] In it she told a story very similar to what happened in Texas:

> From November 1992, until the present, the Ohio State Board of Education has not engaged in discussion, let alone debate, on national content, performance or assessment standards, and/or Certificates of Initial Mastery. I presume no such discussion is taking place in the legislature. The result of this grievous omission is that the necessary groundwork for *The System* continues to be laid in Ohio without the *informed consent* of the elected representatives of the people. And all

the while, control of education is shifting from state and local school boards to NCEE and company. (Page 29)

She issues periodic follow up reports titled, "School-To-Work: It's The Law." In the November 1997 issue she tells how good people "go along" in adopting programs about which they know too little. She wrote:

Many business and industry leaders, legislators and even members of the general population have accepted STW without knowing what it is or its impact on our nation. Many, myself included, have unwittingly supported STW because we have not been fully informed concerning the STW system. To my shame, when the matter came before the Ohio State Board of Education in September 1996, based on the information available at the time, I voted in support of the resolution.

My current understanding of STW is a result of personal research conducted over the last twelve months. Not everyone has the time for exhaustive research and decisions must be made on the best information at the time that a decision must be made. It is for those reasons that I fully understand why many local board members and others may have given their support to STW efforts in their communities. (Page. 9)

As a result of her year-long "exhaustive study" how does Diana Fessler now understand School-To-Work? In her report she writes:

Based on federal law [totaling over 2000 pages], work-based learning is mandatory. By its very nature STW integrates occupational and academic training. The notion of opting out is completely incompatible with the totality of STW. The result: our schools are being converted to job-training centers. This job-training, beginning in kindergarten, will reduce our children and grandchildren to dependent, intellectually stunted laborers. (Page 9)

Fessler added these words which should be read and heeded by all elected and appointed officials:

Once informed about what STW really is, those of us sworn to uphold the Constitution will be hard pressed to support a national system that regulates our children's future employment and education.

Abolishing STW will take the kind of political courage demonstrated by Craig Hagen, North Dakota's elected Commissioner of Labor. After serving for three years on the state's STW management team, he resigned as a matter of principle because he could no longer support STW. (Page 9)

The resignation letter North Dakota's Commissioner of Labor, Craig Hagen, sent to his governor, Ed Shafer, included a detailed three-page attachment explaining his reasons for resigning. He told the governor:

There is no sound rationale for North Dakota's plan which calls for career guidance counseling from kindergarten through sixth grade or the provision in the federal law stating that children should be helped to "select or reconsider" careers not "traditional" to their sex, race or ethnic background which could result in "outright value manipulation." As for selecting career majors by 11th grade, what about those students who are not interested? Will a career major be selected for them by instructors and counselors who have been giving them career interest tests since kindergarten? There are many people who do not choose a career major until their second or third year in college and they are not mature enough to do so earlier. Yet STW would force them into a career track at an early age.[24]

Another area of concern was the STW emphasis of using "portfolios" for each child. Hagen said:

North Dakota's plan calls for developing career portfolios for each pupil "containing notations of skills, hobbies, talents, and personal goals, as well as records of work experiences, inter- and extra curricular activities, training programs and significant accomplishments. The state is to train teachers in implementing portfolios, which will be "sources of information for future employers." Essentially, these all-inclusive files will follow an individual throughout life.[25]

Hagen criticized the STW portfolio system which ultimately is to be stored in an electronic file available for access by prospective employers saying, "Kids make lots of mistakes growing up and maturing. These mistakes don't need to be recorded to haunt them the rest of their lives." He added that permanent records should only contain objective material and not subjective judgments made by teachers or counselors at some point during twelve years of schooling. Of the required "political correctness" he said:

> North Dakota's plan states that in the seventh and eighth grades students will be put through a "sex equity experience" and "multiculturalism will be included in curricula developed for STW programs.[26]

As he resigned from North Dakota's STW board, Hagen asked the questions that parents, school board members and legislators across America should be raising. He wrote:

> When did we decide the school, the former provider of knowledge to our children, would become the job training center of America? When did we mandate the schools with the task of ensuring our children's psychological, physical, and emotional health according to some subjective norm we've never seen?

> Ask yourself: Did the Founding Fathers of this nation, dedicated to ensuring the freedom of all citizens and a free enterprise system, envision schools that would socialize values, opinions, knowledge, training, skills, and jobs? Isn't that what ultimately happens under this plan?[27]

Diana Fessler of the Ohio State Board of Education had earlier come to the same conclusion. When she learned of Hagen's resignation from the North Dakota STW Management Team and his reasons for doing so, she commented:

> May others also have the wisdom and courage to take steps needed to disengage from STW.[28]

All states don't use the School-to-Work name or the STW acronym. In Illinois it's called *Education to Careers* (ETC). In California it's *School to Career* (STC). North Carolina calls it the *JobReady* program. Virginia doesn't like the STW label so has a program for "professional-technical studies." Whatever name is used, it is still School-to-Work.

STW gets major support from educational organizations, associations and think tanks, nonprofit foundations, manufacturers of educational products and business groups, and quasi-government groups including...

...the National Governor's Association, Education Commission of the States, The National Education Association, the American Federation of Teachers, the National PTA, National Association of School Boards, the Carnegie Corporation, the DeWitt Wallace Reader's Digest Foundation, Pew Charitable Trusts, the Committee for Economic Development, the National Alliance of Business, the Association of Manufacturers, the U.S. Chamber of Commerce, the U.S. Conference of Mayors, the National Conference of State Legislators, etc., etc., etc.[29]

As Diana Fessler explained, many of these groups and the executives in them have gone along with idealistic sounding programs without doing the personal research needed to separate rhetoric from fact. Unfortunately, once they get committed, they defend their decision and fail to do on-going research on the dangerous program. Others, she says, knew full well what they were giving their support to.

How does it all work in actual practice? The St. Louis Career Academy opened in July 1996. After only six months in operation, the school was recognized by U.S. Secretary of Education Richard Riley as one of the five top "New Urban High Schools" in the nation. The award was presented by Missouri Congressman Richard Gephardt.[30]

During its first year news articles and editorials in the *St. Louis Post-Dispatch* gave rave reviews saying:

> Early reports from the academy already show students gaining more than three grade levels with African-Americans doing better than whites....The Career Academy is a textbook example of success—one the region should study and emulate....a national model....[31]

The Career Academy should have fulfilled the dreams of even the most futuristic-minded reformer. In an interview with a St. Louis Christian newspaper, Dr. Larry Hutchins, Chief Executive Officer for the Career Education District, said he had worked with Marc Tucker and the National Center for Education and the Economy. For twelve years he headed the Mid-Continent Regional Education Laboratory.[32] (Dr. Shirley McCune, who gave the speech on using schools "to build a new kind of people" at the Kansas Governor's Conference, was on Hutchins' staff.)

In April 1998, faculty and staff at the school were asked to respond to a glowing 11-page dissertation about the school titled "Building the Foundation for Life-Long, Self-Directed Learning." A teacher, Christine Burns, submitted a cover letter titled "St. Louis Career Academy—Reality Check" with a scathing 24-page paragraph-by-paragraph response.

When asked by the *MetroVoice* what prompted her, a 25 year teacher, to take such action, she said:

> I've been teaching at the St. Louis Career Academy for eight months. I have been witness to the most chaotic, unprofessional and deceitful situations I've ever seen in my professional career.

> I've gone home sick, literally sick. I've watched as the administration has paraded visitor after visitor into school and

successfully bamboozled them (apparently) into believing educational experiences of some value were taking place at the Academy. I have listened to countless presentations about the Academy that absolutely turned my stomach because of the blatant lies and exaggerations expressed about what was happening there.[33]

She had already informed the school administration that she would not accept a teaching contract for the next year. When she was asked to read, critique and sign off on the glowing dissertation which she says was...

...full of lies, suppositions and half truths, something snapped. I realized that I could not walk away without someone, somewhere knowing what I believed to be the truth about what is happening, or rather what is not happening at St. Louis Career Academy."

Among the charges in Mrs. Burns' 24-page response to "Building the Foundation for Life-Long, Self-Directed Learning" she had been asked to critique are:

An escalating amount of violence in school including fights and riots....Destruction and theft of computer equipment....Students roam the halls at will disrupting other classes due to lack of passes or class bells....unrestricted access to the Internet and E-Mail results in the accessing of on-line pornography through school computers...."Team Learning" is hated or disliked by a large number of students because brighter students do all the work while other team members cheat....Students cheat on Destination Tests to advance to the next "tier" (The CED term for grade levels), and are not required to take a written test to confirm their skill levels....No homework is allowed to be given despite complaints by teachers, parents and students.[34]

That's how one teacher sees the St. Louis Career Academy, a "model school" which U.S. Secretary of Education says is one of the top five in the nation. The complete 11-page dissertation Burns was asked to critique, her 24-page response and the administration's attempt to answer her and the questions of the newspaper can be found on the *MetroVoice* web page at http://www.brick.net/stlmv.

While paying regular lip service to the "voluntary" aspects of Goals 2000, Improving America's Schools Act and STW Opportunities Act all the bills repeatedly use language which says "...all students...." When laws say *all students* the meaning is that ultimately "all students" (public, private or homeschooled) will be included. Here are examples from the Goals 2000 and Improving America's Schools Acts which refer to *all students:*

> ...by the year 2000, <u>all students</u> will leave grades 4, 8, and 12 having demonstrated competency over challenging subject matter...

> ...<u>all students</u> will be involved in activities that promote and demonstrate good citizenship, good health, community service, and personal responsibility.

> ...<u>all students</u> will be knowledgeable about the diverse cultural heritage of this Nation and about the world community.

> ...the term "State assessment" means measures of student performance...which are intended to evaluate the progress of <u>all students</u> in the State toward learning the material in the State content standards...

These goals or requirements may sound good but they should raise many questions. The concern is that the law again and again specifies <u>all students</u>. The National Education Goals spelled out in the first section of the Goals 2000 law have similar all-inclusive language. Achieving the goals will move the government into every home and every child/parent relationship. The law says:

By the year 2000, <u>all children</u> in America <u>will</u> start school ready to learn.

How can that be accomplished unless some governmental agency gets involved in the home between the time a child is born and age 5? The law further states:

> ...<u>every parent</u> in the United States <u>will</u> be a child's first teacher and devote time <u>each day</u> to helping such parent's preschool child learn...

This is a desirable goal, but how far will the government go in determining if parents are fulfilling the requirements of this federal law? Could failing to do so trigger enforcement of state laws which define "child neglect" as failing to provide "education as required by law?" Parents in Idaho, Nebraska, Michigan, Iowa, Missouri and other states have either lost their children or been threatened with loss of their children for homeschooling or enrolling children in non-approved Christian schools in the last fifteen years. The Goals 2000 law raises concerns. How far, for example, will the government go in enforcing the requirement that before starting school at age 5...

> ...children <u>will receive</u> the nutrition, physical activity experiences, and health care needed to arrive at school with healthy minds and bodies, and to maintain the mental alertness necessary to be prepared to learn...

Again, these are desirable goals—but the law says it <u>will</u> be done. How, for example, can the government ensure that children receive needed "physical activity experiences" without intruding into the family? The federal legislation—and many of the state reform bills—will move the government and its schools into every area of family life and living.

Again the Goals 2000 legislation says:

By the year 2000, the high school graduation rate <u>will</u> increase to at least 90 percent.

How will it be accomplished? One way would be to reduce the standards for all graduates. As the next chapter shows, Outcome-Based Education programs in some states have already done this by abolishing the use of traditional credits for graduation and replacing them with "assessment programs" which determine if the student has developed "right attitudes."

Even as the structure is created for nationalizing education in America, the legislation pays lip service to "voluntary participation" and continued local control of schools. The bills include language which legislators can point to as safeguarding local control.

How "voluntary" it all is was shown by Missouri's experience. The Governor submitted the state's voluminous School-to-Work application for a federal "implementation grant." On October 6, 1995 the state's application for STW funds was denied by a letter signed by Timothy Barnicle, an Assistant Secretary of Labor and Patricia McNeil, Acting Assistant Secretary of Education. Their letter said:

> While Missouri's State plan addressed many of the 23 <u>required</u> elements listed in the School-to-Work Opportunities Act, some elements were missing. We cannot, under the law, approve your plan at this time....A detailed discussion of the strengths and weaknesses of Missouri's application, as identified by the review panel, will be sent to you later this month. (Underline added.)

Nine weeks later Missouri received a three-page analysis of how its plan failed to meet the "voluntary" requirements of the federal government. The federal letter told Missouri:

> There are few strategies discussed for overcoming the obstacles that exist in serving <u>all</u> students....The State plan to

support local School-to-Work efforts is not sufficiently proactive....We encourage you to continue momentum toward establishing School-to-Work opportunities for all students.[35] (Underlines added for emphasis.)

Alabama's Governor Fob James and the Alabama legislature decided not to enter the "voluntary" program. They refused an initial federal grant of $14-million. Dick Brewbaker, a key Alabama educator said that when Alabama continued to reject the Goals 2000 money, Michael Cohen of the U.S. Department of Education came to Alabama to "pour oil on our troubled Goals 2000 waters." Cohen met with key members of the governor's staff including Brewbaker who reported:

> He kept telling us that there were no mandates in the Goals 2000 Act. But when you look at it, there are 63 places where the Act says that states who participate *will* do something and 195 places where it says states *shall* do something.[36]

When Cohen was shown the examples, he always said:

> Don't worry, we're not going to enforce those sections of the Act. You don't have to do it. Just take the money.[37]

Brewbaker said:

> I thought the Governor's lawyer was going to have apoplexy when that sort of language was presented to him. The problem is that in Alabama we have tried to ignore federal statutes before and it always lands us in exactly the same place—a federal courtroom with a federal judge telling us we *will* comply with the law.[38]

The state and federal bills channel multiplied billions of dollars into creating a system and the bureaucratic structure to implement it. Goals 2000 appropriates billions of dollars to finance dozens of panels, councils, institutes and commissions. Appropriations of from $1-million up to $400-million annually are authorized for the staff and program of *each* of these bureaucracies.[39] A gigantic new multi-layered bureaucracy is established and financed within the government which also encompasses various think tanks and consulting agencies outside government which grow fat on federal and state grants.

Seeing how all the pieces of the state and federal education reform package fit together and reach into every area of family life validates the shocking judgment of author and veteran education researcher Samuel Blumenfeld. He says:

> ...the cumulative impact of this avalanche of education legislation amounts to a cultural revolution being imposed on the American people.[40]

Hillary Clinton's visionary planners, Marc Tucker and David Hornbeck, said achieving their goals...

> ...will require a change in the prevailing culture—the attitudes, values, norms and accepted ways of doing things....The question is how to bring about this kind of cultural transformation on the scale we have in mind...[41]

Remember that the dictionary says the "culture" which they plan to transform is...

> ...the sum total of ways of living built up by a group of human beings, which is transmitted from one generation to another.

At stake in our schools are the ways of living we will hand down to our children and our grandchildren. In the light of those words, President George Bush's April 18, 1991 speech kicking off the drive for what has become Goals 2000 fits right into the blueprint. Bush said the goal was...

> New schools for <u>a new world</u>.[42]

The destruction of our culture through the schools has not been a partisan political effort. It is bipartisan and both parties share the blame.

CHAPTER 8

USING OUTCOME-BASED EDUCATION TO MODIFY CHILDREN'S BEHAVIOR

The purpose of education is to change the thoughts, feelings and actions of students.
      —Dr. Benjamin Bloom, grandfather of OBE[1]

IN HIS COMMENTS on the infamous "Dear Hillary" letter, Congressman Henry Hyde charged that the Goals 2000/STW education reforms were a planned concept...

> ...for dumbing down our schools <u>and changing the character of the nation through behavior modification</u>.[2]

Other opponents of school reform plans who were quoted earlier made similar charges. The school reformers them-selves acknowledged that behavior modification—"changing people"—was their goal. Dr. Shirley McCune was quoted in Chapter 6 saying:

> We no longer see the teaching of facts and information as the primary function of education....Building a new kind of people must be a part of the curriculum.[3]

Congressman Sonny Bono in his letter said that behavior modification was already being done. In the letter to a constituent quoted in the previous chapter he said:

> Our schools will be restructured to teach labor skills and to focus on changing attitudes and social behavior.[4]

Lynne Cheney, former head of the National Endowment for the Humanities, showed in her *New York Times* article that:

School-to-Work programs don't just direct job choices. They also seek to inculcate attitudes.

The chairman of the Education Committee in the Oregon House of Representatives said that through school "reform" Oregon shifted...

from effective education (reading, writing and arithmetic) to affective education where the emphasis is on attitudes, behaviors, and socialization. Academic subjects become secondary.[5]

The vehicle the reformers have used to accomplish this "behavior modification" was initially called "Outcome-Based Eucation." OBE, as it came to be known, provoked widespread controversy, legislative reactions, and teacher concerns in many of the more than 25 states where it was proposed, studied, advocated or adopted. Parents, educators and legislators expressed concerns that OBE placed more emphasis on developing attitudes than on academic achievement. OBE became so controversial by the mid-1990s that the term was dropped, but the OBE cycle for in-school behavior modification has continued under other names. Among them are competency-based education, high-performance education, and performance-based education.

Liberal educators have traditionally used good sounding words to describe or label experimental programs. Often, rather than solving programs, the innovations contribute to lowering academic achievement and the "dumbing down" of the students. When failures become evident, rather than dropping a controversial program, its name is changed.

Outcome-Based Education (OBE) became the buzzword in education in the early 1990s. All education should have goals (or outcomes) the teacher, the school, the district or the state work to achieve. A first grade teacher, for example, has the goal of teaching her students to read.

William Spady, one of the developers of what came to be called "Outcome-Based Education,"[6] claims on that basis that all education is outcome-based. Spady adds, however, that there are three kinds of OBE. Traditional OBE works toward academic "outcomes" or goals. Transitional OBE adds attitudinal goals (usually liberal) to traditional academic ones. Transformational OBE places major emphasis on attitudes the graduate should possess about himself, others, world peace, the environment, AIDS, etc. The question of course is: Who determines what are the "right" or passing attitudes?

An OBE program or cycle involves (1) establishing goals (outcomes), (2) planning instruction to achieve these goals, and (3) developing tests or "assessments" to determine if goals are being met. (4) Those who do not measure up (academically or attitudinally) are "remediated" until they finally meet the goals or achieve the "outcomes"—no matter how long it takes.

There can be two problems with the OBE blueprint. First, the goals must be right—and with OBE they aren't. Family Research Council issued a report on OBE in 1994 saying:

> ...the outcomes that the gurus of OBE have in mind have less to do with whether Johnny can comprehend the Federalist Papers or place the Civil War in the correct half-century than with his acquisition of the desired attitudes on such issues as global resource inequality, multiculturalism, homelessness, alternative lifestyles, and environmentalism. Under OBE, political correctness goes to grade school. The new outcomes are supposed to make education "relevant" to "real life problems."[7]

The second major problem with OBE is that its advocates say, "No student will fail—all will measure up."

That sounds appealing. Yet all students do not have the same basic abilities. To insure that <u>all</u> achieve the targeted outcomes there must be a leveling down of the goals.

The problem was spelled out in a September 1992 publication of the Missouri Department of Elementary and Secondary Education (DESE). In answering the question, "What are some of the major challenges in the process of converting to OBE?" DESE said:

> The first and most critical challenge is changing our beliefs and attitudes. We must stop believing that a few students will do well in school, that most will be "average" and that some will certainly fail. That belief or expectation will be difficult to change because, in all our experience, that is what we have observed. A successful conversion to OBE requires us to believe that virtually <u>all students can learn at a satisfactory level.</u> They can if our schools are organized and conducted to achieve that goal.[8] (Underline added.)

In other words, we have to decide to disbelieve what we have observed to be true.

Phyllis Schlafly, in a May 1993 report on "What's Wrong With Outcome-Based Education?" said:

> OBE is based on the unrealistic notion that every child in a group can learn to the designated level and must demonstrate mastery of a specific outcome before the group can move on. The faster learners are not allowed to progress, but are given busy work called "horizontal enrichment" or told to do "peer tutoring" to help the slower learners, who are recycled through the material until the predetermined behavior is exhibited.[9]

In a traditional classroom situation, it's true that every student doesn't "get it" at the same rate. However, as a math class, for example, moves on and concepts are reviewed, applied and used, the light "turns on" for the slower student. It happens without the rest of the class being hindered.

Kentucky was one of the earliest states to adopt the entire reform package incorporating OBE when, in 1990, it passed the Kentucky Education Reform Act (KERA). OBE, like School-to-Work, has moved at varying paces sometimes under other names. In Idaho, for example, the label was ODDM for Outcome Driven Development Model. Parts of the OBE program are referred to as mastery learning, restructuring, relearning, or cooperative learning. By using different names, educators can say, "We don't have OBE."

Actually, Outcome-Based Education is just a recycled, renamed version of an earlier failed program called "mastery learning." The "father" of OBE, Dr. Bill Spady, acknowledged the relationship. In an article titled, "On Outcome-Based Education: A Conversation With Bill Spady," in the December 1992-January 1993 issue of *Educational Leadership*, Spady said:

> In January of 1980 we convened a meeting of 42 people to form the Network for Outcome-Based Schools. Most of the people who were there...had a strong background in Mastery Learning, since it was what OBE was called at the time. But I pleaded with the group not to use the name "mastery learning" in the network's new name because the word "mastery" had already been destroyed through poor implementation.

Mastery Learning was the brainchild of Professor Benjamin Bloom. It was a colossal failure when tried in Chicago schools in the 1970s. Illiteracy increased and students' achievement test scores dropped dramatically. Even so it was widely promoted and adopted across the nation in the 1980s. Bloom taught that...

> ...the purpose of education is to change the thoughts, feelings and actions of students.[11]

The OBE name, but not the system, has almost vanished as a result of controversy and setbacks in

Pennsylvania and other states in the early 1990s. The *Washington Times* said:

> Pennsylvania has become the first state in the nation to scrap traditional high-school graduation requirements for a set of "learning outcomes" that may include "appreciating and understanding others."

> Under recently approved regulations, a high-school diploma will no longer be awarded for taking and passing four years of English, three years of mathematics, science and social studies, two years of arts and humanities, a year of health and physical education and five electives. Instead, students will have to demonstrate their proficiency in meeting 51 "learning outcomes" that critics complain are based more on developing particular attitudes about such issues as the environment and cultural differences than about academics.[11]

The newspaper story quoted a spokesman for the Education Commission of the States saying that Minnesota, Washington, Colorado and Connecticut among others were the states then moving to adopt "learning outcomes" aimed at influencing feelings or emotions. The story explained that Pennsylvania's Board of Education had set five broad "goals of quality education" that local school districts must consider in revising the curriculum. The goals included:

> ...self worth, information and thinking skills, learning independently and collaboratively, adaptability to change, and ethical judgment.

To achieve those five goals the Pennsylvania Board of Education formulated a list of 51 academic and attitudinal outcomes. The newspaper reported:

> One outcome under "environment and ecology" would require students to demonstrate that they "make environmentally sound decisions in their personal and civic lives." Under "appreciating and understanding others," students must demonstrate that they can "work effectively with others,

recognizing the intrinsic uniqueness, worth and rights of each person."

Peg Luksik, a leader of the Pennsylvania Coalition for Academic Excellence which fought the changes, asked:

> How do you measure someone's attitude? What standards are to be set for proper attitude and how do you remediate attitude?[12]

Thousands of people turned out for meetings across the state protesting OBE outcomes. As a result, in early 1993 the Pennsylvania House of Representatives by a 139-61 vote called for the state Board of Education to take its outcome-based proposal back to the drawing board. The State School Board of Education basically ignored the legislative efforts. The *Washington Times* reported:

> A spokeswoman for the state school board said the House action was "outside the regular regulatory process" and has "no immediate impact."

Other states had been moving similarly. Missouri's 1992 proposal for implementing OBE in Missouri listed 40 other states which were already moving on OBE either by actions of state legislatures or boards of education.[13] Phyllis Schlafly's report "What's Wrong With Outcome-Based Education?" reported that the state of Washington's Performance-Based Education Act of 1993 called for a new performance-based assessment system to "replace the current standardized achievement tests."

The word "assessment" appears numerous times in this chapter and the one on School-to-Work. Understanding the difference between "assessing" and "testing" is essential. "Testing" measures a student's performance against established absolute standards of right or wrong, true or false, good or bad. An "assessment" is just someone's best judgment or evaluation of a student's attitudes, accomplishments, beliefs and behavior. It can be very biased, influenced by "political correctness."

Mrs. Schlafly said that Washington's "performance goals" were extremely vague and gave these examples:

> Under Goal 1, students are to communicate "effectively and responsibly in a variety of ways and settings." No indication is given of what is meant by "responsibly." Under Goal 2, students must know and apply the core concepts and principles of "healthful living." What constitutes "healthful living" is not disclosed. Goal 4 instructs students to "function as caring and responsible individuals and contributing members of families, work groups and communities." "Responsible" and "caring" are undefined. "Citizenship" is redefined from its traditional sense to include "a multicultural and world view."[14]

Phyllis Schlafly sums up her concerns by saying:

> OBE involves a major change in the school's avowed mission. Henceforth, its mission is to conform student beliefs, attitudes and behavior to prescribed school-mandated social norms, rather than to provide an academic education. Parents are concerned about what methods will be used to change behaviors that are deemed incorrect.[15]

She discussed terms or "buzzwords" OBE educators use:

> When educators talk about "higher order thinking skills" or "critical thinking," they mean a relativistic process of questioning traditional moral values.

> Parents who are trying to rear their children with strong traditional values are concerned that willingness to go along with the crowd is taught by OBE as a positive rather than a negative attitude. Since "tolerance" is a major attitudinal outcome demanded by OBE, parents are concerned that this includes "tolerance" for extra-marital lifestyles of all kinds. The non-directive "decision-making" classroom approach leads children to believe they are mature enough to make

decisions about sex and drugs that parents believe are unhealthy and may even be illegal.[16]

OBE has been imposed on schools across America without most parents being aware of it. In July 1990, for example, the State Board of Education in Missouri issued a report saying:

> By the end of the decade, all school districts will adopt outcome-based education practices. This effort should include widespread adoption of mastery learning strategies...and reduced dependence on textbooks as the primary basis for organizing instruction.[17]

The State Board of Education mandated OBE for Missouri in 1990. Three years later when the legislature considered and passed SB380, the Marc Tucker-developed plan for restructuring Missouri schools, the bill never used the words "Outcome-Based Education." By then OBE was controversial, so the words weren't used—but the OBE system was imposed by law on the state's schools.

Actually, the legislature just rubber-stamped the State School Board/Marc Tucker plan which was in place—and added a $300-million annual tax increase to pay for it.

After issuing the 1990 edict mandating OBE for Missouri schools, the State School Board had followed up with its *Universal Outcomes* in September 1992. They were similar to those the Pennsylvania legislature tried to reject. The Missouri publication had almost seven pages of "outcomes" devoted largely to attitudes with only three pages on academics. The Missouri "outcomes" require students...

> ...to demonstrate that they can "make informed, rational decisions on social issues" and that they can "identify, investigate, discuss and take reasoned positions on major public policy issues." (Who will decide what is a "rational" or

"reasoned" position on a social or public policy issue?) Other potentially explosive required "outcomes" include understanding "relationships between environments and people's well-being," "using rational decision-making processes to make informed health-related decisions...and behaviors which can prevent life-style-related deaths and diseases."[18]

These "outcomes" open the door to classroom advocacy of condoms for "safe sex," abortion, etc. In addition to imposing outcomes, the Missouri State School Board guidelines require schools to...

> ...develop and use new assessment techniques (essays, <u>portfolios</u>, interviews, etc.) which go beyond traditional pencil-and-paper testing methods. (Underline added for emphasis.)

The concerns that North Dakota Labor Commissioner expressed in the previous chapter about dangers of the STW "portfolios" parallel the concerns of Phyllis Schlafly. She charged that computers and electronic portfolios will...

> ...track the child's efforts to master the learning outcomes. These "electronic portfolios" will take the place of traditional assessments and test results....The portfolios will include all school, psychological and medical records, and are to be available to prospective employers after graduation....The computer records how the child responds to behavior modification, what is his threshold of resistance to remediation, and whether he develops positive attitudes toward mandated outcomes.[19]

Like the North Dakota Labor Commissioner, she asks:

> Will the child be able to get a job if he has not demonstrated the OBE values and Politically Correct attitudes?

With no absolutes on which to base judgments, a conservative student might not get a good "assessment" (and graduation) from a liberal teacher—or vice versa.

Imposing attitude outcomes is not the only tragic result of OBE. Bad "outcomes" deprive children of the basic tools needed for the "lifelong learning" to which OBE and education reformers pay lip service. Phyllis Schlafly analyzed the five volumes of "Learner Outcomes"[20] for Grades One through Twelve issued in 1992 by the Oklahoma State Department of Education. She wrote:

> The Foreword in each volume makes clear that the changes in the school system do not mean teaching the basics (usually defined as reading, writing and arithmetic). The Foreword states: "Oklahoma has joined a national movement in education—not a *back-to-basics* approach, but an effort to focus and organize all of the school's educational programs and instructional efforts around clearly defined outcomes we want all students to demonstrate when they leave school."

The instructions for one "clearly defined outcome" dooms most children to lifelong reading problems and frustrated school careers. Mrs. Schlafly explains:

> The Oklahoma Learner Outcomes dictate total subservience to the discredited "word guessing" method of teaching reading to first graders, and do not allow the use of the proven phonics method. Instead of teaching children to read by learning the sounds and syllables of the English language so that the child can sound out words, the child is taught by endless repetition to memorize a few dozen "sight" words, to guess at new words by looking at the pictures on the page, to "predict" the text instead of reading it, and to skip over words they can't read.

Teachers are instructed *not* to have the child focus on sounding out actual words, but to let the student substitute any words that seem to fit. The ability to read a simple story that a child has never seen is *not* on the list of Oklahoma "outcomes."

Direct quotations from the official *Oklahoma State Competencies, Grade One, pages 15-22* confirm that first-graders will reach their OBE "Reading Learner Outcome" by guessing rather than reading:

> The student attends to the meaning of what is read rather than focusing on figuring out words....Uses the context, pictures, syntax, and structural analysis clues to predict meanings of unknown words. Develop a sight vocabulary of high frequency words....Predicts unknown words....Uses predictions in order to read pattern books (stories with a repetitive element)....Uses fix-it strategies (predicts, uses pictorial cues, asks a friend, skips the word, or substitutes another meaningful word)....The student will interpret the story from illustrations. (Underlines added for emphasis.)

In her analysis Phyllis Schlafly said, "Predicting is *not* reading, nor is asking a friend, nor is guessing at the meaning from the illustrations!" For Grade 2, Oklahoma reinforces the guessing game approach rather than teaching the child to read. Quotations from pages 7-15 include:

> Use context clues and nonverbal clues to aid comprehension (pictures, type faces, word placement, illustrations)....Predict outcomes....Makes, verifies, and/or revises predictions while reading.

The Oklahoma Learner Outcomes for Mathematics, Grade One (pages 25-27) make clear that children will not learn ordinary math skills that will enable them eventually to make change at the grocery store. Instead they are given a mish-mash of "higher-order thinking skills" and "facility in applying technology." That means that instead of learning 2+2=4, first graders get calculators. The instructions say:

> The longstanding preoccupation with computation and emphasis on rote activities must change to a focus of fostering mathematical insight, reasoning and problem solving both individually and in collaborative groups.

The mention of "collaborative groups" is another reform "technique," sometimes called "cooperative" or "group learning." In practice the smart or hardworking child in the group does the work and everyone gets the same grade.

It must be recognized that educators face some very real problems trying to educate young people. As families, churches, etc. are failing to be the influence they should be, students come to school with serious attitude problems.

OBE is "sold" as an effort to resolve the problems. However, when schools try to deal with attitudes (beyond encouraging children and convincing them that they can achieve if they try, etc.) who decides what the "correct" or "passing" attitudes are. The door has been opened to those who would create the "new people" they believe will fit into the workforce, political climate, etc. of the 21st Century.

CHAPTER 9

SCHOOLS ARE BEING TRANSFORMED INTO MENTAL HEALTH PROVIDERS

Comprehensive mental health services are being provided throughout the public school system despite the absence of specific legislative authority for such school-based programs.

—Report, Pennsylvania House of Representatives

MOST AMERICANS think Medicaid was started to provide health care for people on welfare. However, Medicaid-financed health coverage and mental health services are being expanded to cover most students regardless of the income levels of their families. School-based health clinics, financed with Medicaid reimbursements, are the backdoor approach to imposing President Clinton's national health reform system on the nation even though Congress, under massive pressure from Americans, refused to pass it. It is being done without direct Congressional approval—and in some cases without the knowledge of the state legislatures. The school-based clinics can get paid for providing health care, including mental health services, for almost all enrolled students. That's one reason why federal Medicaid costs have tripled since 1991—and are on the verge of exploding as more schools learn how to do it.

On October 8, 1996, Jean Rowe, a "Medicaid Consultant" of the Illinois State Board of Education, wrote letters to Illinois school districts which were not yet enrolled as Medicaid providers, encouraging them to sign up. The letter that went to Barrington CU School District #220, reportedly one of the wealthiest school districts in the United States, is an example. It said:

> To date, our records reflect that you are not participating in
> Medicaid initiatives....LEAs (Local Education Agencies)
> have found Medicaid to be a viable funding source. The
> Illinois Department of Public Aid (IDPA) joins the Illinois
> Board of Education (ISBE) in encouraging all LEAs to active-
> ly move towards participating in Medicaid programs....The
> potential for dollars is limitless.[2] (Emphasis added.)

The letter explained that since 1991 participating
LEAs in Illinois had collected over $100-million in
federal Medicaid matching funds. The letter added that
billing Medicaid for school-based health services has
been expanded to cover about 20 "health related" services including...

> ...not only therapies, but also social work and psychological
> services, public awareness, initial health review and evalua-
> tion, and family planning referral.[3]

The Illinois State Board of Education letter explained
that the "limitless" Medicaid dollars had been used by
schools "for purchases ranging from audiometers to
mini-buses, from a closed caption TV for a classroom to
an entire computer system, from contracting with sub-
stitutes to employment of new special education staff..."

Illinois legislators questioned the Medicaid expansion which had never received legislative approval—
and its potential for "limitless dollars." The State
Superintendent of Education Joseph A. Spagnolo explained:

> While I may not have chosen some of the terminology which
> Jean Rowe used in her letter to local school administrators, her
> point of encouraging them to maximize possible federal
> Medicaid reimbursement was and remains valid.[4]

In many cases schools are collecting a second time for
remedial services they've performed in the past—and
for which local taxpayers have already paid. The letter
to Illinois schools told how, saying:

Illinois Department of Public Aid allows LEAs to bill school-based health services for up to two years from the date of service. As a result, all services your practioners can document from 1994-95 and 1995-96 school years are billable. This is an opportunity that should not be overlooked.

Illinois is not alone in encouraging school districts to expand school-based health services with Medicaid funds. By 1998 Ohio, Missouri and other states were opening doors to make almost all students eligible for Medicaid-financed school-based health clinic services. Combinations of executive orders and waivers on Medicaid eligibility granted by federal agencies were used. "Mental health treatments" without parental notification are included.

In Missouri, Governor Mel Carnahan, by executive order in December 1997, decreed that children in families making up to 300% of the federal poverty level would be Medicaid eligible. Under the Governor's order, children in a Missouri family of four (father and mother and two children) making $48,000 a year would qualify for Medicaid.[5] Missouri and Connecticut are the first states to go to the "three times poverty level" guidelines. They are the highest in the nation. Other states will probably get on the bandwagon since Vice President Al Gore announced federal waivers approving the 300% guideline for Missouri. It's all a backdoor step towards adopting the Clintons' national health care.

Pennsylvania went even a step further. Governor Tom Ridge asked the federal government for a waiver of *all* income requirements for Medicaid. The waiver was granted for *all* "children under the age of 21." From that point on, *all* children in Pennsylvania, regardless of their parents' income, qualify for Medicaid benefits.

When the Pennsylvania legislature started processing the proposed 1995 budget, one item attracted attention—and raised questions. Legislators wanted to know why the line item for Medicaid expenses which in 1994 had been $10-million was jumping to $65-million in 1995. When it was determined that most of the added dollars were the result of the "medicalization of the schools" a special committee was established to determine how a 650% increase in Medicaid expenses could have happened without knowledge or action of the legislature.

The final report of a Pennsylvania legislative committee charged with investigating "the use of public schools for mental health school-based programs" determined that schools in that state, like those in Illinois, were being pushed to be Medicaid providers. The report said that...

> ...there has been a systematic attempt by Executive Branch officials to create programs which use the public school system as a means of providing comprehensive mental health and related services to school children and to qualify as many children as possible for these services even though these programs inappropriately subject some students to the stigmatization of being labeled with a learning, emotional, mental or behavioral disorder.[6]

The "benefits" paid for by Medicaid include (1) Early Periodic Screening, Detection, and Treatment (EPSDT) services, (2) mental health/counseling, (3) health education, (4) physical examinations, (5) anticipatory health guidance, and referral/tracking of health problems.[7] EPSDT includes...

> (1) A comprehensive health and developmental history (including assessment of both physical and mental health development; (2) A comprehensive unclothed physical examination; (3) Appropriate immunizations according to age and health history; (4) Appropriate laboratory tests (including

blood lead level assessment appropriate to age and risk; and (5) health education (including anticipatory guidance.)[8]

Pennsylvania's education and welfare people planned to have 900,000 students, half of the state's public school children enrolled in EPSDT by the end of 1997.[9]

The expansion was pushed by tax-exempt charitable foundations. Genevieve Young, an attorney and director of the Center on Exempt Organization Responsibility, investigated how charitable foundations like the Robert Wood Johnson Foundation and the Annie B. Casey, the Rockefeller and the Pew Charitable Trusts were promoting expansion of school-based clinics. She wrote:

> In Pennsylvania, one foundation memorandum to schools describes a list of 20 possible services that could be provided to each child for up to 20 sessions during the school year and billed to Medicaid at $20 per session. This amounts to $8000 per child per year that schools are told they could receive in "additional revenues." [10]

Forbes magazine in December 1996 reported on another approach big foundations have been using to push the medicalization of schools. It said:

> U.S. charitable foundations dole out about $100-million each year to state and local governments....The money comes with ideological strings attached. Pennsylvania was one of the 15 states selected by the Robert Wood Johnson Foundation in 1993 to receive money to craft schemes to push primary medical care. In order to get the $100,000 seed money, Governor Robert Casey and state health officials had to agree to...collect information about hospitals, doctors and patients, and give Johnson the right to use and even sell those data.

Governors Mel Carnahan of Missouri and Brereton Jones of Kentucky were among other governors who signed similar contracts giving the Johnson Foundation access to what should be confidential medical records. Missouri's contract required the governor to push special health care legislation through the legislature. *Forbes* magazine told how it worked in another state:

> Six weeks after Pennsylvania agreed to conditions for getting the first $100,000 RWJF grant, Governor Casey called a special session of the legislature and passed a law providing for free or cut-rate medical care for children whose families are too affluent to get Medicaid but have no insurance—a typical Johnson ploy.

A year after RWJF made its seed money grant in Missouri, the state had gone the same route with children in families making up to $48,000 now eligible for Medicaid and/or low cost subsidized insurance. In Kentucky, Forbes reported that...

> ...Robert Van Hook, a longtime Johnson Foundation operative, headed up the state's new Health Policy Board—at a salary of $80,000 a year, $20,000 of which was paid by the Johnson Foundation. Presumably he would see to it that the board carried out the foundation's big government agenda.

Within a year Van Hook moved back to Maryland and Forbes reported:

> Kentucky bureaucrats recently imposed emergency regulations permitting schools to treat children for both mental and physical ailments and bill everything to Medicaid, all expected to cost taxpayers another $80-million a year.

Attorney Kent Masterson Brown is suing on behalf of Kentucky citizens to void the state's $299,500 contract with RWJF. The Robert Wood Johnson Foundation has assets of over $3-billion, most of it in Johnson & Johnson stock. Johnson & Johnson is a supplier of forty or more medical items ranging from Q-tips to condoms. Other big players in influencing government decisions through grant-making are the Annie B. Casey Foundation and Pew Charitable Trust. *Forbes* reported that in

Kentucky the Casey Foundation, endowed by the founder of the United Parcel Service...

> ...seeded a $74-million program to put social workers in every public school. Among other things, the workers train new parents and make sure the children get all the health and social services they need, including referrals to get pregnancy tests and condoms. Some local officials balked at making referrals for contraceptives without parental consent. But Kentucky educrats cracked down, telling them they had no choice. Thus, without debate, an important new policy was imposed on the state's students.

Foundation involvement in education is not new, although some of the big players are. For much of this century, the Carnegie Corporation, the Rockefellers and the Ford Foundation have financed the education "reformers" who have been using the schools to create "a new social order." Details on their activities, including information on Congressional investigations in the 1950s into the foundation involvement in education, are spelled out in Chapter XI in the book, *None Dare Call It Treason—25 YEARS LATER*.

Representative Sam Rohrer, chairman of the special legislative committee which investigated the expansion of Medicaid into Pennsylvania's schools and the foundation involvement in it cited two "horrible examples" of what has happened as a result of the Medicaid-financed initiatives. He said that in both cases parental rights were violated, pupil privacy was invaded and sensitive data was collected.[11] His examples included:

> In several Pittsburgh area schools, psychological profiling was conducted by an outside psychiatric clinic without parental knowledge or permission on 1000 elementary age children. This process sought personal information on both the child and the family. Once caught by the parents, the program was

halted, but the collected data has still not been turned over to the parents.[12]

A second case received national headlines. Rohrer said:

The second infamous example occurred in East Stroudsburg, Pennsylvania in March 1996. Almost 50 sixth grade girls were given unclothed gynecological exams without the permission of the parents and against the objections of many of the girls.[13]

Katie Tucker, a mother, told the *Washington Times* that when the embarrassed disrobed girls learned that they would be forced to submit to genital exams...

...they were scared. They were crying and trying to run out the door, but one of the nurses blocked the door so they couldn't leave. My daughter told the other nurse that "My mother wouldn't like this. I want to call her." And they said, "No." My daughter said, "I don't want this test done." And the nurse said, "Too bad."[14]

Parents are finding increasingly that they have no rights. The doctor, when asked if some of the girls were crying said, "I don't remember." The *Pocono Record* in its report added that the doctor, Ramlah Vahanvaty, said:

Even a parent doesn't have the right to say what's appropriate for a physician to do when they're doing an exam.[15]

Pennsylvania Family Institute's research director, Tom Shaheen, commented that with President Clinton's push for national standards, including in-creased in-school medical treatment for all children, parents in Pennsylvania and beyond might expect more incidents resembling the one at J.T. Lambert.[16]

Such incidents are not limited to Pennsylvania. *Forbes* magazine in its December 16, 1996 issue reported:

In the summer of 1993 Betsy Grice of Owensboro, Kentucky took her 11-year-old daughter to the local elementary school for the checkup she needed before starting sixth grade. Grice was shocked to learn that the doctor intended to give the child a genital examination. Turns out it's required by the Department of Education. Why? "The reason they said was to catch abuse at an early age," recalls Grice (not her real name). Who authorized the intrusive program? Not the state legislature. The program, imposed by state bureaucrats, was bankrolled by the private Annie B. Casey Foundation.[17]

Camille Wagner, leader of a grassroots movement of Kentucky parents and teachers opposed to school officials usurping parents' rights asked:

They abuse them (the girls) to see if anybody else is abusing them?

Representative Samuel Rohrer chaired the Pennsylvania committee which did the year-long investigation. The committee turned out a detailed 100-page report supported by over 500 pages of corraborating documents. Rohrer became a real expert on how Medicaid is being continually broadened and often misused. Medicaid started as a program providing health services for the poor. It can now cover all segments of the student population. Rohrer discovered how two longtime education and health programs were subtly changed to open the door so schools in Illinois and other states could be told...

...the potential for dollars is limitless.

Changes in Medicaid and in Title I of the Elementary and Secondary Education Act of 1965 (which originally provided "extra" education services in the poorest areas) opened the door for schools to get billions of dollars. They could be used, Rohrer said, to finance the combining of workforce development, education "reform" and health care in the classroom. He explained how it was done:

> In October 1994, President Clinton signed the "Improving America's Schools Act." Title I was changed so that children who do not meet a state's OBE "outcomes" can be designated as "at risk" and "educationally deprived" even though they are not "economically deprived" which was the original Title I purpose.[18]

Rohrer said similar changes or loopholes have been opened in Medicaid legislation which, at least in Pennsylvania, have been used to drop poverty guidelines completely for ages 0-21. He explains:

> Through the exploitation of a loop-hole in the Omnibus Budget Reconciliation Act of 1989 (OBRA 89), terms have been redefined. Disability now includes reading and math deficiencies and such things as "breaking up with one's boyfriend or girlfriend." Other terms have been expanded like "at risk" which now means "at risk of becoming at risk."[19]

Rohrer said this assures that every child can be "identified" as being "at risk" under OBE/Goals2000 or Title I. Once "identified" as being "at risk" or "at risk of being at risk" they can then be "remediated" under Medicaid mental health "wraparound services with federal tax dollars paying the bills."[20] Rohrer detailed how outrageous some of the "treatments" are for which Medicaid makes reimbursement to the school. He said:

> For instance "mobile therapists" can bill $42 per hour for the time they spend riding the bus home with Johnny if Johnny is "stressed" by a bully on the bus.[21]

In order to provide these mental health remedial services (and be reimbursed for them by Medicaid), the school must have its school-based health clinic obtain "partial hospitalization provider" status from the Health Care Finance Administration. This status allows the school to provide all health-related services—

and be reimbursed by Medicaid.[22] Most school districts, when they learn about the potential financial windfall, go along. Pennsylvania has 501 school districts. Over 475 of them have applied for and received the "Medical Hospital Provider Number" needed to apply for reimbursement for supplying "medical treatment" under Medicaid. Only 20 full-scale, true school-based clinics were actually operating in Pennsylvania at the time.

To receive reimbursement from Medicaid or other third party insurers, a person rendering mental health services must establish that a child has a psychiatric or psychological disorder listed in the American Psychiatric Association's *Diagnostic and Statistical Manual (4th Edition)*. As a part of the transition to allow Medicaid reimbursement for "treating" a child with a reading problem, the definition for "medical problems" had to be broadened. The American Psychiatric Association *Diagnosis Statistical Manual* was revised dramatically. The number of codes for psychiatric "ailments" used for insurance purposes was increased from less than 50 to almost 350. Basically, "mental disorder" was redefined to include what once would have been considered variations in ability or talent like "has difficulty in reading or math—or "growing-up" behaviors such as "talking back" or "breaking up with girl or boy friend."[23]

Since Medicaid rules require a code designation from the *Diagnostic and Statistical Manual of Mental Disorders*, every child billed through Medicaid will have a mental disability code permanently assigned to his medical record. The Pennsylvania legislative committee's report said:

> This diagnosis of a psychiatric or psychological disorder
> becomes a part of the child's record with potentially adverse

consequences for that child in the future as far as employment.[24]

In Pennsylvania, some psychiatrists and psychologists protested the Medicaid-financed, in-school "mental health" services. They claimed that unqualified teachers and counselors were practicing medicine and making what could be questionable and dangerous diagnoses. Rohrer said:

> The potential for this disability designation haunting the child throughout his future is frightening. One current example is that children labeled, sometimes fraudulently, with the mental disorder designation of ADD or ADHD and who are placed on Ritalin or equivalent and receive the drugs through age 12 are already being denied entrance into the military.[25]

Similar concerns that notations in school records could jeopardize a child's future were raised by North Dakota Labor Commissioner Craig Hagen when he resigned from his state's School-to-Work management agency. He said:

> North Dakota's STW plan calls for developing career portfolios for each pupil "containing notations of skills, hobbies, talents, and personal goals, as well as records of work experiences, inter and extra curricula activities, training programs and significant accomplishments. The state is to train teachers in implementing portfolios, which will be "sources of information for future employers." Essentially, these all-inclusive files will follow an individual throughout life. (See Chapter 7.)

The STW portfolio system Hagen mentioned is to be stored ultimately in an electronic file available for access by prospective employers. Hagen said, "Kids make lots of mistakes growing up and maturing. These mistakes don't need to be recorded to haunt them the rest of their lives." This is particularly dangerous when designations of "mental disorder" are made so schools can be reimbursed for treating a reading problem. Hagen added that permanent records should only contain objective material and not subjective judgments made by teachers *or counselors* at some point during twelve years of schooling. Genevieve Young, who investigated the problem for the Center on Exempt Organization Responsibility, confirmed the problem. She said:

> Children can now be labeled in permanent records for life, with physical and mental disorders identified by school personnel. [26]

The term "mental disorder" means different things to different people. What do the mental health "experts" who apply the label mean? Listen to the words of Dr. G. Brock Chisholm, first head of the World Federation of Mental Health. Later he became head of the World Health Organization of the United Nations. His address, sponsored by the William Alanson White Psychiatric Foundation, was delivered in October 1945, in Washington, D.C., to a large group of psychiatrists and high government officials. Chisholm said:

> What basic psychological distortion can be found in every civilization of which we know anything? The only psychological force capable of producing these perversions is morality—the concept of right and wrong. The reinterpretation and eventual eradication of the concept of right and wrong are the belated objectives of nearly all psychotherapy.
>
> If the race is to be freed from its crippling burden of good and evil, it must be psychiatrists who take the original responsibility. [27]

Anticipating an objection, Chisholm added:

> The pretense is made that to do away with right and wrong would produce uncivilized people, immorality, lawlessness, and social chaos. The fact is that most psychiatrists and

psychologists and other respected people have escaped from
moral chains and are able to think freely.

Fifty years after Chisholm made those "mental
health" pronouncements, society is plagued by "uncivil-
ized people, immorality, lawlessness and social chaos."

Chisholm had been obsessed for years with the idea
that instilling concepts of right and wrong, love of
country, and morality in children by their parents is
the paramount evil. In another speech, he said:

> The people who have been taught to believe whatever they
> were told by their parents or their teachers are the people who
> are the menace to the world.[28]

It was this same concept which Harvard psychiatry
professor Chester Pierce enunciated at the Childhood
International Seminar in 1973 in Denver. As has already been quoted in Chapter 4, Pierce told educators:

> Every child in America entering school at the age of 5 is
> mentally ill because he comes to school with certain allegian-
> ces to our founding fathers, toward our elected officials,
> toward his parents, toward a belief in a supernatural being, and
> toward the sovereignty of this nation as a separate entity. It's
> up to you as teachers to make all these sick children well—by
> creating the international child of the future.

That's what will result from in-school mental health
programs, the "behavior modification cycle of OBE, the
Medicaid-financed programs for "at-risk" students,
School-to-Work, multiculturalism, diversity training
and the NEA-promoted counseling sessions. They all
contribute to "creating the international child of the
future."

Drs. Chisholm and Pierce cannot be written off as
"two isolated crackpots." After expressing these views
widely and frequently fifty years ago, Chisholm became
head of the World Federation of Mental Health and the

World Health Organization. Is it any wonder that Chisholm's appointment as head of the World Health Organization was warmly sponsored by his friend, the communist spy, Alger Hiss?[29] As detailed in the Mental Health chapter in *None Dare Call It Treason—25 YEARS LATER*, other psychiatrists and psychologists have similar views, officially expressed.

How did Chisholm and the other experts like him hope to achieve control over Americans they say need "care"? Chisholm provided the answer:

> We may begin to speculate on the advisability that psychiatrists, once the necessary one, two, or three million are available, should be trained as salesmen and be taught all the techniques of breaking down sales resistance.[30]

The growing field of "school counselors" is filling the "need." Even counselors with sound beliefs, those who recognize that most metal health "problems" are rooted in spiritual needs cannot by law give truly troubled students real answers.

The two drastic changes made in Title I and Medicaid guidelines broaden the definitions of what "treatments" can "earn" reimbursements under the two federal programs. Waivers are the third factor which has allowed government-sponsored in-school mental health treatments to be imposed on hundreds of thousands of school students. Waivers have been a key factor in the medicalization of schools without the approval of Congress or state legislatures. Representative Rohrer's committee learned how it works. He said:

> It's a bureaucracy-to-bureaucracy transaction. Simply have the state executive branch and Department of Welfare apply to the [federal] Health Care Finance Administration and waivers will be granted. Once granted these waivers allow all types of things to occur.

There is a major problem with waivers...the very purpose of waivers is to allow that which is not permitted by law.[31]

The federal Government Accounting Office (GAO) pointed up the danger of waivers in testimony presented to the Congressional Committee on the Budget on April 4, 1995. The testimony was:

> ...allowing the waiver process to be used to expand coverage to hundreds of thousands of additional individuals without the consultation and concurrence of Congress appears inappropriate. The result of these waivers could lead to a heavier financial burden on the federal government.

The states are impacted as well because all Medicaid money must be matched on some basis by the state. That's what alerted the Pennsylvania legislature to what was happening in the Keystone state. From 1994 to 1995, the proposed budget jumped Medicaid expenses from about $10-million to $65-million. That prompted the legislature to authorize its year-long investigation.

Dr. Jane M. Orient, M.D. practices internal medicine and serves as the Executive Director of the Association of American Physicians and Surgeons. While the general public for the most part has not given much attention to the "medicalization of the schools" and the growing "mental health treatment" of students, Dr. Orient writes:

> Some attentive parents have been very concerned about the program, especially when they perceive that certain aspects have been deliberately concealed. Surveys asking intrusive psychological questions have been done without parental consent.... The "consent" process for the school-based clinics may really be just notification, at best, or an attempt at notification of possible treatment. If a permission slip is sent home and placed in the student's file, and a refusal is not returned within seven days, treatment is deemed to be "authorized." There is not even a requirement to show that the form actually

arrived at the student's home. Parents need not be notified if treatment (e.g. psychotherapy) is actually rendered, and Medicaid does not send them an Explanation of Benefits form.[32] No restrictions are placed on the treatment except that it must be "deemed advisable" or necessary by the student's examining or attending physicians and/or other professional employees at the hospital.[33]

Dr. Orient added, "Treatment may be prescribed, not only for students who are *at risk* for substance abuse, suicide, antisocial behavior, etc. but also for those who are *at risk of being at risk*"[34]

What can concerned parents do? How can they determine whether the school district which their children or grandchildren attend is providing "treatment" for conditions designated as "mental health disorders" so they can qualify for Medicaid reimbursement? One concerned Pennsylvania parent suggested a series of questions, including:

> Has your school obtained "partial hospitalization provider status" and/or a Medicaid provider number? Does your school counsel students in group therapy type sessions where family and personal matters are discussed? Do intrusive personality "tests" ask personal questions which may induce insecurity or undermine family relationships and values? Does your school have a procedure for labeling students "at risk" or "at risk of being at risk" because of certain things in their backgrounds or attitudes? Does your school have anger management or conflict resolution lessons? Who is paying for these programs in your school?

Those questions are appropriate and need to be asked. Pennsylvania, Illinois, Missouri, Connecticut and Kentucky have all been shown to be involved in the medicalization of their schools. They are not alone. Medicaid funds are now available to any state wishing to tap into them. The questions need to be asked whether children are in public or private schools. In some states like Missouri, even parochial schools have obtained Medicaid status for their school-based clinics.[35]

It's all part of a backdoor approach to a universal national health care system. Documents obtained under the Freedom of Information Act from the Hillary Clinton White House Health Care Inter-Departmental Working Group show the connections. Even before Congress, under massive pressure from across America, killed the Clinton proposals for a socialized universal health care plan for all Americans, plans had been made to institute the plan piecemeal starting with children.[33] School-based clinics financed by making children from higher and higher income families eligible for Medicaid was the key. It is being done now.

CHAPTER 10
POWERFUL TECHNIQUES ARE USED
TO MANIPULATE SMART KIDS

...the evidence collected so far suggests that a single hour of classroom activity—a time of peak learning experience—under certain conditions may bring about a major reorganization in cognitive as well as affective behaviors.
— *Benjamin Bloom, grandfather of OBE*

AS WAS STATED EARLIER, "dumbing down" rightfully gets attention. However, some students do learn in spite of all the falling college entrance scores, complaints from colleges about poorly prepared students, and statistics on functional illiteracy. They learn and excel no matter how faulty the curriculum or poorly prepared a teacher may be.

Students who are "born bright" are taught to think and they do excel. However, with emphasis on developing what educators call "higher-order thinking" or "critical thinking skills," these students are encouraged and taught to question everything, including the traditional values of their families and churches. They are being conditioned and trained to be the leaders of "the new social order"—a world with a new culture and new way of life.

In some states the best and brightest of them get special attention. Since started by the Clintons in 1979, Arkansas has had its Governor's School, a six-week summer program for the "Gifted and Talented." Other states have either summer programs or year-round boarding academies with emphasis on math and science, the arts or other specialities.

In Arkansas, the Governor's School has enrolled about 400 of the top juniors from high schools across the state every summer since 1979. The program is based at Hendrix College, an elite Methodist liberal arts school in Conway, Arkansas. Students live on campus and are forbidden to have visitors except on Sundays or to leave the college grounds except for the 4th of July weekend.

The Washington newsletter *Human Events* did a series of articles[1] on the Arkansas Governor's School in 1992 when Clinton was running for president. The paper reported:

> The program is divided into three areas—academic (with concentration based on the student's talents such as math, science or English), "conceptual development" and "personal and social development."

Bruce Haggard, a biology professor at the college and the director of the Governor's School, said the "personal and social development" segment is the most controversial part of the school as it teaches students to "look into the implications of knowledge."

The *Human Events* article quoted Chris Yarborough, a Governor's School student who left the school midway in 1991 out of disgust for its teachings. He said:

> ...there was a running joke among the faculty at the school that the "area two" portion of the school (conceptual development) is designed to "take you (the student) apart" and "area three" (personal and social development) is designed to "put you back together."

Mark Lowery, a member of Clinton's staff at the time, served as the school's publicity director in 1983-84. He became concerned and disillusioned as he watched the program unfold. He said:

> It's almost a mind-bending process during those six weeks. It was an attack on Christianity, but more so it was an attack on

conservative thought. They very strongly put out the implication that if you want to be considered an intellectual by your peers, you have to be a liberal. You can't be conservative.[2]

Human Events obtained a copy of the "textbook" put together for the 1991 Governor's School. Its report said:

> The book, a collection of readings called the "Tree Book," states the school's intention is to promote "reflective thinking" by its young "gifted" attendees. But a review of the book's essays, as well as the program's guest speakers and the films shown, suggests the real purpose of the Governor's School is to "uproot" whatever traditional beliefs the students bring into the program and replace them with liberal skepticism and secular relativism.[3]

The newsletter added: "The 1991 teaching materials, readings and speakers cover the full gamut of the left....There is also a heavy anti-Christian element to the school, as if special care was taken to shed impressionable teenagers of their Bible Belt past." The story then gave examples:

> A blatant anti-Christian diatribe from a radical feminist "witch," who likens Jesus Christ's death on the cross to necrophilia and sado-machochism.

> A lecture from the attorney who defended "Jane Roe" in the Roe v. Wade Supreme Court case (with no balancing speaker from the pro-life side).

> A reading praising pacifism lavishly praised a Mennonite who refused to register for the draft because he didn't want to send a "hostile signal" to the Soviet Union.

> Other readings condemned capital punishment; depict euthanasia as a human response to suffering; promote radical environmentalism, and satirize marriage as hopelessly unfair to women.

Pro-homosexual readings, films and discussions were presented. An essay in the "Tree Book" argues

philosophically for "The Morality of Homosexuality."
Author Michael Ruse writes:

> There are, then, four independent rejoinders to the "unnatural
> argument" that has dominated both classical and modern
> discussions of homosexuality: it is false that animals are not
> homosexual; it is false that homosexuality must be an-
> tireproductive and nonbiological; it is false that
> homosexuality is to be judged without taking note of the
> cultural nature of humans; and it is false that what is unnatural
> is necessarily immoral.[4]

The "Tree Book" had an article by the 19th Century
philosopher Ludwig Fuerbach. Karl Marx based his
atheistic materialism on Fuerbach. Fuerbach's essay
showed:

> His chief aim in life was to change the "friends of God into
> friends of man, believers into thinkers, worshipers into
> workers, candidates for the other world into students of this
> world" and to assail the "supranaturalistic egoism of Chris-
> tianity."

Such assaults on traditional beliefs seem to do more
than encourage kids to "think critically." Therefore,
they provoked controversy. Governor's School Director
Bruce Haggard acknowledged that the school's approach would alienate "religious fundamentalists," but
said they would likely be offended by much that is
taught in public education anyway. (That's a significant admission.) He added that to think critically
and openly, students need to be exposed to views they
don't normally get at home or in some traditional
classroom settings. He added:

> I don't think a good education requires a balanced treatment
> of everything.[5]

Haggard directed the school for a number of years.
Ms. Martha Bass, administrator of Gifted and Talented

Programs of the Arkansas Department of Education supervised the curriculum.[6]

When two former Governor's School students committed suicide, the controversy grew. A critical professional video titled, *The Guiding Hand,*[7] presented interviews with parents and former students, some of whom said:

> They're taking the cream of the crop...the leaders of the next generation and pushing them into values that Governor Clinton has—that the leftist media has—the values that go totally against what this nation was founded on. This is what I was exposed to. There wasn't any warning, there wasn't anyone that said, "Okay, now you are going to have to take all the values you grew up with and put them on a shelf and be exposed to this." If my parents had known what was going on there, they wouldn't have let me go.

> We watched movies like Harvey Milk (the homosexual San Francisco supervisor who was murdered by a city councilman in the 1970s). We learned about gay life style—those things your parents say, "This is wrong...You shouldn't see this type of thing because, hey, that's just not right."

> They're bringing a political agenda in the guise of academic excellence....It was something that was well-orchestrated, well-organized, it was mind-bending and manipulative. And the faculty knew what was going on.

The *Arkansas Gazette* quoted Ellen Gilchrist, an author, who told the 1985 Governor's School students:

> I ask you to start ignoring your parents. Be really nice to them, and forget them. At the age you are now, it's time to start using your stuff, your real stuff.[8]

Mark Lowery, the Clinton staff member who became disillusioned, said:

> The instructors tear down the student's authority figure system and help establish another one—the student himself. They convince the students that "You are the elite. The reason why you are not going to be understood when you go home, not by

your parents, your friends, your pastor or anybody is because you have been treated to thought that they can't handle." This intellectual and cultural elitism gives students the "right" to say, "We know better than you."

After two former students committed suicide, the Joint Interim Education Committee of the Arkansas legislature held limited hearings on September 15, 1994. Shelvie Cole, a trained school psychologist testified. Her son Brandon committed suicide after attending the Governor's School. She said she was appearing both as a professional and as a parent. She also made it plain that she was not a religious zealot or a conservative, adding that, "The reason I am saying this is because anytime anyone seems to have a negative comment toward the Governor's School, they are automatically categorized into one of those groups, somehow negating their comments."[9] *WORLD* magazine said her car had a Clinton-Gore sticker.[10] She said:

> I had no idea the impact that Governor's School had on Brandon until I read his log after his death. I knew that he had begun to change; but when I began reading his log, I understood some of the things that had gone on within Brandon that were the result of some of his experiences at Governor's School. I am not going to give you secondhand information. I am going to let Brandon talk for himself because I am going to read directly from his diary that he kept while he was in Governor's School.

She then read from his log words written at the school:

> We have truly been plucked out of our world. We live in the Governor's School world. I don't think I will be able to leave after this is over. Let me warn you that I am changing inside. I hope you will like me as I am, but I am learning a new outlook on life and reality....I feel sorry for people who aren't here. The outside world is so blind toward world events.

His final entry in the log said:

Governor's School helped me to separate myself from most of the people around me. The absence of being who I was known for gave me a chance to look inside of my real self. After I came back from the [3-day July 4th] break, my friends and I could tell that we had suddenly been transformed into free thinkers.

His mother then said, "There's a false sense of security in Brandon's statement because when he completed Governor's School, he doubted friendships and support he had most of his life. And he questioned values and relationships that in the past had been extremely important to him. But most of all he began to question himself."

Mrs. Cole continued her testimony by reading the first entry written into Brandon's log at Governor's School and then one that was written three weeks later. The first one said:

Moms are the best people around, and my mom is the best mom on earth. As a child she cuddled me and showed me the way like a guardian angel watching my moves, supporting me through times of confusion and lifting me up off the floor of desperation. My mom is great!

Three weeks later Brandon wrote in his diary:

My mom is so closed minded I feel like we will have a standoff soon over issues, She doesn't see people for who they are, only for the way they act.

Mrs. Cole, a psychologist, closed her testimony to the legislative committee with these challenging words. She said:

I had to ask myself what could happen during a young person's life during these short weeks to make such a drastic change in his attitude toward a parent, and I think that is a question you need to ask yourselves today. Thank you.

Another mother of a Governor's School graduate had professional expertise also. Iris Stevens in her tes-

timony answered Mrs. Cole's question as to how a
young person can be so changed in just a few weeks.
Mrs. Stevens had taught Gifted and Talented students
for eighteen years in Arkansas public schools. After
reciting her impressive credentials and experience she
said:

> I am telling you this to refute the assertions of those who say
> that we who oppose some of the tactics utilized by the Arkan-
> sas Governor's School are semi-literate, wild-eyed, religious
> fanatics who resent children being exposed to anything other
> than the rudiments of the three R's. I assure you that couldn't
> be any farther from the truth. I have spent most of my adult
> life trying to get children to think and that is not what is going
> on at the Governor's School.[11]

She detailed for the legislators the six-week program
promoting abortion, feminism, homosexuality, les-
bianism, attacks on Christianity, animal rights, etc.
Then she told the joint education committee:

> ...if I have heard it once I've heard a thousand times, "When
> you have raised your child for seventeen years, they're not
> going to change him in six weeks." Unfortunately, that is not
> quite true. Let me give you some quotes by Benjamin Bloom
> and Abe Maslow. If you've been in education, you know
> these people are the pillars of modern education theory....Lis-
> ten to what they say about that idea of not being able to change
> people in a short period of time.

> Maslow has suggested that "a peak experience" may have a
> powerful influence on major change in an individual...a single
> powerful experience (and I think you will agree that every time
> you hear a Governor's School student talk that it is the most
> wonderful thing—the most profound experience they have
> ever had) may have much more impact on the individual than
> many less powerful experiences....the research collected so far
> suggests that a single hour of classroom activity under certain
> conditions may bring about a major reorganization in cogni-
> tive as well as affective behaviors.

Her next quote from the educational theorists said:

> It does seem clear that to create effectively a new set of attitudes and values, the individual must undergo a great reorganization of his personal beliefs and attitudes, and he must be involved in an environment which in many ways is separated from the previous environment in which he has developed.

Mrs. Stevens asked the legislators, "Does that sound familiar? We get them down there for six weeks and basically isolate them from outside influences." All the quotations confirm that education "experts" have the goal of changing attitudes, beliefs and values. The final quote she read indicates that while the techniques the "experts" use change attitudes and values in a general classroom situation, it happens much faster in a totally controlled situation. She read:

> The changes produced in a general academic atmosphere which is not deliberately created are of smaller magnitude than the changes produced where the entire environment is organized with a particular theme at work. Learning experiences which are highly organized and interrelated may produce major changes in behavior related to complex objectives in both the cognitive and affective domain. Such new objectives can best be attained where the individual is separated from earlier environment conditions and when he is in association with a group of peers who are changing in much the same direction and who thus tend to reinforce one another.

These quotes merit careful study. They came from *Taxonomy of Educational Objectives* by David Krathwohl, Benjamin Bloom and Bertram Masia, pages 56, 84, 85, 88 and 89. Bloom is regarded as the father or grandfather of Outcome-Based Education." The quotations confirm the interest of modern education reformers in changing the values and beliefs of students—whether they are in "a general academic atmosphere" or "where the entire environment is organized with a particular theme at work."

The process the educators described can be and is used for good or for evil. In her testimony Mrs. Cole related:

> During the six weeks of Governor's School the students are really encouraged to disassociate themselves from the outside world. This in itself has its effect on students. A friend of mine who was in the Marine Corps said that it reminded him of boot camp when they separate young men from their parents and their friends so they can get them thinking in a military way.

The techniques can be used for good or evil. Cults use them in seducing people into their "elite group." Such a setting is also used effectively by Christian groups which minister intensively to those addicted to drugs or alcohol. Young people often make life changing decisions during a week in a good Christian camp where they are isolated from many of the worldly influences they face at home. However, unless they are brought to understand the dangers in old habits, entertainment, etc. they can suffer "relapses."

Another mother, Carol Haynes, also testified.[12] Her concern and testimony was typical of most who appeared. She said:

> My son, Scott, attended Governor's School in 1991. He has always been a very smart, very bright student, someone I am very proud of. We've put a lot of time and effort into him, so I was very flattered when he was nominated to attend Governor's School. Unfortunately, I had not checked into it...Until a year ago I had not talked with any other parents whose child had attended Governor's School, but I knew the problems we were seeing started shortly after he returned.

> My son came back from Governor's School and his favorite line was, "There are no absolutes; there are no absolutes." Every time you would say something to him, you would get the same line, "There are no absolutes."

One day I just said, "Scott, what do you mean?"

He said, "Mom, I've just figured out in life there are no rights and wrongs. It's just whatever you see. It's a gray area." Well, we didn't raise him this way. I imagine that most of you didn't raise your children that way either. There are rights and wrongs.

Mrs. Haynes added, telling the legislators: "The last time we were here in June, I spoke with three different parents in the lobby and we all had the same story as to what had happened to our children."

What has happened in Arkansas has been more thoroughly documented than experiences with Governor's Schools and Academies in other states—probably because of President Clinton's involvement. Indiana opened its Academy for Mathematics, Science and Humanities in 1988. This state-supported two-year residential school for gifted and talented high school juniors and seniors describes itself as "an elite institution." The 1991-92 School Profile states:

Among the intellectual processes to be emphasized in the academy's curriculum are critical thinking, creativity, problem solving, investigation and decision making.[12]

An article on the Academy commented, "These are the Higher-Order Thinking processes that can bring about despair and mental breakdown." In a six-week period in the spring of 1994, three of the 300 gifted and talented students committed suicide. The researchers who did the article said:

...in 1994 the suicide rate at the Indiana Academy was 1 in 100 or 100 times the national rate—and these were students who had everything seemingly going for them. Add to these the unknown number of mental breakdowns and those seeking psychological counselors and the picture does not look like an advertisement.[13]

In Missouri, a legislator received a letter from a student who attended the three-week Missouri Scholars Academy in 1994. He praised the program but said, "...there was one incident that occurred that disturbed me and caused the Academy to be less than it could have been."[14] He wrote:

> Dr. ___ _____ was leading one of our nightly discussions. After the lecture he opened for questions. The last question he was asked was if he thought homosexuality was genetic, learned, or if it mattered. He replied that he certainly did not think it mattered and then went on to relate that, when he was in Boy Scouts, he had a scoutmaster who sneaked into his bed at camp one night and introduced him to one of the most beautiful experiences of his life. He then finished with the statement that no one could tell him that was wrong.

> It concerns me that this instructor to whom many of the Scholars were looking up to as a role model and teacher would say that there was nothing wrong with a scoutmaster committing a felonious act against him as a child. I am not trying to harm or destroy M.S.A., but only trying to let you know what I observed so that M.S.A. may be improved.

The Governors' Schools and Academies reflect the prevailing philosophy in the State Education Departments which establish them. The Arkansas Governor's School, for example, was state funded and was conducted under the authority of the seven-person State Board of Education which was appointed by then Governor Clinton. In a one-hour public television presentation on the Governor's School, Clinton said:

> It would be impossible for me to describe how exciting this experiment is to me.

As the inaugural speaker at the opening session one year Clinton described the Governor's School as "a dream come true."[15] Bruce Haggard, Governor's School director, said:

Clinton takes a very active interest in the program. On occasion he even gives guest lectures to the students.[16]

Every American and every parent should be aware. The same Clinton who started the Arkansas Governor's School in 1979 was responsible for education "reform" in Arkansas. After twelve years of promoting education in Arkansas, the state's schools still ranked 45th in the nation. Then Governor Clinton was also the key figure in the 1989 education summit which produced Goals 2000, School-to-Work, Outcome-Based Education and much of the education "reform" which has swept across the nation in the 1990s.

CHAPTER 11

NATIONAL EDUCATION ASSOCIATION PUSHES RADICAL AGENDA

The NEA will become a political power second to no other special interest group.
    —*NEA Executive Secretary Sam Lambert, 1967*

OVER SIXTY YEARS AGO the early education "reformers"—people who planned to use the schools to "create a new social order"—gained the prestige and power of the National Education Association, the largest professional teachers organization. In 1934, a year before he became the NEA executive director, Dr. Willard Givens, then a California school superintendent, in a report entitled, *Education for a New America,* told the NEA's 72nd annual convention:

We are convinced that we stand today at the verge of a great culture...But to achieve these things many drastic changes must be made. A dying laissez-faire must be completely destroyed, and all of us, including the owners, must be subjected to a large degree of social control.[1]

After delivering this call for the destruction of free enterprise and individual freedom (laissez-faire) and the creation of a new culture, Givens was named executive secretary of the NEA. He held the post for 17 years.

Resolutions passed annually at the NEA conventions demonstrate that the NEA is committed to leftist political activism, abortion, gay and lesbian causes and destruction of support for traditional morality. A resolution passed by the 1995 convention is typical. It said:

The National Education Association recognizes the importance of raising the awareness and increasing the sensitivity of staff, students, parents, and the community to sexual orientation. The Association therefore supports....the celebration of a Lesbian and Gay History Month as a means of acknowledging the contributions of lesbians, gays, and bi-sexuals throughout history.[2]

The *Washington (D.C.) Blade*, a homosexual weekly newspaper, rejoiced that the 8,000 NEA convention delegates passed the resolution by a 2 to 1 vote.[3] NEA resolutions regularly advocate AIDS education and other pro-gay policies.

Since at least 1992, the teacher delegates have approved "reproductive-rights" resolutions which support a woman's "right" to abortion.[4] The 1997 convention defeated an effort by pro-life teachers to prohibit use of NEA funds for pro-abortion lobbying activities. The vote was 5,748 to 2,408.[5]

The NEA has a split personality. It's demonstrated by Resolution E-9 which passes annually. E-9 demands total academic freedom for teachers and students to "explore and discuss divergent points of view"—but then adds:

> The Association further believes that legislation and regulations that mandate or permit the teaching of religious doctrines and/or groups that promote anti-public-education agenda violate student and teacher rights. The Association urges its affiliates to seek repeal of these mandates where they exist.[6]

While the NEA says it is for quality education, it also stands firmly against efforts to check teacher competency. Since 1994, the annual conventions have passed Resolution D-19 which says:

> The National Education Association believes that competency testing must not be used as a condition of employment, license retention, evaluation, placement, ranking, or promotion of licensed teachers.[7]

After 56% of prospective teachers failed a Massachusetts test for certification in 1998, Governor Paul Cellucci proposed that basic literacy and subject matter tests be given to current teachers before they were recertified. The *Washington Times* in a July 2 editorial said:

> The teachers' unions went ballistic, accusing the Governor of "finger pointing" and "teacher-bashing" and "bashing the system."

The newspaper added:

> Given that nearly 60 percent of prospective teachers failed these exams the first year they were required, it's a safe bet that theMassachusetts current teaching core is littered with teachers who are failing their students.

But the NEA consistently says, "No testing of teacher competency." NEA convention resolutions also erode parental rights. They consistently call for programs for controlling children from birth on and for providing comprehensive health care to children in schools without parental notification or knowledge. In 1997 Resolution C-23 said about health care:

> The National Education Association believes that every child should have <u>direct and confidential access</u> to comprehensive health, social and psychological programs and services. The Association believes that programs in schools should provide....comprehensive school-based, community-funded student health care clinics that provide basic health care services (which may include diagnosis and treatment). If deemed appropriate "by local choice," the clinics would provide family-planning counseling and access to birth-control methods with instructions in their use.[8] (Emphasis added.)

The NEA also leads the drive of education reformers and some politicians to get control of children from birth on. Since at least 1992, the annual convention has passed Resolution B-1 which reads:

The National Education Association supports early childhood education in public schools from birth through age eight....The Association further believes that early childhood education programs should include a full continuum of services for parents and children, including child care, child development, developmentally appropriate and diversity-based curricula, special education, and appropriate bias-free screening devices. The Association believes that federal legislation should be enacted to assist in organizing the implementation of fully funded <u>early childhood education programs offered through the public schools.</u> These programs should be available to all on an equal basis <u>and should include mandatory kindergarten with compulsory attendance</u>.[9] (Emphasis added.)

For at least twenty years the NEA has promoted educator control of children at ever earlier ages. *Today's Education,* the official NEA Journal, in its January 1969 issue, published its "Forecast for the 70s." Teachers were told to expect and work for the day when...

...educators will assume a formal responsibility for children when they reach the age of two....we will offer such services as medical-dental examinations, early identification of the handicapped and deprived, attacks on nutritional needs, and— of major importance—early referral to cooperating social agencies for treatment of psychobehavioral problems.

New programs for two-year-olds will involve the coordination of community resources, under school auspices, to equalize educational opportunity for these children before cultural deprivation makes inroads on their social and mental health.

The basic role of the teacher will change noticeably. Ten years hence it should be more accurate to term him a "learning clinician." This title is meant to convey the idea that <u>schools are becoming "clinics" whose purpose is to provide individualized psychosocial "treatment" for the student,</u> thus increasing his value both to himself and society.[10] (Emphasis added.)

What sorts of "treatments" are planned. The official journal of the National Education Association predicted:

> New drama will play on the educational stage as drugs are introduced experimentally to improve in the learner such qualities as personality, concentration and memory [Ritalin, etc.]. The application of bio-chemical research findings, heretofore centered in infra-human subjects, such as fish, could be a source of conspicuous controversy when children become the objects of experimentation.[11]

What happens when controversies arise and parents resist such "help?" The NEA article anticipated parental resistance and hinted at the "solution," saying:

> ...there could be a tinderbox quality to the introduction of <u>mandatory foster homes and "boarding schools" for children between the ages of two and three whose home environment was felt to have a malignant influence</u>.[12] (Emphasis added.)

Such articles in the *NEA Journal* condition teachers and other educators to accept the statement of Harvard psychiatry professor Chester Pierce quoted already in Chapter 4. Recall that at the Childhood International Seminar in 1973 in Denver, Pierce told educators:

> Every child in America entering school at the age of 5 is mentally ill because he comes to school with certain allegiances to our founding fathers, toward our elected officials, toward his parents, toward a belief in a supernatural being, and toward the sovereignty of this nation as a separate entity. It's up to you as teachers to make all these sick children well—by creating the international child of the future.

Many would say that NEA proposals like "the introduction of mandatory foster homes and "boarding schools" for troubled children could never happen. However, it's already starting to happen. On April 10, 1998, the *St. Louis Post-Dispatch* published a syndicated *Washington Post* news service story which said:

MINNEAPOLIS– Minnesota lawmakers voted Thursday to build state-run boarding schools to house and educate children from poor families and troubled neighborhoods....housing anywhere from 150 to 900 school children. Gov. Arne Carlson, the plan's author, described the three institutions planned for Minnesota as hybrids between orphanages and preparatory schools.

The press account said, "The measure's passage made Minnesota *the first state* to return to the old-fashioned notion of providing publicly funded living and schooling called orphanages in their era."

In addition to attacks on the family and its rights to rear its own children, NEA convention resolutions over the years have also supported a wide assortment of leftist positions having no relation to education. The Equal Rights Amendment, the Clinton universal health care program, nuclear freeze and nuclear disarmament have all gained NEA support. During the 1980s, the NEA also opposed any U.S. plan that "would have destabilized Nicaragua" which at the time was controlled by the Communist Sandinistas.[13] That's probably why, in both 1986 and 1987 the Communist Party U.S.A. praised the actions and resolutions of the NEA conventions.[14] The communist journal, *Daily World*, said:

The National Education Association, established originally as a professional association to promote public education, lobby for funds and advance high standards, has become over the years a bona fide, progressive union....The union's progressive and united actions indicate that the 1987 convention will continue to provide leadership for its membership and set an example for the labor movement as a whole.

Communist use of the term "progressive" in describing NEA actions would signal Communist readers that the Reds had real influence in the organization. Earlier in the 1980s the Communist *Daily World* used similar

Aesopian language to tell of their growing influence in the teachers' union. One paragraph in the article points up Communist success in influencing the NEA. It states:

> Nowhere in the basic documents of the NEA, in their resolutions or new business items, are there any anti-Soviet or anti-socialist positions. This is susceptible to change, of course, if progressive forces are not vigilant.

The NEA has become one of the most powerful lobbying organizations in Washington and state capitals across America. Its clout is built on the activists and money it can turn loose to influence elections. Dues from the 2-million teachers who are NEA members provide an annual budget of $200-million nationally. The total reaches $750-million when state and local income is added in.[15]

The NEA move into political activism was announced by the NEA executive secretary, Sam Lambert, in the *NEA JOURNAL* in December 1967. Lambert said:

> NEA will become a political power second to no other special interest group....NEA will organize this profession from top to bottom into logical operational units that can move swiftly and effectively with power unmatched by any other organized group in the nation.[16]

That political clout has developed. In the January-February 1974 *Today's Education* NEA President Helen Wise told the teachers:

> Teachers are 2-million strong, and any politician who can count knows how much power an active, determined group of that size can generate.[17]

The leftist ideological commitment of the NEA's leadership was demonstrated by endorsements of liberal presidential candidates since at least 1980. The support has been overwhelming. For example, in 1980 the NEA board of directors endorsed the Carter-Mondale presidential ticket over Reagan-Bush *by a vote of 118 to 4.* The leadership's leftist leanings do not represent the views of many NEA members. *Forbes* magazine reported that in spite of top-down leftist control, the NEA's own figures show that one-third of its members are Republicans and well over 40% voted for Ronald Reagan and George Bush.[18]

NEA money goes almost totally to liberal candidates. In the 1996 elections a review of the Federal Election Commission's records showed that...

> ... the NEA's Political Action Committee made contributions of $1,213,230 to candidates for Congress. Of this, $1,202,880 went to 298 Democratic candidates, while just $5,350 went to 11 Republicans.[19] In the 1994 election cycle, the NEA-PAC gave candidates $2.26-million, 98.5% of it to Democrats. The American Federation of Teachers gave $1.29-million, 99.1% of it to Democrat congressional candidates.[20]

The *Washington Times* in an editorial titled "Educators or Lobbyists?" said:

> Even the $3.5-million donated to congressional candidates by the two national teacher association PAC's is dwarfed by the total contributions from the NEA's state and local affiliates.

In some states teachers, ex-teachers, and teacher spouses hold 40% to 50% of the seats in state legislatures.[21]

Since about 1985 the NEA has been working in concert with the Carnegie Corporation to control teacher certification in the United States. By controlling requirements for teacher certification, the NEA would ultimately control what teacher training institutions would have to offer to qualify their graduates for certification. The push was kicked off in 1986 by the Carnegie Task Force on Teaching as a Profession. The 140-page report, "A Nation Prepared: Teachers for the

21st Century" called for establishment of a National Board for Professional Teaching Standards.[22]

NEA President Mary Hatwood Futrell boasted of the growing NEA political power and NEA involvement in teacher certification at the 1988 convention.[23] She said:

> Today, for the first time in the history of the United States, there is a fully operational National Board for Professional Teaching Standards. And not just any board, but a Board governed by a working majority of classroom teachers! The new Board—which includes 18 NEA members—has already met several times. By 1991 the Board will draft national standards, design assessment instruments, and develop voluntary certification procedures.

Of course, once the "voluntary" national standards were developed, the NEA has worked in the states to make them mandatory.

The effort continues. An NEA "model bill" has been introduced into the Missouri legislature four or five times in recent years. The bill would transfer control of teacher certification from the Department of Education to a seventeen- member board. The teacher-dominated board would be appointed by the governor. Most of the language specifies public schools, BUT the penalty provision says:

> Any person who performs duties as a professor educator in the schools of this state without a valid license as required pursuant to the provisions of sections 168.600 to 168.654 shall be guilty of a Class A misdemeanor.[24]

Teachers and administrators in private and parochial schools and homeschool parents who were not licensed and certified by the NEA-dominated board would face fines of $1000 and up to one year in jail. The bill hasn't passed *yet*.

In addition to pushing its leftist causes and efforts to totally control America's schools, NEA resources are also committed to fighting the leaders and activities of groups opposed to its leftist agenda. Those who support pro-American, pro-family, anti-Communist positions are labeled "enemies of public education."

Starting over 50 years ago the National Education Association's *National Commission for the Defense of Democracy Through Education* rushed its trained propagandists to the scene whenever public education programs were challenged. *The Pasadena Story* was typical. It was an impressive publication issued by the NEA Defense Commission when parents in Pasadena, California, rebelled at the indoctrination of their children. Of the Pasadena parents, the report said:

> They apparently claim that this country has already moved into, or is rapidly moving toward, some form of socialism, collectivism, or statism. They contend that subversive elements have sifted into public education and that many teachers are seeking to change the American way of life. They charge that John Dewey's progressive education is an instrument designed to break down American standards and weaken the fabric of American society...They oppose certain educators who they assert are seeking to indoctrinate the youth of the country for a changed social and economic order.[25]

That report was issued in June 1951 by the National Education Association. The NEA executive secretary at the time was Willard Givens who had confirmed the parents' charges when, as quoted in the start of this chapter, he publicly stated:

> We are convinced that we stand today at the verge of a great culture...But to achieve these things, many drastic changes must be made. A dying laissez-faire must be completely destroyed, and all of us, including the owners must be subjected to a large degree of social control.

Through the years, the NEA's Defense Commission and its successors have maintained a "blacklist" of individuals and organizations which publicly question or criticize the quality of education. The NEA Commission for "Defense of Democracy" in its 1961 annual report admitted:

> About 1000 requests for information concerning individuals or groups thought to be causing trouble for the schools or the profession were received during the year. Several new fact sheets and information bulletins concerning critics of education were prepared. The Commission has, probably, the most complete files of their kind of critics of education.[26]

The *Tulsa Tribune*, after determining that a dossier on its editor was in the NEA files of "critics of education," asked editorially:

> What is the function of the National Education Association— to improve the education of America's children or to stifle criticism of present educational methods?[27]

Other "establishment" education organizations line up against parents who question school "reforms," explicit sex education and other abuses. For example:

School Board News published "How To Defuse Far-Right Attacks On Schools" by Erica Sorahan of the National School Board Association in its Jan./Feb. 1993 issue.

The California PTA issued "Guidelines For Handling Extremists" in March 1989.

The American Association of University Women Pennsylvania Division issued a revised edition of its 44-page guide titled, "The School Censorship Movement—Is Your School Prepared?" in June 1987.

The Upstate New York Coalition for Democracy, composed of teachers' unions like the New York NEA, the New York State United Teachers-AFL-CIO and liberal groups like the People for the American Way and Planned Parenthood Services of New York, disseminated surveys to school superintendents. The *Wall*

Street Journal noted that although the survey supposedly dealt with...

> ...groups like the KKK and neo-Nazis...there are no questions about swastikas, cross burnings, racial incidents, hate crimes or weapons stashes.

The paper asked, "Just what sort of activities were of interest to the coalition?"[28] The survey identified members of the Radical Right, yoked by implication to the KKK and neo-Nazis, as...

> ...individuals, groups, churches, or "faith-based organizations" who spoke about "the moral decline of America" and "the need to return to family values;" involved themselves in school-board races or public budget debates; attempted to reduce public funding of the arts; spoke about such issues as "back to basics," "phonics only," "parental rights," or "abstinence only sex education."

The labeling of such concerned parents as "radical" or "extremist" was not new. In the early 1980s, the Western States Regional Staff of the NEA developed a 50-page training manual for teachers and NEA leaders titled "Combating The New Right." It targeted as enemies the leaders and activities of just about every conservative, pro-God, pro-America political and educational organization in America. Phyllis Schlafly, Rev. Jerry Falwell, Pat Robertson, the Heritage Foundation, black conservative economist Thomas Sowell and Senators Jesse Helms, Bob Dole and Paul Laxalt were among the many conservative leaders spotlighted as part of the dangerous "new right."[29]

In 1994, the NEA joined a coalition which brought together the near-porn *Penthouse* magazine and an assortment of gay and lesbian organizations such as the National Gay and Lesbian Task Force and the Gay and Lesbian Victory Fund with over sixty seemingly

respectable "mainstream" education, religious and
political groups.

The coalition produced a manual titled, *How To Win:
A Practical Guide for Defeating the Radical Right in
Your Community.*[30] An examination of its 252 pages
and eight sections shows that...

> ...(1) over half of its 43 sections deal with support for gay and
> lesbian issues and causes, and (2) that what they try to label
> as the "radical right" is really an attack on any evangelical or
> Biblically-based effort or organization.

According to the *How To Win* manual, all those who
have a Christian World View—a view which holds that
Biblical principles extend to every area of life and not
just the matter of how to get to heaven someday—are
enemies who must be stopped. Other education organizations which joined the NEA in sponsoring the
How To Win manual included the National Associations of both Elementary and Secondary School Principals, the National Council of Teachers of English, The
National Center for Science Education, the American
Library Association, and the National PTA.

Citizen protests labeled "extremist" or "radical" often
result when two resolutions which NEA conventions
endorse annually are applied in local situations.
Resolution E-9 demands total "academic freedom" for
teachers. Resolution I-22 says it supports "freedom of
expression in the creative arts and deplores any efforts
to suppress, directly or indirectly, such expression."

Three recent incidents in the St. Louis metropolitan
area illustrate what results when efforts are made to
have schools uphold traditional morality. When a local
school board, under parental pressure, decided that
sexual nudity had to be edited out of movies shown in
the classroom, the *St. Louis Post-Dispatch* under the

headline, "Belleville Teachers Gird To Fight New Film Policy"[31] reported:

> A legal fight may be the next step for Belleville high school teachers, who have decried a new classroom movie policy as censorship and grounds for a challenge to the First Amendment. The board for the Belleville Township High School District voted 4-3 on Monday to state that sexual nudity must be edited out of movies shown in class. Tom Steinmann, president of the union that represents 230 teachers said he would call a membership meeting. "We're going to fight. We think it's wrong. This is censorship at its highest," he said.

Another 1997 *St. Louis Post-Dispatch* story carried the headline "Profanity Rule Irks Teachers In Collinsville."[32] The story said:

> School administrators in Collinsville say they're having a bit of a problem with profanity. But it's not the students who are the problem—it's the teachers.

> Unions representing the city's public school teachers and assistants are balking at a policy that bans cursing and declares that they should act as role models. "Whose definition of role model applies?" asked Mike Cook, regional director of the Illinois Education Association. "Does that mean a teacher cannot go down to the Horseshoe Lounge and have a beer?" The same goes for swearing, he said.

> School officials say the administration adopted the (no cursing) policy during the summer because of numerous complaints last school year about teachers swearing around students.

Teacher groups demanding total classroom authority in fulfillment of NEA resolutions were encouraged for a time by another St. Louis area happening. In 1996 a federal court upheld the right of a teacher in a St. Louis suburb to allow her students to use any type of profanity and filthy language including the "f" word in class writing assignments. Some in-class "writings" became the basis for class-produced R-rated videotape productions. When the principal objected, the woman teacher claimed her right to "academic freedom." The school board fired her for violating school policy and she sued. She claimed that she was the target of racial and gender discrimination. The principal who tried to uphold traditional decency and classroom decorum was a black male and the teacher was a white female. A federal judge and jury gave her a $750,000 damage award.[33] After two more years of court battles, in June 1998, a federal appeals court reversed the earlier ruling. With the support of teacher organizations, the case will likely end up in the U.S. Supreme Court. What message does the support of classroom profanity by a teacher and teachers' organization send to students?

Over the years as the NEA developed its left-leaning, anti-traditional values political machine, the education of American children has suffered a tragic decline. Headlines have told that scores on the SAT and ACT college entrance exams were dropping. Functional illiteracy in cities has reached epidemic levels. The crisis in education has steadily worsened. The solution the NEA and its political supporters offer regularly is "Give us more money!"

CHAPTER 12

REBUILDING SOUND FOUNDATIONS IN A SECULARIZED NATION

If the foundations be destroyed, what can the righteous do? —*Psalms 11:3*

HUNDREDS OF YEARS BEFORE CHRIST, Sun Tzu, the Chinese military genius wrote his classic book, *The Art of War.* In it he said...

> The basis of victory in war is to know your enemy and the basis of the conflict.[1]

Those who become concerned about what has happened to America's schools need to recognize that there is a war going on. It's a war for our culture and the way of life we will hand down to our children and grandchildren. As Sun Tzu said, in a war it is essential to "Know Your Enemy."

The enemy is not the classroom teacher or the principal. The enemy is not the education reformers or the National Education Association. The enemy is neither the knowing leftists nor the seemingly blind people serving on school boards or in state legislatures or Congress. The Scripture tells why, saying:

> ....we wrestle not against flesh and blood, but against principalities, against powers, against the rulers of the darkness of this world, against spiritual wickedness in high places. (Ephesians 6:12)

The "war for our culture"—the war about how we live our lives and the way of life we will pass down to our children and grandchildren—is a spiritual one. Recognizing that is what Sun Tzu called knowing "the basis of the conflict." The longtime director of the FBI, J.

Edgar Hoover, recognized that all conflicts have a spiritual basis. Upon receiving an award at the Freedom Foundation at Valley Forge on February 22, 1962, Hoover said of the war with communism:

> The basic answer to communism is moral. The fight is economic, social, psychological, diplomatic, strategic—but above all it is spiritual.

Likewise, at its heart, today's war for our culture is a war between the forces of light and the forces of darkness—between Christ and Satan. That's why the Bible says:

> Put on the whole armour of God, that ye may be able to stand against the wiles of the devil. (Ephesians 6:11)

Before He went to the cross, the Lord Jesus told His apostles:

> I am the vine, ye are the branches: He that abideth in me, and I in him, the same bringeth forth much fruit: <u>for without me ye can do nothing.</u> (John 15:5)

NO HOPE HUMANLY SPEAKING

Any realistic evaluation of the control exerted by humanistic forces in the schools and other culture-shaping institutions makes the battle appear humanly impossible. But when things look hopeless God always has a promise. In Isaiah 59:19 God says:

> When the enemy shall come in like a flood, the Spirit of the Lord shall lift up a standard against him (KJV).

The enemy has come like a flood into the schools and into every facet of our society. The standard which God's Holy Spirit wants to raise is triune—a three-in-one standard. It's made up of three institutions He established for the administration of a stable society. They are: Godly homes, power-endued churches and righteous government. Without Godly homes, churches can never be what they should be—and without the right kind of churches, homes will never be Godly. When both the church and the home function as God envisioned, righteous government can result.

MAKING A PERSONAL INVENTORY

To be a part of God's "standard," individuals must first see that the battle is spiritual and then determine where they stand personally. As a part of that "inventory," the twelve foundational concepts in Chapter 5 should be checked. Before those concepts can be the foundations of a stable society, they must first become foundations in the lives of those who would be part of the "standard."

Many "good" people brought up in traditional-values homes generally accept and try to base their lives and families on those foundational concepts. However, every individual is born as a sinner. (What parent ever had to teach a little child to do wrong? It just comes naturally.) Sin separates man from God and deserves punishment. That's why God, in the person of Jesus Christ, became a man so He could die for the sins of all men.

JUDGMENT IS COMING

Foundational Concept #11 points to the time of judgment when each individual will answer to the Lord. To be ready for that day an individual must recognize his own sin and then be able to say in faith, "Jesus didn't just die for the sins of the whole world. He died for my sins and arose again and I've asked Him to be *my* Lord and Savior." To anyone who, in faith, comes to the Lord that way, He promises:

...him that cometh to me I will in no wise cast out. (John 6:37)

Once an individual is "yoked" by faith to the Lord who died to satisfy the penalty for the individual's sin and arose again to be the new life of those who believe, wisdom and guidance concerning the education of children and grandchildren (and everything else) becomes available.

In a growing movement several millions of parents have left government schools. They fulfill their God-given responsibility to "train up their children in the *way* they should go" in either Christian schools or by homeschooling them. (Private, parochial, Christian or homeschooling doesn't guarantee the teaching of a true Biblical world view if public school textbooks, methods or philosophy are used.)

Providing a Christ-centered education for children would be essential even if government schools provided strong academics in a safe, disciplined atmosphere. The decision to withdraw should be based not on what may be wrong in a public school but in recognizing what, by law, is missing from government schools. The Bible gives at least three reasons why a Bible-based education is mandatory.

TRUE BASIS OF ALL THINGS CAN'T BE TAUGHT

In Colossians 1:15-17, St. Paul's epistle shows that true education must recognize Christ's role in everything. Speaking of the Lord Jesus, those Scriptures say that...

> ...by him were all things created, that are in heaven, and that are in earth, visible and invisible, whether they be thrones, or dominions, or principalities, or powers: all things were created by him, and for him: And he is before all things, and by him all things consist.

If those words are true (and they are) then it is impossible to teach true science, or true history or true government—or even give a true understanding of mathematics—without recognizing the place of Jesus Christ. For example, how would it be possible in history or government class to teach the vitally important foundational concept that man's rights come from God if God can't be mentioned in school?

Colossians 1:18 makes a Christ-centered education mandatory for the child of any parent who believes and wants to obey the Bible. It says of the Lord Jesus...

> ...that in all things he might have the preeminence.

Even if a secular school offers good academics in a disciplined orderly setting, the courts make it impossible for the Lord Jesus to have first place—His deserved "preeminence" there.

FOR CHILDREN TO BE HAPPY AND PROSPER

Additionally, if Christian parents want their children to be happy and to prosper, the Bible shows the way. The first three verses of Psalm 1 set forth the complete requirements for "blessedness" and "prosperity." Psalm 1:1-3 says:

> (1) Blessed is the man that walketh not in the counsel of the ungodly, nor standeth in the way of sinners, nor sitteth in the seat of the scornful. (2) But his delight is in the law of the Lord; and in his law doth he meditate day and night. (3) And he shall be like a tree planted by the rivers of water, that bringeth forth his fruit in his season; his leaf also shall not wither; and whatsoever he doeth shall prosper.

God's word first says that to be blessed [happy, satisfied, complete, fulfilled] children cannot be under the "counsel" or teaching of the ungodly. In Bible terms, the "ungodly" are those who do not actually know and trust the Lord Jesus—in short, they have not been "born again" even though they may be moral, caring people.

There are many fine Christians teaching in government schools. However, their schools are controlled by a humanistic philosophy of education and court decisions which are hostile to God. Therefore, they cannot legally challenge children to fulfill the second condition Psalm 1 sets for being happy and prospering in all things. Only in a Christian school or homeschool can children be challenged to "meditate in the law of the Lord day and night." Verse 3 says that's the prerequisite for prospering in whatever they do.

Therefore, for children to be truly educated, to be happy and to prosper, the Bible says they must (1) have Christian teachers who (2) give them a Bible-based, Christ-centered education where Christ is given "preeminence" and (3) their lives must be saturated in the Word of God.

DON'T WITHDRAW FROM SOCIETY

Making the decision to enroll children or grandchildren in a Christian school should not result in abandoning the system. Unfortunately less than 25% of America's children are likely to ever receive a Christ-centered education (unless God works miraculously to transform the nation as He has done several times in the past). So, unless some measure of sanity is returned to the public sector, children who get a Christ-centered education will grow up to live in a world where a majority of people have been "educated" in government schools. The majority will be people who have never learned the twelve foundational concepts of a stable society. Therefore, reversing the worst of the dumbed down, amoral and immoral results of humanism in schools is essential. Christians who work to overturn what the education "reformers" have accomplished are the "salt and light" God leaves us here to be.

Can it be done—and how? A very essential first step is ending federal involvement in education. Until 1965, the federal government had almost no involvement in or control over education. There was (and is), of course, no Constitutional authorization for the Congress to legislate or the federal government to be involved in any way in education.

As in so many areas into which the federal government has moved without Constitutional authority, money was used to get states and local school districts to accept control of their schools. To get the federal "aid," states and school boards had to accept the federal "guidelines."

BOUGHT WITH OUR OWN MONEY

After thirty years of federal "aid" to education, the federal tentacles reach into every school district in the land. The federal government supplies only six percent of the dollars spent for education in America. It has used those dollars to impose the controls of Goals 2000, the Elementary and Secondary Education Acts and School-to-Work on the schools and children of America. For twenty years Republicans have promised to abolish the federal Department of Education—while they annually increase its funding and federal controls.

To either abolish the federal Department of Education—or eliminate its funding—work must be done at the local level. Congress must be pressured to stop federal involvement and control over America's schools—or a President committed to using his veto pen on un-constitutional appropriations must be elected. It won't happen until America's neighborhoods and parents awaken to what is happening in the schools their children attend. It won't happen until State legislatures and local school boards resist federal mandates, even if it means refusing the "federal money."

LOCAL SCHOOL BOARDS BEING ELIMINATED

In 1930, there were 150,000 local school districts in America. Many of them operated just one school.

Parents could have a real input. Massive efforts were made during the 1930s to sell the idea that "consolidation" would improve education. By 1960 over 100,000 local school districts had been eliminated. The number of districts had been reduced to 40,000. By the late 1990s there were only 15,000 school districts left—and education "reform" measures passed in state after state made provision for eliminating more "marginal" districts. By definition "marginal" could mean a district where student "assessments" indicate that the student population is not sufficiently politically correct. Missouri's 105-page Senate Bill 380 enacted in Missouri in 1993 is typical. Titled the "Outstanding Schools Act," the bill mandated the Outcome-Based Education cycle (without ever using the term). It raised taxes $300-million annually and initiated OBE procedures by authorizing...

> ...the state to establish a "framework curriculum" and "performance standards"....school districts could be abolished if they did not measure up when the state made its "assessment" of how the district's students were conforming to the state's standards....Contracts of certified teachers could be suspended, and recall elections ordered for members of the local school board.[2]

To further weaken local school boards and exert more top-down control, the reform measure provided for...

> ...training of members of boards of education in areas deemed important for the training of effective board members as determined by the state board of education.[3]

Stopping further centralization and returning control to local school boards which are truly responsive to parents will require a massive reorientation of citizen and parental thinking. It will also take changes in state and federal laws.

A first step is finding examples of how education "reform," Goals 2000, Outcome-Based Education, School-to-Work and sex education have impacted on the local school and its students. Use examples of what is happening locally to awaken people and get them organized to return the school curriculum to what parents and the community want.

WHAT ONE COMMUNITY HAS DONE

Can it be done? Rick Scarborough is pastor of First Baptist Church of Pearland, Texas (a suburb of Houston). His book, *Enough is Enough—A Call to Christian Involvement,*[4] shows what can be done. He wrote:

> In the spring of 1992, I visited our local high school to attend a high-school assembly that was promoted as an AIDS Awareness Assembly. Throughout the presentation, I became increasingly angered over what I was hearing. Finally after about thirty minutes, I decided, that is it! I have had it..."Enough is Enough!"[5]

An HIV-infected woman had conducted assemblies through the day for 2200 students in the high school. Scarborough attended the day's last session. In his book he said:

> I was able to constrain my inner feelings as she described normal intercourse, anal sex, and oral sex, which she announced to be the safest way to have sex in the world of AIDS, outside of masturbation. Predictably, she displayed a condom, today's amoral solution for the host of afflictions that accompany illicit sex. She stretched it, made jokes about the male anatomy, and announced, "Condoms are ninety-seven percent effective in combating AIDS when used correctly." (Page 205)

Scarborough related his reaction. He said:

> I cannot describe to you how incensed I was as I listened to this young lady. She was giving license to hundreds of stu-

dents, including two of my own, who were in high school at the time, to commit any wicked act they chose. (Page 205)

Scarborough raised his hand and was recognized. He quoted facts from the Federal Centers for Disease Control to challenge the presentation that "condoms were ninety-seven percent safe." One teacher shouted a defense of the statistic. When the program ended, Scarborough said he experienced quite a bit of hostility from some who thought he was being mean to the speaker. Other students, including his daughter, thanked him for speaking out.

INFORM THE COMMUNITY

After checking with an attorney, Scarborough decided to transcribe a recording he made of the session and offer it to the community. The church sign on a major boulevard announced, "This Sunday learn what students heard about AIDS." The community was stirred—and the church was full on Sunday. Following the regular service, Scarborough read the twelve-page transcript to the church family and friends. Scarborough said:

> Our senior ladies heard their pastor say words, I am certain, they never expected to hear him say. I decided if our kids could hear them, their parents and grandparents needed to hear them. That day, the members of First Baptist Church of Pearland decided "Enough was Enough."[7]

Scarborough requested permission to address the school board. Over 500 citizens showed up. Seven speakers were scheduled—Scarborough and six people who supported the program presented in the assembly. The "supporters" of the assembly included faculty members, the wife of a faculty member, one student and a local pastor.

In the months and years which followed, Christians
became involved in politics. The composition of the
school board was changed, some school staff was
replaced—and the Pearland city council and government were changed.

ONE PERSON CAN MAKE A DIFFERENCE

It all happened when one man with determination
and a right attitude stood up for what was right. Others
followed his strong and righteous leadership and positive changes were made. The undermining of traditional morality was stopped in Pearland, Texas.

However, erroneous court decisions of the last fifty
years prevent the Pearland, Texas school district and
any public school from giving students the real answers
for life even if they have a Christian school board and
Christian school administrators. Students cannot be
given the true knowledge and wisdom which results
when Jesus Christ is given His deserved preeminence
"in all things." Biblical principles are banned from
textbooks.

God leaves Christians here to be "salt and light."
Those who try can expect to be attacked—as Chapter
11 showed. In Pearland, Texas, for example, the struggle to return morality to the public schools resulted in
several Christian activists being sued[9] before the
righteous cause prevailed. The NEA and the modern
day "reformers" know they are in a war. Actually, they
believe they were victors in a 50-year stealth revolution. Anyone who stands up for traditional values and
morality is regarded as a counterrevolutionary who
must be destroyed. However, someone must take the
risk and pay the price to return decency to the public
arena.

ATTEND SCHOOL BOARD MEETINGS

Taxpayers, whether they have children enrolled in public school or not, should attend school board meetings. At board meetings look for board members who try to stand for traditional values, strong academics and a back-to-basics approach. They need support and may be the key to linking up with other concerned parents and citizens. School board meetings can also be a good place to ask board members, superintendents and administrators publicly the two questions mentioned in page iv of the foreword. They are:

(1) What do you believe man's purpose to be?

(2) What is the nature of man and of the children you are teaching?

Most educators will reply that they don't deal with questions like that. Of course, it is impossible to formulate a system of education without consciously or unconsciously answering those questions. For centuries the Catholic Catechism, Martin Luther's, the Shorter Catechism based on the Westminster Confession of the Presbyterians and Charles Haddon Spurgeon's Baptist Catechism agreed on man's purpose. The first question a child faced in each generally was, "Why did God make me?" The answer:

> God made me to know Him, love Him and serve Him in this life and to be happy with Him forever and ever in the next.

It was on that truth that western civilization and its education were based. Each of those denominations also agreed that man is born a sinner. Catholics call it "original sin." Luther spoke of "The Bondage of the Will." Baptists see man as having "a fallen nature." Calvinists speak of man's "total depravity." (Parents soon realize they never have to teach a child to do wrong. It's just comes naturally.) The separation of powers built into the U.S. Constitution stemmed from this view of man. The founders believed that dividing powers between the executive, legislative and judicial and the state and federal governments would keep each from getting too much power. Each branch would jealously guard its own area of jurisdiction and right to rule.

That Biblical view of man's nature is in sharp conflict with humanism which teaches that man is basically good. The humanist believes that any evil man does or seems to do is the result of evil influences in his environment. The way, therefore, to change man is to change whatever in his environment influences him. Jesus, of course, said man needs to get a new nature "from above" by being born again spiritually. Every system of education is, consciously or unconsciously, built on one philosophy or the other.

LEARN HOW THE SYSTEM WORKS

Get informed and learn the workings of the political system which elects school board members, legislators, etc. Then support good people—or become a candidate yourself. The "What Can I Do?" chapter in the book *None Dare Call It Treason—25 YEARS LATER* told how an obscure county chairman named Abraham Lincoln trained effective political workers for the Whig Party in 1840. Lincoln said:

> ...the following is the plan of organization...divide (your) county into small districts, and...appoint in each a subcommittee, whose duty it shall be to make a perfect list of all the voters in their respective districts, and to ascertain with certainty for whom they will vote...keep a constant watch on the doubtful voters, and from time to time have them talked to by those in whom they shall have the most confidence... on election days see that every Whig is brought to the polls.[10]

Lincoln knew that elections are won by the candidate whose organization gets its voters to the polls. Issues and beliefs of a candidate are important—but they cannot win unless they are backed by a functioning organization geared to locate friendly voters, register them, and get them to the polls.

ISSUES MOTIVATE THOSE WHO WILL WORK

Issues, properly used, can motivate average, apathetic citizens to work to elect principled candidates using the process Lincoln described. A dozen concerned motivated activists who start early can multiply themselves tenfold. They can turn the tide in a school board or legislative race. The concept can grow to win a congressional race.

Distributed selectively this book can be effective in awakening, informing and recruiting those who will become the campaign hardcore. (It's not wise to hand someone a book and say, "Here's something you must read!" It's often more effective to say, "Here's a book I found interesting and alarming. I'd be very interested in your opinion of it. I'd like to check with you after you've read it.")

Those who get involved will find that the education reformers are already well-organized. All sorts of education organizations from the NEA to the PTA have guides for organizing the community. One of the most comprehensive is the six-and-one-half-pound Community Action Toolkit produced and distributed to activists by the National Education Goals Panel[11] in 1994. It tells how to motivate and organize a community and its leaders, how to use the media and work elections. It's available on the Internet. The techniques and methods are valid and can be used for good or "bad" causes.

HOW COMMUNITIES ARE MANIPULATED

The individual who gets involved will soon encounter the way educators, civic leaders, businessmen, the clergy and parents are manipulated using the Delphi Technique. Delphi is a method for obtaining a predetermined "consensus" among a diverse group of individuals who may or may not be knowledgeable about a field of endeavor or problem.

The Delphi Technique was developed by the RAND Corporation, a liberal think tank, in the 1960s.[12] It was developed originally as a way of using repeated surveying of a group of people to bring them to agreement or "consensus." The original survey technique has been adapted for use in controlling and manipulating meetings or study groups called to get public input for issues in education, police community relations, state control of child care, etc.

The survey approach, when used, is supposedly anonymous. It is done with a group of people who may never come face to face. A knowledgeable person has little opportunity to get exposure of his or her views or ideas to the entire group. It is a technique used by the educational establishment (often financed by the U.S. Department of Education) for reaching a supposed consensus on curriculum goals, content or instructional methods.

Widely used as a technique for developing programs "to meet the needs of an individual state or community" the results often turn out to be almost identical, even in wording, to those adopted in other communities or states.

HOW DELPHI WORKS

Using a series of surveys to develop a "consensus" was the original technique. A 100-page report using a Delphi technique survey done in 1989 is typical. The study was titled, <u>Teacher Perceptions of the Effects of Implementation of Outcome-Based Education.</u>[13] It was financed and distributed by ERIC (Educational Resources Information Center) of the U.S. Department of Education. The report described the method used. It said:

> A random sample of 60 teachers was selected from 600 teachers in an Iowa SCHOOL DISTRICT. The 60 teachers were given a "survey" which included 39 "statements" concerning educational goals and implementation of OBE. Those surveyed were given a choice of six responses from Strongly Disagree to Strongly Agree. Space was provided for writing any comments or reactions to each statement.

When the surveys were returned, those conducting them tallied the results and analyzed the comments. An effort was made to determine the degree to which at least 75% of those responding would accept each of the statements. On the first "try" 75% or more of those responding agreed to (or would go along with) twenty of the original thirty-nine statements or premises. Those twenty statements became a part of the "consensus."

TRY, TRY AND TRY AGAIN

A month later the sixty participants were surveyed again. They were asked to rethink their positions and then were again given the nineteen statements on which there had been no "consensus." When these tabulations were done, there was a consensus on twelve of the nineteen. Thirty days later, a third survey was done on the last seven points. By the time the third round was completed and the written comments were tabulated, it was found that a consensus was achieved and at least 75% of the participants were "in agreement" on the pre-determined package of statements.

When the Delphi "consensus" is achieved, a lengthy and comprehensive report can be prepared and released using the "consensus" to support the goals and techniques of OBE—or a tax increase or some other new project. When experienced teachers, or citizens, or business leaders, etc. have come to a "consensus" anyone disagreeing, must obviously be uninformed or out of step and may be an odd ball. The technique avoids the possibility of informed people with conflicting views influencing others.

Ultimately, depending on how big the project is, the "consensus" may be packaged beautifully (expensively) for dissemination to parents, teachers, legislators, and media.

TECHNIQUE USED TO CONTROL MEETINGS

Delphi has been adapted for use in meetings where participants are present. Panels, groups and community meetings are manipulated to develop a community "consensus" which is then sold to the public. Here's how it works:

A group of interested citizens, community leaders, pastors, labor and business leaders, etc. are invited with the announced goal of "getting input" to develop a community "consensus on the problem of XYZ." The session starts with a general assembly addressed by an "expert" from Washington, a college, etc. He or she sets forth the "problem," the "opportunity" and general goals all can agree upon. There may be 50, 75, 100 or 250 in attendance in the general session.

When the general session ends, attendees may be instructed to check the package of materials they received when they registered to find a numbered or colored card—red, blue, green, orange, etc. This determines the breakout session they will attend with 10 to 40 others.

There will be a "facilitator" running each breakout session. There may be a panel of lesser experts to help in the discussion. When the time comes for input (comments and suggestions from the group), a call may be issued for a volunteer to serve as the "recorder" or "secretary." Normally one has already been chosen to "volunteer." This person may work at a chalkboard. As suggestions and proposals are made, the "recorder" will say, "I think we can simplify that to say ....." Or "I think what you are saying is...." Or "Can we say it this way..." An unwelcome comment or question can be disregarded by the recorder who says "That's outside the scope of what we are dealing with today."

They will usually get five to eight such suggestions, at which time there is a break before going back to the general session. The "recorders" from each group get together and construct a joint "consensus" of the ideas and agreements from their sessions. A list of "agreed upon" goals, etc. is presented to the entire group. There will not usually be opportunities given for additional comments or disagreements in the general session when the "consensus" is presented.

Through the entire process, of course, care is taken to isolate the informed, opinionated individual who could sway the entire group if given an opportunity to speak. If there are half a dozen such people in attendance, the odds are they will be in different breakout sessions so they cannot support one another.

In the final report on "consensus," a conservative or traditional answer may be thrown in. However, it will be presented in a way which indicates it was probably a joke. Everyone will laugh at how impossible that approach would be. This will serve to further intimidate other right thinking people. Many in attendance may be uneasy with the "consensus"—but they don't want to appear stupid or out of step so they go along with the group's "consensus."

SELLING THE "CONSENSUS"

In due time the community or state is flooded with a fancy, pretty "toolkit" selling the tax increase or promoting OBE, School-to-Work or a new approach to meeting the health "needs" of the community. The "consensus" may be joined or supported by the American Association of University Women, the state or local affiliate of the National Education Association, the local ministerial association, or the state or local Catholic Conference, the Chamber of Commerce, the Labor Council, etc.

The steamroller gets media support. When concerned citizens form a group for "Excellence in Education" or "Taxpayers for Fiscal Responsibility," they will be ignored or pictured as enemies of public education or "progress."

Goal of the entire process is the changing of beliefs and attitudes. That isn't difficult today. After 50 years of progressive education and the liberalization of most mainline churches and religious denominations, many people aren't sure about what they believe. Even if they have a "gut" reaction that something is wrong, they have no solid foundational beliefs on which to base opposition or from which to offer creative constitutional solutions if there is a real problem.

WHAT CAN BE DONE WHEN FACED WITH DELPHI?

Recognizing the technique and how to combat it is important. It may be possible to disrupt the process or enable a knowledgeable individual to locate others in the meeting who are uneasy but do not realize how they are being manipulated. Here are six simple steps:

1. Know what you believe. Go to such meetings prepared.

2. If possible ask in the first general session, "Will we have an opportunity here to discuss or question any *consensus* brought in from the breakout sessions?"

3. If a group of concerned friends attend, don't all sit together. Then if when one person speaks, those in other parts of the room can rise in support.

4. When speaking or disputing, face and speak to the audience and not the "facilitator" or panel. Have friends who will speak up and agree or say, "We want to hear more from...."

5. If necessary, afterwards issue a "Dissenting (not a minority) Report." In the big meeting, if the announced consensus is out of line, try to get the floor to ask anyone who disagrees and wishes to participate in a dissenting report to contact you. Get names, addresses and phone numbers.

6. Enlist supporters in Service Clubs, Veterans Groups, Senior Citizens Groups, labor unions, etc. to question the announced consensus and distribute any dissenting report.

DON'T PUT HOPES IN THE COURTS

Concerned citizens frequently think they can look to the courts for justice. It doesn't usually happen on major issues. The 1925 decision of the U.S. Supreme Court in *Pierce v. Society of Sisters* was an exception. It held that parents have the basic right to educate their children. Another is *Wisconsin v. Yoder* which in 1972 upheld the right of the Amish to educate their children in accordance with their religious beliefs and culture. Otherwise, Christian conservatives haven't had much success in court on fundamental issues—and it costs a fortune. There are, however, a growing list of Christian law firms which handle some cases.

In the early 1980s, Alabama parents sued in federal court to have 44 textbooks banned because they promoted the religion of secular humanism. The National School Board Association's Council of School Attorneys' Annual Law Seminar in 1988 told what happened ultimately after U.S. District Judge Brevard Hand in his ruling said...

> If this court is compelled to purge "God is great, God is good, we thank Him for our daily food" from the classroom, this court must also purge from the classroom those things that serve to teach that salvation is through oneself rather than through a deity.[14]

That was good reasoning and Judge Hand banned the 44 textbooks which promoted secular humanism. He wrote:[15]

1. The systematic exclusion of references to religion from the 44 textbooks in question, in fact, establishes or supports the religion of secular humanism.

2. Inclusion in those books of information which is antitheistic, hedonistic, antiparent, or which supports subjective value judgment, establishes or supports the religion of secular humanism.

3. John Dewey was the founder of the public education system as we know it today. In 1933 he, along with 33 other individuals, signed the Humanist Manifesto. It is his philosophy which permeates our schools of education.

4. Our system of public education is doing a poor job of educating our young.

Judge Hand supported the parents and banned 44 state-adopted textbooks used in home economics, history and social studies classes. It could have been a real turning point in the cultural war. However, the Court of Appeals in a unanimous opinion, overruled Judge Hand.

OTHER "QUICK FIXES" WON'T WORK EITHER

School "choice" through vouchers, tuition tax credits and charter schools are among the proposals of those concerned about the decay of government schools. Supporters of choice believe that...

...competition will put pressure on public schools to improve. They also argue that vouchers will allow low-income families to give their children the better private education which today only the well-to-do and career politicians can afford.

Charter schools and vouchers both have pitfalls:

(1) Federal "school choice" vouchers would continue the unconstitutional federal involvement in education. (2) Government control always follows government money, either immediately—or eventually.

President Bush, in his speech announcing America 2000—the forerunner of Goals 2000—proposed vouchers. In his presentation, he said that vouchers would make all schools part of the public system—and bring public accountability. What President Bush said is all too true. Government aid in any form will result ultimately in the school reformers' programs being imposed on private education. The answer? Raise the dependency allowance for *all* children. People keep their money. If they wish, they may spend it for an alternative to public education for their children—or they can spend their money for whatever other purpose they desire.

A POSSIBLE SAFER APPROACH

In 1999, steps were taken to encourage individuals and corporations to provide scholarships to enable more children to attend private, parochial or Christian schools. The effort got attention and impetus when an heir to the Wal-Mart fortune and a friend each contributed millions of dollars to a fund which provided scholarships to 40,000 children in private school grades K-8. Their efforts and the attention it received probably contributed to passage of a measure in the Arizona legislature in early 1999 which gives tax credits to individuals and corporations contributing money to charitable organizations which provide scholarships for private or public school tuition payments. By having the monies distributed by private groups, it is hoped that state control over private education can be avoided. Since the Arizona law passed, legislators in other states are considering similar measures.

WHAT CAN BE DONE?

Implement the seven steps set forth earlier in this chapter:

(1) Make sure where you stand with the Lord so you can be used by Him.

(2) Evaluate why millions are fleeing government schools. Even if you have to teach them yourself, make sure your children learn to read by using systematic phonics to teach them yourself no matter where they attend school.

(3) Become informed and develop an understanding about the proper and Constitutional role of government. Then evaluate what is happening in your community, state and nation. Consider which of the listed resources on the following pages can be of help to you.

(4) Oppose programs and teaching methods in your community which weaken academic standards and achievement or anything which is ungodly. Learn about state and federal laws, regulations and programs which impose such programs on local communities.

(5) Find and support individuals, elected officials and groups and organizations that are working in your community, state and nation to rebuild Biblical foundations for the nation.

(6) Inform and awaken others and encourage and help them to get involved in the same efforts.

(7) Pray for wisdom, direction and strength personally, for those who need to be awakened and for those you might regard as enemies or part of the "problem."

These steps will enable you to fulfill the role and enjoy the blessings God promises to you and your children and grandchildren in Isaiah 58:11-12. Those verses say:

> And the Lord shall guide thee continually, and satisfy thy soul in drought, and make fat thy bones: and thou shalt be like a watered garden, and like a spring of water, whose waters fail not.

> And they that shall be of thee shall build the old waste places: thou shalt raise up the foundations of many generations; and thou shalt be called, The repairer of the breach, The restorer of paths to dwell in.

That's what the nation needs—and what God can do in and through us when we yield ourselves to Him and His Holy Spirit.

Other Works By John Stormer

- **None Dare Call It EDUCATION—Hardcover**
  Get hardcover copies of this book for special friends, your pastor, your legislators, and the local library. Single copies are
  $21.95 plus $3 for shipping—or you can get six copies including shipping for just $100.

- **None Dare Call It Treason—25 YEARS LATER**
  The updated version of John Stormer's 1964 bestsller. Over
  7-million copies are in print. The 1992/1998 update reprints
  the original without change and adds 350 pages of updates including the so-called deaths of communism and the Soviet
  Union, and the Red China threat. An invaluable resource
  which documents the influence communists and other
  humanists have attained over the last 75 years in America's
  culture-shaping institutions.Single copies are $9.95—or get 5
  copies for $29.95 including postage.

- **Growing Up God's Way**
  A guide for getting children ready for school and life. Over
  600,000 copies of this bestseller have helped multitudes to get
  their homes, their marriages and their finances on a Biblical
  foundation while giving children a right start in life. Single
  copies are 6.95—or get 10 copies (for shower, new baby or
  wedding gifts) for $29.95. All prices include postage.

- **Understanding The Times—A periodic newsletter**
  John Stormer analyzes news developments in education,
  religion, politics, foreign policy and economics. Published by
  Liberty Bell Press, the price is $29.95 for ten reports issued pe-
  riodically as significant news demands.

LIBERTY BELL PRESS

P.O. Box 32   Florissant MO 63032

Information You Can Use
...from sources you can trust!

- **RESEARCH MANUAL: Goals 2000—Moving the Nation Educationally to a "New World Order."**
  Compiled and edited by James R. Patrick, this 824-page manual reproduces the actual text of laws, UNESCO and Soviet documents on education, a chronology of important happenings in education over a 50 year period, etc. Order from Citizens for Academic Excellence, P.O. Box 11164, Moline IL 61265. Price including postage is $23.00.

- **Crisis in the Classroom—Video, 58 minutes**
  Produced by Phyllis Schlafly and the Eagle Forum, this comprehensive video features top members of Congress and the press speaking out on what schools are doing to our young people. A real eye-opener. Send check or money order for $25.00 to Eagle Forum, P.O. Box 618, Alton IL 62002.

- **Child Abuse in the Classroom, Schlafly**
  Phyllis Schlafly produced this 450-page paperback by editing the text of testimony given in Congressional hearings on educational abuses. Over 250,000 are in print. Columnist Thomas Sowell says it is must reading for every parent. Order from Eagle Forum at the above address for $8.00.

- **First Reader System by Phyllis Schlafly**
  Everything a parent or grandparent needs to teach children to read phonetically. The package includes a 192-page, 4-color hardbound reader, 128-page workbook, and two instructional audio cassettes. Order from First Reader System Inc., P.O. Box 495, Alton IL 62002, 1-800-700-5228.

Books and other resources on specific problems in education too numerous to mention here are available and will be soon located by those active in the program outlined in Chapter 12.

REFERENCES

CHAPTER 1
What's Happened to Academics?
1 Congressional Record, 6/9/97
2 Secondary Math: An Integrated Approach, Addison-Wesley, 1997, p. 1
3 U.S.News & World Report, 5/27/97
4 Readers Digest, 12/97, p. 182
5 Speech, Education Policy Conference, St. Louis, January 1995
6 Milwaukee Journal-Sentinel, 11/10/97
7 Ibid., 11/19/97
8 Washington Times, 9/7/94, p. A8
9 Ibid., 10/19-21/97
10 San Francisco Chronicle, 7/10/95
11 Ibid.
12 Ibid.
13 Washington Times, 9/7/97, p. A1
14 Ibid., 10/20/97, p. A12
15 St. Louis Post-Dispatch, 6/12/94, p. 8A
16 Ibid., 10/3/93,p. 5B
17 Ibid.
18 Idaho Statesman, 10/21/89, p. 8A
19 Gallup Poll, 1989
20 St. Louis Post-Dispatch, 7/11/97, p. 7B
21 Ibid.
22 Washington Times, 10/20/97, p. A1, A12
23 Ibid., p. A12
24 Ibid.
25 Ibid., 6/25/95
26 Ibid., 1/25/97
27 St. Louis Post-Dispatch, 6/21/83, p. 4A
28 Washington Times, 6/28/98, p. A6, 7/2/98, p. A18
29 Blumenfeld, NEA: Trojan Horse in American Education, 1985, p. 211
30 Dallas Morning News, 3/16/91, pp. 21-22
31 Washington Times, 9/22/96, p. B1
32 Ibid., 11/13/92, p. A5

CHAPTER 2
What's Happening Morally In Schools?
1 Speech, Dr. Shirley McCune, Kansas Governor's Education Conference, Wichita, 11/2/89
2 Washington Times, 9/30/94, p. A20
3 Ibid., 5/6/97, p. C4
4 Ibid.
5 Ibid., 6/1/92, p. E1
6 Ibid., 9/9/92, p. A3
7 Anti-Bias Curriculum: Tools For Empowering Young Children, National Association for the Education of Young Children, Washington DC, 1989- 7th Printing, 1993
8 National Review, 5/25/92
9 Human Events, 10/20/95
10 Washington Times, 8/21/97, p. A1
11 National Review, 5/27/96
12 Citizen, Focus on the Family, 8/1/97
13 California Assemblyman Steve Baldwin, Report on AB101, March 1997
14 Los Angeles Times, Updated clipping in California legislative file
15 Ibid.
16 Ibid.
17 Ibid.
18 Ibid.
19 Ibid.
20 Reiff, Harper & Row, 1966
21 Ibid., pp. 159-60
22 Ibid., pp. 160-61, 187
23 The UnReported News, 4/30/96, p. 8
24 Ibid., 1/25/97
25 Detroit News, 10/1/90
26 Ibid.
27 Ibid.

CHAPTER 3
Creating A New Social Order
1 Rugg, The Great Technology, p. 32
2 Ibid., p. 271

3 Ibid., p. 278
4 Report, Special House Committee To Investigate Tax Exempt Foundations, 83rd Congress, 1954, pp. 137, 153
5 Ibid., p. 137
6 The New Republic, Jul. 29, 1936, p. 343
7 Progressive Education, April 1932, pp. 261-62
8 Ibid.
9 Ibid.
10 Counts, The Soviet Challenge to America, p. 324
11 Counts, Foreword to translation of New Russia's Primer, Ilin, Houghton, 1931
12 Ibid.
13 Counts, Dare The Schools Build A New Social Order, pp. 28-29
14 Ozman, Philosophical Foundations of Education, Fourth Edition, 1990, Merrill Publishing, p. xix
15 Hearings, Special House Committee To Investigate Tax Exempt Foundations, 83rd Congress, 1954, p. 482
16 See Chapter 10
17 The Tablet, Brooklyn NY, 8/11/59
18 Humanist Manifesto I
19 Ibid.
20 Dworkin, Dewey on Education, pp. 19-32
21 Ibid.,p. 22
22 Ibid., p. 25
23 Elementary Curriculum Staff, Contra Costa County Schools, First Grade Social Studies, 1963, p. xiii
24 See Chapter 3
25 Human Events, 10/18/96
26 Gordon, What's Happened To Our Schools?, p. 16
27 Ibid.
28 Schlesinger, The Age of Roosevelt, pp. 156, 176, 563
29 British Fabian Society, 49th Annual Report, 1932; See also The Great Deceit, Zyman Dobbs, Veritas Foundation

30 Report, Special House Committee To Investigate Tax Exempt Foundations, 83rd Congress, 1954, p. 150
31 Ibid.
32 Frontiers of Democracy, 12/16/42, pp. 75-81
33 Report, Special House Committee To Investigate Tax Exempt Foundations, 83rd Congress, 1954, p. 154
34 Ibid.
35 Ibid. p. 155
36 Communist Indoctrination—Its Significance to Americans, Maj. William E. Mayer, Psychiatrist, U.S. Army, 1959, pp. 14-15
37 Ibid., pp. 11-12

CHAPTER 4
Textbooks Destroy Foundations

1 Humanist Manifesto I, pp. 8-10
2 Humanist Manifesto II, pp. 13, 15-16
3 1828 Webster Dictionary
4 First Grade Social Studies, Elementary Curriculum Staff, Contra Costa County Schools, 1963, p. 38
5 1968 Edition, pp. 14-16
6 Congressional Record, 10/10/62
7 Washington Times, 9/18/97, p. A11
8 Quoted by James Dobson, August 1994, Focus On The Family news letter
9 Ibid.
10 Guidelines for Comprehensive Sexuality Education, National Guidelines Task Force, Sex Information and Education Council of the U.S., 1991
11 Humanist Manifesto II, p. 18
12 SIECUS Report, June/July 1994, p. 14
13 Report, Taxpayers for Excellence in Education
14 Copley News Service, 6/2/98, 1959PST
15 Nicole Ziegler, Associated Press, 6/3/98, 8:23 p.m. ET
16 NEA Journal, Today's Education, Nov. 1964

17 The Social Frontier, Feb. 1936, pp. 134-35

18 Ginn and Company, 1950

19 Harper and Brothers, 1951

20 D.C. Heath & Company, 1951

21 Scott Foresman, 1983, p. 534 (SE)

22 Allyn & Bacon, 1978, p. 45

23 Houghton-Mifflin, 1980, p. 70

24 Introduction, Teachers Manual, Butler County, Pa. Schools, 1992-93, pg. 1, cited Rohrer,Speech, St. Louis, 9/27/97

25 Silver Burdett, 1972, pg. 10-11; TM, p. 10

26 The Barna Report 1994-95: Virtual America, Regal Books, p. 85

27 Textbook Review, A More Perfect Union, Michael J. Chapman, Eden Prairie MN.

28 Report, President's Commission on High Education, 1947, Vol. 3, Pg. 48

29 UNESCO, Towards World Understanding, Vol. 1, p. 6

30 Applying Basic Principles, IBYC, Vol X, 1984, pg. 17; Rep. Sam Rohrer, St. Louis, September 1997.

31 St. Louis Post-Dispatch, 1/16/86, p. 16A

32 Republished, Human Events, 10/23/65, p. 10

33 Reader's Digest, Jan. 1995

34 Ibid.

35 Wall Street Journal, 12/31/94, p. A8.

36 Washington Times, 11/27/96, p. A14

37 Ibid.

38 Wall Street Journal, 12/30/94, p. A8

39 Reproduced, Gabler Newsletter, March 1992

40 Houston Chronicle, 11/9/91

41 Sidewalk, Gunboats and Ballyhoo, Promise of America Series, p. 136

42 Congressional Record, 3/1/62, p. 2906.

43 St. Louis Post-Dispatch, 5/9/92

44 Ibid.

45 Humanist Manifesto II, p. 19

46 Ibid.

47 Ibid., pp. 16-17

48 Human Events, 5/17/86

49 Associated Press, Houston Chronicle, 10/6/85, p. 21

50 New York Times, 6/3/86

51 Vitz Report, p. 16

52 Ozmon, Philosophical Foundations of Education, Fourth Edition, 1990, Merrill Publishing Co., p. xix

53 Quoted, Chalfont, Abandonment Theology, p. 53

54 Footnote, p. 12

55 Unfinished Story volume, Scott Foresman Promise of America series, p. 87

56 Struggling for the Dream volume, Scott Foresman Promise of America series, p. 169

57 New York Times, 6/3/86

58 Colson, Prison Fellowship, Breakpoint broadcasts, Numbers 219, 61223, 61226, 61229

CHAPTER 5
The Revolution We Lived Through

1 Denton, When Hell Was In Session, Traditional Press, 1982, p. 183

2 Huckabee, Character is the Issue, Broadman & Holman Publishers, 1997

3 Barton, To Pray Or Not To Pray, Wall Builder Press, 1988, p. iv

4 Ibid. pp. 9-49

5 Ibid. pp. 107-142; Chicago Daily News, 9/3/76, p. 9

6 St. Louis Post-Dispatch, 7/5/77

7 Washington Times, 3/10/92, p. F1

8 St. Louis Post-Dispatch, 3/26/98

9 St. Louis Globe-Democrat, 4/16/77, p. 6B

10 Ibid.

11 St. Louis Post-Dispatch, 1/8/78, p. 1B

12 St. Louis Globe-Democrat, 2/27/76, p. 12A

13 Cheating In Our Schools, Reader's Digest, October 1995

14 Ibid.

15 Ibid.

16 Spock, Baby and Child Care, 4th Edition, Simon and Schuster, 1976, p. 11
17 Ibid.
18 de Tocqueville, Democracy in America, Anchor Books, Doubleday & Co., 1966
19 Quoted, Magruder, American Government, 1952, p. 13
20 Huxley, Brave New World, Foreword, p. xv

CHAPTER 6
The New Generation of Reformers
1 Transcribed from videotape of speech
2 Ibid.
3 Ibid.
4 Ibid.
5 Clinton and Magaziner, Education Leadership, March 1992
6 NCEE 1992 Letterhead listing of Board members
7 Proposal for Restructuring Education for the State of Washington, NCEE, p. 1
8 Ibid., p. 33
9 Ibid., p. 13-14
10 Report, Goals 2000: Restructuring U.S. Society Through Education, The Winds, 1997, p. 2 (Internet at http://www.The Winds.org)
11 Letter, To all members of Congress, Congressman Henry Hyde, 3/6/96, (Internet at http://www.sover.net/~nbrook/Hillary.html)
12 Ibid.

CHAPTER 7
School-to-Work Will Transform America's Future
1 Speech, Holland, Goals 2000 Conference, Washington DC, 2/12/97
2 Ibid.
3 Letter, Jenny Potochnik, Wichita Eagle, Feb. 1996, quoted, Holland, Richmond, VA Times-Dispatch column

4 Ibid.
5 FAX Alert S. 1186, Donna Hearne, Constitutional Coalition, March 1998
6 Letter to constituent, Cong. Sonny Bono, 12/10/97
7 The Secretary's Commission on Achieving Necessary Skills, Skills and Tasks for Jobs, A SCANS Report for America 2000, U.S. Dept. of Labor, April 1992, pp. 3-197
8 Ibid.
9 Speech, Virginia Miller, Goals 2000 Conference, Washington DC,, 2/12/97 text published EDUCATION REPORTER, December 1997
10 School to Work Opportunities Act of 1994, Section 3(a)(C)
11 U.S. Department of Education, ERIC REVIEW, Volume 4, Number 2, Spring 1996, p. 2
12 Report to Congress Cover Letter, pg. 1 and Report, p. 16
13 Ibid., pp. 21-22
14 Report, 25 pages, School-To-Work: The Coming Collision, Texas Education Consumers Association, (Internet: http://www.fastlane.net/~eca)
15 Text, Speech, Phyllis Schlafly, 1996 National Conference of State Legislators, Philadelphia, PA, September 1996
16 Report, The Coming Collision, TECA, pp. 6-7
17 Ibid., p. 7
18 Ibid.
19 Press Release, Texas AFL-CIO, 9/9/97
20 Letter, Missouri Legislators to Missouri Congressional delegation, 3/6/96
21 Report: STW: The Coming Collision, TECA, p. 10
22 Ibid., pp. 10-11
23 Fessler, Report to Ohio State Board of Education on Work Toward National Standards, Assessments and Certificates, 12/10/96, p. 26 (Down

load from the Internet at
http://www.fessler.com)

24 Hagen, 1997 Letter of Resignation
to North Dakota Governor Ed Shafer

25 Ibid.

26 Ibid.

27 Ibid.

28 Fessler, STW: It's The Law, Oct.
1997, p. 9

29 Ibid.

30 St. Louis MetroVoice, June 1998,
p. 1

31 St. Louis Post-Dispatch, 3/10/97,
3/13/97, 7/15/97, 8/11/97

32 Resume, 4 pages, Dr. C. Larry
Hutchins

33 MetroVoice, June 1998, pp. 1, 4, S2

34 Ibid., p. 4

35 Letter, Janice Perry, Grants Officer,
U.S. Department of Labor, 11/29/95,
to Steve Alexander, Missouri
Department of Education

36 Speech, Brewbaker, Goals 2000
Conference, Washington DC,
2/12/97, text published EDUCA-
TION REPORTER, January 1998.

37 Ibid.

38 Ibid.

39 Federal and State Education
Measures Will Nationalize
America's Schools, Understanding
The Times, June 1994, pp. 4-5

40 The Blumenfeld Education Letter,
March 1994, p. 1

41 NCEE proposal to New American
Schools Development Corporation,
p. 33

42 President Bush, Speech, America
2000, An Education Strategy, April
18, 1991

CHAPTER 8
Outcome-Based Education Modifies
Children's Behavior

1 Bloom, All Our Children Learning,
p. 180

2 Chapter 6

3 Chapter 7

4 Ibid.

5 Sunseri, Letter to Missouri Legislators, 2/12/98

6 Spady, Beyond Traditional Outcome-Based Education, Educational
Leadership, October 1991, pp. 49,
67-72

7 Policy Report, Outcome-Based
Education: Dumbing Down
America's Schools, Family Re-
search Council, 1994, p. 5

8 Q & A About Outcome-Based
Education, Missouri Department of
Elementary and Secondary Educa-
tion, September 1992, p. 6

9 Phyllis Schlafly Report, May 1993,
p. 2

10 Bloom, All Our Children Learning,
p. 180

11 Washington Times, 4/11/92

12 Ibid.

13 A Proposal to Implement Outcome-
Based Education in Missouri
Schools, Draft, 12/28/92, Appendix
C, p. 24

14 Phyllis Schlafly Report, May 1993,
p. 4

15 Ibid., pg. 2

16 Ibid.

17 Missourians Prepared, Department
of Elementary and Secondary
Education, July 1990

18 Universal Outcomes, Missouri
Department of Elementary and
Secondary Education, September
1992

19 Phyllis Schlafly Report, May 1993,
p. 3

20 Ibid., p. 4

CHAPTER 9
Schools Become Mental health
Centers

1 Final Report on House Resolution
#37, Select Subcommittee on Educa-
tion, Pa. House of Representatives,
11/19/1996, p. 15

2 Letter to Barrington, IL School District #220, Jean Rowe, Medicaid
Consultant, 10/8/96, p. 1,2

3 Ibid.
4 Letter to Rep. Lee Daniels, Illinois House of Representatives, Joseph Spagnolo, Illinois Superintendent of Education, 2/4/97, p. 2
5 St. Louis Post-Dispatch, 12/14/97, p. C5
6 Final Report on House Resolution #37, Select Subcommittee on Education, Pa. House of Representatives, 11/19/1996, pp. 15-16
7 Ibid., p. 46
8 Ibid., p. 46-47
9 Ibid., p. 14
10 Young, EDUCATION REPORTER, January 1997
11 Rohrer, Medicalization of the Schools, Medical Sentinel, Volume 3, Number 1, January/February 1998, p. 14
12 Ibid.
13 Ibid.
14 Washington Times, 4/27/96, p. A1
15 Pocono, Pa. Record, 3/22/96
16 World, 8/17/96, p. 1714 Forbes, 12/16/96, p. 123
17 Forbes, 12/16/96, p. 123
18 Rohrer, Speech, Public Schools As Nurse and Nanny, Goals 2000 Conference, Washington DC, 2/12/97, text published in EDUCATION REPORTER, November 1997, p. 3
19 Ibid.
20 Ibid.
21 Ibid.
22 Rohrer, EDUCATION REPORTER, November 1997, p. 3
23 Ibid.
24 Final Report, p. 18
25 Rohrer, Speech, The Modern Child, Text, pp. 9-10, Eagle Forum 1997 National Leadership Conference, St. Louis
26 Young, EDUCATION REPORTER, January 1997
27 Chisholm, Psychiatry, February 1946
28 Speech, Chisholm, Conference on Education, Asilomar, CA, 9/11/54

29 Preface, Conference Proceedings, International Conciliations, March 1948
30 Psychiatry, February 1946
31 Rohrer, Medical Sentinel, Vol. 3 Number 1, January/February 1998, p. 14
32 Orient, Speech, The Clinton Plan: Entering Through the Back door, AAPS, p. 6
33 Hearing, Pennsylvania Select House Committee on HR 37, Nov. 30, 1995
34 Consent form requested from parents of minor students, Central Dauphin School District, Harrisburg, PA cited by Orient.
35 Smith, Health & Education Reform: Freedom's "Voluntary" Demise, pp. 162-63, 245
33 Clinton Presidential Records, 44 USC 22.31 #1447

CHAPTER 10
Manipulating Smart Kids

1 Human Events, September 12 & 26, 1992
2 Ibid, 9/12/92, p. 7
3 Ibid., p. 1
4 Ibid., p. 7
5 Ibid.
6 WORLD, 11/21/92
7 Video, Geoffrey Botkin, Prime Time Design, 22 minutes, 1992
8 Arkansas Gazette, 7/23/85, p. B1
9 Hearing Transcript, Joint Education Committee, 9/15/94, p. 1
10 WORLD, 11/21/92
11 Hearing Transcript, p. 8
12 Ibid., pp. 13-14
13 Boyer, Volkman, Georges, The Indiana Academy, Media Bypass, September 1994, pp. 22-19
14 Student Letter to Rep. Delbert Scott, 2/11/95
15 Human Events, 9/12/92, p. 1
16 Ibid.

CHAPTER 11
NEA Advances Reformers Agenda

1 Hearings, Special House Committee to Investigate Tax-Exempt Foundations, 83rd Congress, p. 482
2 Resolution B-9, 1995 NEA Convention, NEA Today, September 1995
3 The Washington Blade, 7/21/95
4 Resolution I-13, NEA Conventions, 1992, 1993, 1994, 1995, 1996, 1997
5 Phyllis Schlafly Report, August 1997, p. 2
6 Resolution E-9, NEA Conventions, 1994, 1995, 1996, 1997
7 Resolution D-19 NEA Conventions, 1994, 1995, 1996, 1997
8 Resolution C-23 NEA Conventions, 1994, 1995, 1996, 1997
9 Resolution B-1 Every NEA Convention, 1992-1997
10 Today's Education, January 1969, pp. 29-31
11 Ibid., p. 30
12 Ibid.
13 Phyllis Schlafly Report, February 1985
14 Peoples' Daily World, 7/10/86 and 6/25/87
15 Forbes, 6/7/93
16 NEA Journal Today's Education, December 1967, p. 34
17 Blumenfeld, NEA: Trojan Horse in American Education, p. 161
18 Forbes, 6/7/93
19 Washington Times, 9/20/96, p. A10
20 Ibid., 9/1/96, p. B2
21 Ibid., Forbes, 6/7/93
22 Congressional Record, 2/7/90, p. S956
23 Speech, Futrell, NEA Convention, 7/4/98,
24 SB 843, Missouri General Assembly, 1998, p. 16
25 The Pasadena Story, NEA Commission For Defense of Democracy, June 1951, p. 23
26 Editorial, Tulsa, Oklahoma World, 3/27/62
27 Ibid., 4/26/62
28 Wall Street Journal, 5/20/97
29 Combating The New Right, Western States Regional Staff, NEA pp. 3-11
30 How To Win: A Practical Guide for Defeating the Radical Right in Your Community, 1994, National Jewish Democratic Council, 711 Second Street N.W. Washington DC 20002
31 St. Louis Post-Dispatch, 11/27/96, p. 10A
32 Ibid., 9/25/97, p. 13A
33 Ibid., 11/20, 22-23/96

CHAPTER 12
Rebuilding Destroyed Foundations

1 Sun Tzu, The Art of War
2 Missouri General Assembly, 1993, SB380, pp.4-6, 17, 33
3 Ibid., p. 13
4 Liberty House Publishers, Lynchburg, VA. 1996
5 Scarborough, p.8
6 Ibid., p. 205
7 Ibid., p. 207
8 Ibid., p. 210, 221-230
9 Ibid., p. 227
10 Stormer, None Dare Call It Treason—25 YEARS LATER, p. 314
11 1850 M Street NW, Washington DC 20036
12 Teachers' Perception of the Effects of Outcome-Based Education, ERIC Center, U.S. Department of Education, July 1989, p. 11
13 Ibid.
14 Quoted, National School Boards Association Council of School Attorneys Annual School Law Seminar, New Orleans, LA March 1988, p. 10
15 Ibid., p. 11

INDEX

- - - - - - CUT OUT OR COPY AND MAIL - - - - - -

LIBERTY BELL PRESS
Post Office Box 32
Florissant MO 63032

Send me _____ copies of the paperback edition of *None Dare Call It Treason—25 YEARS LATER*

Payment of $ _____ is enclosed. (Send check or money order in U.S. funds. Missouri residents please add 6.75% for sales tax.)

NAME: _____

COMPANY OR ORGANIZATION (if any): _____

ADDRESS: _____

CITY: _____ STATE: _____ ZIP: _____

------- CUT OUT OR COPY AND MAIL -------

LIBERTY BELL PRESS
Post Office Box 32
Florissant MO 63032

Send me _____ copies of the paperback edition of *None Dare Call It Education*

Payment of $ _____ is enclosed. (Send check or money order in U.S. funds. Missouri residents please add 6.75% for sales tax.)

NAME: _____

COMPANY OR ORGANIZATION (if any): _____

ADDRESS: _____

CITY: _____ STATE: _____ ZIP: _____